LAND LAW IN LESOTHO:
THE POLITICS OF THE 1979 LAND ACT

For Mattie Morinia Franklin

Land Law in Lesotho: The Politics of the 1979 Land Act

ANITA SHANTA FRANKLIN

Avebury

Aldershot • Brookfield USA • Hong Kong • Singapore • Sydney

Published by
Avebury
Ashgate Publishing Limited
Gower House
Croft Road
Aldershot
Hants GU11 3HR
England

Ashgate Publishing Company
Old Post Road
Brookfield
Vermont 05036
USA

British Library Cataloguing in Publication Data

Franklin, Anita Shanta
    Land Law in Lesotho: Politics of the 1979
    Land Act. - (Making of Modern Africa
    Series)
    I. Title II. Series
    346.8850643

ISBN 1 85628 976 1

Library of Congress Catalog Card Number: 95-77722

Typeset by
K.F. May
7 Lambton Terrace
Leeds
LS8 5PG

Printed and bound in Great Britain by
Ipswich Book Co. Ltd., Ipswich, Suffolk

Contents

Tables

Acknowledgements

Significant financial support for this research was provided by a Leeds University Studentship.

I would also like to record my gratitude and thanks to the many friends and colleagues in Lesotho, USA and Britain who stimulated, supported and helped me to begin and finish this thesis, especially Steve Lawry, Shubi Ishemo, Chris Corrin, Rose Ayuru, Pauline Feltham, John Douglas, Haunani Kay-Trask, Constance Cole, Hugh Fox, Caroline Wright, Gavin Williams, Ray Bush and my supervisor Lionel Cliffe.

About the author

Anita Franklin is a senior lecturer in sociology at Sheffield Hallam University. She teaches in the areas of "Race" and Black Studies, Gender, and Development Studies.

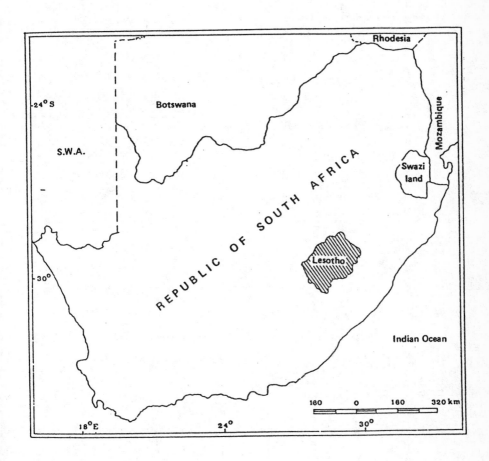

Source: Makhanya (1979): 2

Introduction

In June 1980 a new land law took effect in Lesotho: the Land Act of 1979. The significance and implications of this law for the legal, economic and political institutions of the country up to now have remained largely unexplored. The central aim of the thesis is to analyse the Land Act of 1979 and so fill lacunae in the literature on contemporary land policy in Lesotho. Although Lesotho's so-called communal land tenure system has fascinated scholars over the years, the post-colonial state's attempts at transforming property relations on the land have received relatively little attention. In setting out to achieve the central aim of the thesis I have adopted two paths of inquiry. The first path deals with the exposition of the law; its provisions, antecedents, also what the law advocates and opponents say about the Act and its origins, purposes and the nature of change that it is sought to bring about by the law, and the likely social implications if it were implemented. The second path of inquiry focuses on the actual transactions taking place on land. The second path is concerned with currently existing property relationships as they have developed on rural and peri-urban arable land in Lesotho. It is in the context of relating the first path of inquiry to the second wherein the main challenge of the thesis lies.

It is intended to link an explanation of the law with an understanding of the limitations of law when used ostensibly to facilitate development in post-colonial states. This particular legislation has been seen as a crucial prerequisite to development efforts in Lesotho. Government and donor agency documents have been produced extolling a wide range of benefits available to the nation upon the full implementation of the 1979 Land Act. As yet the law has not been fully implemented. The Act's main feature, the conversion of traditionally allocated holdings to state authorized leaseholds, has been achieved in the urban areas. However, in the rural areas where 90% of the population is based, the Act remains largely unimplemented. The inheritance

1

provision of the Act is the only one which as yet touches the lives of the majority of rural residents, allowing as it does a legal right of the landholder to bequeath his holding to an heir, or in the absence of a will, allowing the holding to remain the property of a family member, usually the eldest son.

I went to Lesotho in January 1987. During the seven months I was there I did four kinds of research.

First, I spent time in various villages in the lowland areas of Berea and Mohale's Hoek doing surveys and in-depth interviews with sharecroppers and local chiefs. Typically I would contact the chief of a village before arrival. On arrival potential respondents would visit. I talked with all who wanted to speak including the chiefs of the area. Because I have chosen to name the district and areas within which I worked, I cannot further identify the respondents for the sake of their privacy. Contact with entrepreneurial farmers was made unofficially. Again, because information about their occupation and business operations are given in the text, I have not identified them by name.

Secondly, I attended two important conferences, one at the National University of Lesotho, Institute of Southern African Studies on Food Security, and the other, the Land Policy Review Seminar, at Quthing. The latter conference was crucial in several ways: it provided me with information about the Act, the proponents and opponents of the law, and gave me insight into the interministerial rivalry between the Ministry of Agriculture and the Ministry of the Interior.

I also spent time working in Lands, Surveys and Physical Planning, helping with the backlog of lease applications. This experience enabled me to understand the various steps involved in processing lease applications, the conditions which contribute to delay in processing them and the conditions which contribute to difficulties in training and maintaining qualified staff. I journeyed with the Land Policy Review Commission on several occasions also during their tour of the country to assess public opinion of the Act. This involved attending *pitsos*, i.e. village meetings called by local chiefs, wherein Commission members would address those village residents who attended: talking about land policy nationally and in particular the 1979 Land Act. Residents were given the opportunity to express their views and question the Commission members.

Finally, the Documentation Centre of the Institute of Southern African Studies at the University provided me with access to numerous studies and reports on the country, in particular on Basotho women, agriculture and previous land legislation.

In the final analysis it was the gap between law and reality which interested me more than a technical assessment of the law as an appropriate spur to agricultural economic growth.

Floating in the spaces between law and on-the-ground experience were bubbles of rumour and anecdote attributing the actual timing of the 1979 Land Act to then Prime Minster Jonathan's attendance at an important international conference where he could impress representatives of external sources of income. Rumour also had it that Jonathan was attempting to prevent a mooted cutback in aid.

However, representatives from USAID and SIDA deny that Lesotho's aid would have been reduced but for the execution of the Act. Nevertheless there is no denying that *more* assistance is likely to be forthcoming now that the law (and partial implementation) exists. Certainly two key government officials with opposing views on the efficacy of the Land Act have both said to me (unofficially) that implementation in the rural areas *will not* and *can not* happen without increased external funding.

Another rumour linked with popular Basotho perceptions explains the Act as a preventative measure, discouraging Asian businesses from accumulating land. But counter-rumour blames the law for the increase in such accumulation by non-Basotho.

Finally the law has been justified as being capable of preventing land sales (which is illegal) but there are many within the government and outside of it who privately believe that land sales have actually increased since the 1979 Act.

The gap between reality and law is a recognized phenomenon in social policy. But in so far as any explanation for the gap is given, policy makers blame the lack of adequate resources and personnel. Nonetheless, I argue in the book that the gap between law and reality is defined by other factors besides those associated with lack of resources in staffing and financing. Along the first path of inquiry, research suggests that the introduction of a particular leasehold mechanism and therefore of a limited market in land is the radical intention of the law. In order to explain the significance of this new departure it will be necessary to explore: In what ways has land been administered prior to the Land Act? To what extent is the law a discernible part of a trend in post-colonial policy? What economic, social and political factors provoked the enactment of the legislation? How has the Act been justified? How can we explain its 'hybrid' (not fully freehold) character? How can we explain its only partial implementation after a decade? In what ways do the Act's provisions serve the interests of different social groups in Lesotho? In what ways are the Act's provisions related to cropland transactions currently taking place in rural areas?

Insight into some of the more complex questions are found along the second path of inquiry, where experience in the field suggests that the gap between law and reality is filled with unofficial tenurial forms which seem to fulfil some of the intentions behind the Land Act 1979, i.e. encouraging capitalist development on arable land through allowing for the transfer of cropland from smallholders to supposedly more efficient entrepreneurial farmers with the capital to maximize production — but in a different form to that allowed for under the Act, and one not formally sanctioned by law. At the same time the unofficial tenurial forms are fulfilling these aims independent of state regulation and with potentially enormous consequences for the agrarian social system and its role as social security in Lesotho.

Four recurring themes pattern our investigation into the nature and significance of the Land Act 1979.

Firstly, there is the changing role of chiefly administrative authority over land of chiefs *vis-à-vis* the state and how the rise and decline of such chiefly powers has shaped access to arable land in particular, and affects agrarian life more generally.

Secondly, another pattern that emerges is the series of shifts which have occurred in development orthodoxy on the issue of land tenure and its relationship to social progress.

A third major theme concerns the 'unreality' of certain kinds of law, which fail to regulate or control behaviour 'on the ground'.

The fourth and final theme is the continued partial nature of the Act's implementation after a decade.

In summary, our aim is to explore the relationships between the state, law and society in a case study that involves an attempt by a state to transform social relations on land.

There are at the very least three different narratives that could be pursued in the Lesotho case, three avenues into exploring the significance of the 1979 Land Act. First of all the Land Act of 1979 can be understood as the outcome of external pressures exerted by various international agencies. It is possible to argue that the Lesotho state, as evidenced by the haste with which the law was drafted, unwillingly had at long last acquiesced to demands that modifications be made to the land tenure system. In order for this argument to effectively explain the existence and partial nature of the law, it would be useful to advance an analysis of the Lesotho state as a state desperate to protect and further its own interests through shaping its policies in such a way as to maximize foreign aid. Was the Land Act then simply a device to ensure that Western money would continue to flow in and help prop up an unpopular and illegitimate regime? Another avenue different from the inter-state focus of the first, reaches into the past for a historical focus on the struggle over access to land, specifically the social conflicts among those who would be allocators of land rights. Such a focus allows the Land Act to be seen as part of an ongoing but contradictory process to strip traditional authorities, i.e. chiefs, of their administrative rights over land and the simultaneous increase in civil or secular authorities over land administration. Still a third avenue takes as its primary focus the transformation of relations on the land as it currently is, with a view towards addressing the relevance or lack thereof of the law on the 'ground'.

Somehow these three 'narratives' need to be woven into the texture of the book. They are all important elements that help to explain the nature of the Land Act 1979 and the actual land patterns. Any discussion of Basotho society must take sufficient account of the country's unique geo-political circumstances. Totally surrounded by the Republic of South Africa, Lesotho is a predominantly mountainous area totalling 11,716 sq. miles (Cobbe and Bardill 1986, p. 1), only 9% of which is considered cultivable (Tshabalala and Holland 1986, p. 4). It has a population of approximately 1.4 million legally resident in 1985 (Winai-Strom 1986, p. 15) in the country although the *de facto* population is considerably less owing to the migration of men and women to the mining, manufacturing and other employment opportunities in the neighbouring Republic. It has been estimated by C. Colclough (1980) that 33% of the total labour force is employed in South Africa. In contrast only 5% of the employed population has formal employment inside Lesotho. Furthermore Lesotho's arable areas are densely populated, with the population heavily concentrated in the crescent-shaped area that extends from Butha Buthe south-west along the Mokhare River (Caledon) to Mafeteng and Mohale's Hoek and east along the banks of the Senqu River (Orange).

The terrain is a poor one for agriculture. Although the average rainfall is, in the words of John Bardill and James Cobbe, 'theoretically adequate' for crops in the lowlands and foothills, nevertheless the sudden and violent nature of the downpour can do more harm than good to crops. Hail, frost, soil erosion and drought combine to make crop cultivation a risky venture at best (Bardill and Cobbe 1986, p. 2). In the face of these statistics powerful agencies such as the World Bank persist in describing Lesotho as a predominantly rural nation (International Bank of Reconstruction: *The Economy of Lesotho,* Report No. 331 a-LSO 1974, p. 1). On average there is very much less than an acre of arable land per rural person in Lesotho (Winai-Strom 1986, pp. 12-18).

Indeed the character of Lesotho's land tenure system prior to 1979 has contributed to this image held by international agencies. On one level the Basotho seem to be a nation of subsistence farmers, closely guarding their traditional rights of access to cropland and pasturage. At the same time it is also clear that neither Basotho households nor the government of Lesotho relies solely or even primarily on income from agriculture.

In Southern Africa commoditization of African labour has preceded the commoditization of the lands Africans occupy. The Land Act 1979, more than

5

any other single piece of legislation, encourages commoditization of land in Lesotho, a *de facto* labour enclave of the South African national economy. Study after study (e.g. Van der Wiel 1977, Spiegal 1979, Gay 1980, Murray 1981) has shown that it is the migrants' earnings in South Africa which constitute the main source of cash income for most households in rural areas. Bardill and Cobbe have shown that since independence in 1966 the country's reliance on migrant earnings has 'more than tripled'. 'By the early 1980s migrant earnings contributed directly over $3 for every $4 produced at home ...' (Bardill and Cobbe 1985, p. 59). Within the context of Lesotho's labour reserve and enclave status there are other ties of a formal and institutionalized nature that link Lesotho with its hostile neighbour. There is the Labour Agreement, the Rand Monetary Area Agreement, and the South African Customs Agreement. There are also what the authors characterize as more informal links as well, '... of commercial and transport links, family ties, migrant movements, broadcasting, the press and magazines, and a largely common culture' (ibid., p. 69). At any rate most writers interested in the political economy of Lesotho recognize the important place South Africa has in Lesotho's past and present circumstances. The data collection and analysis was completed before 1991 and thus does not reflect the changes that have occurred in Lesotho and South Africa since then.

In the book I will, in Chapter 1, explore some of the theoretical perspectives that may prove useful in exploring the Land Act, previous land policy and legislation, and how these inter-relate with other, especially agrarian, social relations. This section explores some of the debates in the literature on custom and law and concludes that in some cases custom is and has been a product of colonial construction at least as much as being of indigenous origin. Such an insight is useful in the Lesotho case because it helps in developing a perspective on the role and function of the laws of Lerotholi, Sotho customs which were codified by the colonial state which include the customary rules and regulations of land use, administration and allocation. This section also introduces an alternative perspective which does embrace the notion of legal pluralism in underdeveloped societies but which I find useful for its perspective on relating different kinds of law to various, i.e. household, workplace, national and international, levels of analysis. The model also is able, I feel, to help focus on the problem and the significance of the gap between law and reality.

In Chapter 2, I outline the origins of the Basotho nation, and describe the political institutions of the pre-colonial, colonial and post-colonial eras. I will argue that the chieftaincy and in particular the Koena clan of the Moshoshoe dynasty consolidated administrative rights over land with the support of the colonial power. This consolidation of chiefs' rights through, among other

6

things, the colonial construction of customary law, was central to the simultaneous weakening of commoners' rights of access to land. However, after independence, moves were made on the part of government to limit chiefly administration of land (but it should be noted, not so much with a populist intention as a desire on the part of government leaders to strengthen the basis of the latter's support).

Moreover, as will be made clearer in Chapter 3, this political state of affairs and the migrant labour system has led to landlessness which in turn drove ever-increasing numbers of Basotho over the border in search of cash income. The main purpose of this chapter will be to investigate the links between migrant labour and land issues, or how the contemporary political economy affects land use.

This will form a basis for the discussion in Chapter 4 which will look at the academic debates which have taken place in the region and in Lesotho on the issue of tenure and how the state has partaken of a particular 'line' on tenure used subsequently to justify the enactment of the legislation.

Chapter 5 explores the Land Act of 1979 in detail, including its predecessors and illustrates in what ways the Land Act 1979 is part of a post-colonial trend in policy.

Chapter 6 attempts to assess the actual and likely impact of current trends in land transactions on various groups in society — chiefs, civil servants, migrant workers, women, etc. — given the current types of cropland transactions which are occurring in lowland areas.

1 Discussion of land and law in Lesotho

Introduction

One central purpose of the book is to examine the variety of land transactions on the ground and relate these social relations to developments in land legislation. Such an investigation should include a theoretical understanding of the relationship between legally prescribed norms and actual (and changing) realities. Also required is a perspective on the transformation of property relations and relations of agricultural production between pre-capitalist and capitalist social relations and between various conceptions of property. In addition the Land Act must also be discussed within the specific context of the debate in literature on land policy and development, but that is beyond the scope of this chapter. The issue will be dealt with in some detail in Chapter 4.

In this chapter I set out to trace the theoretical framework within which the argument on the politics of the Land Act 1979 and actual changes in land tenure is cast and developed in subsequent chapters. The essential theoretical dilemma that I am dealing with here concerns, on the one hand, the nature of property in societies where social and productive relations do not fit the conventional model of capitalist relations; and on the other hand, the uneasy fit between law and reality.

The framework, as a result, has to be informed by several theoretical fields and levels of analysis; each I argue is crucial for explaining and more importantly assessing the trends in land policy in Lesotho, especially the 1979 Land Act. There are two main sections to the chapter: Explanations of the Persistence of Non-Capitalist Social Relations; and Law and Custom in Underdeveloped Societies. I conclude at the end of the first section that the persistence of non-capitalist relations of production does not and has not impeded capitalist development; indeed in the Southern Africa context, non-capitalist relations have subsidized capitalist enterprise in the form of apartheid through the bantustanization of Africans in South Africa, and the economically similar (in the sense that 'bantustans' are also sources of inexpensive labour) but politically different cases of Lesotho, Botswana and Swaziland. I also conclude that non-capitalist social relations are not all necessarily echoes of the pre-capitalist mode of production of Sotho peoples. Some of the non-capitalist social relations are more expressions of changing patterns of gender — power relations between men and women between and within households — rather than pre-capitalist modes of production.

1.1 Explanations of the persistence of non-capitalist social relations from modernization to modes of production

How do social scientists concerned with Development explain the continuation of what seem to be non-capitalist social relations of production in a global economy dominated by a capitalist system? The post World-War II Modernization theorists described the phenomenon in terms of a dual economy: traditional and modern sectors that function separately and statically within a developing country. Marxists, on the other hand, seek to analyse the dynamic of capitalist penetration in, and transformation of, previously viable and autonomous political economies. The key concepts that I have found of particular use within the Marxist school include: social formation, mode of production, reproduction and articulation.

Modes of production first became a useful concept in the discussion of the causes and cures of underdevelopment as part of the Marxist critique of Dependency Theory (Foster-Carter 1978, pp. 44-74).

The modes of production school has had its own problems and debates (Banaji 1973, pp. 2498-2502, McEachern 1975, pp. 444-457, Terray 1972, Meillassoux 1972, pp. 93-105, Rey 1971). As much as the school has benefited from its Althusserian heritage, it has also suffered from grossly reified language, making some of the literature nearly impenetrable.

There are as well critiques of the use of modes of production and articulation, some rejecting the concepts, others modifying them. Here I set out to outline the basic arguments.

The work of Claude Meillassoux (1972, 1975) and P.P. Rey (1971, 1973, 1976) set the groundwork for discussion around the concept of mode of production. In the early 1970s their anthropology focused on how 'circulation' or exchange of certain goods allowed for the encroachment of mercantile capitalist relations and ultimately to other colonial and neo-colonial variations of capitalism. Meillassoux reviews the work of Rey in the latter's comparison of the African and European capitalist transitions. Rey argues that

9

bride price played a crucial role (not unlike that of ground rent in Europe) in the articulation of the lineage mode with the capitalist mode of production. It is the conversion of bride price into money form, its commoditization, that opens the gates to one half of the defining characteristic of capitalism, i.e. free wage labour (Meillassoux 1981, pp. 96-7).

Once bride wealth became a commodity the labour power of young men could be all but guaranteed. The commoditization of bride wealth allowed young (migrant) men more 'independent' access to wives, in that young men were not as dependent on elders providing bride wealth. Access to wives carried with it access to the means of production and reproduction, i.e. land, labour (of women and their offspring) on the land and in the homestead. We will return to this issue on the Section 'Gender and Property' in Chapter 2, when we look at the lineage mode in Lesotho. During this stage it is trade which leads to commoditization of status goods, like bride wealth. This commoditization then becomes a mechanism which triggers a supply of free wage labour. However, in the African context, particularly in the southern region, proletarianization has not been complete even in the later stages of transition. 'Peasants' have not been totally 'freed' from their means of production, and wage (migrant) labour is still tied in many ways to the residues of pre-existing relations of production.

Capitalist production exploits the non-capitalist modes by stripping the latter of labour, and by levying upon it the costs of the reproduction of exhausted labour. What makes migrant labour cheap, according to Meillassoux, is the maintenance of the obsolete organization of agriculture through the employment of so-called surplus labour on the sale of agricultural products at prices below those necessary to insure the full costs of reproduction of that labour. If 'customary' practices on land are necessary for the domestic reproduction of labour, then it would be in the interest of the (colonial) state to preserve 'custom', not transform agrarian relations with the institution of a market in land.

In *Maidens, Meal and Money* (1981, pp. 89-135) Meillassoux argues that imperialism developed its strength and maintains its hold because of its special linkages with the domestic community, whether the site of the domestic community is the nuclear family or the extended one. Pivotal to the exploitation of the domestic sector is the exploitation of women 'who despite the dominant place which they occupy in agriculture as well as domestic labour ... are not granted the status of procedures.' The work a woman does in the domestic sphere and agriculture does not strictly speaking belong to her, except as mediated through a man, i.e. husband, son or father. A further indication of alienation is according to Meillassoux the fact that the other exploited group within the domestic community, junior men, win emancipation from elders (Meillassoux 1981, p. 78). At any rate capitalism preserves the domestic sector which produces subsistence (use value) goods. And that quality of preservation on the one hand and dissolution on the other defines the concept of articulation between modes of production.

At the same time, articulation is not simply a matter of the economic bases of two modes, rather articulation finds its expression in the superstructure as well, in ideology: politics, law, religion. The ruling classes of indigenous societies clashed head on initially in an often violent struggle to preserve their autonomy. However, as the capitalist mode asserted its dominance, the ruling classes were more or less co-opted into undermining the viability and autonomy of the pre-existing modes of production while at the same time seeking to preserve their material and ideological advantage. Lionel Cliffe (1982) has shown how two sets of variables, the first concerning the indigenous modes of production, the second concerning the quality or character of capitalist production, link, with attendant consequences for class formation and struggle. Harold Wolpe's (1980, 1988) contributions to the discussion include a formalization of the term 'articulation' with capitalism, and a clarification of the expression 'mode of production', which had been used in two ways, (1) as the sum total of forces and relations of production which Wolpe calls 'restricted' mode, and (2) the latter plus 'missing elements' which may account for the 'reproduction' of the mode which Wolpe termed the 'extended' mode. Wolpe has employed the concept of extended modes of production, which allows for the possibility of analysing articulation at the level of superstructure which includes law and judiciary. Paramount to Wolpe's most recent position (1988) though is that he defines the nature of capitalism's dominance over other modes. That dominance is tied to the ability of capitalism to reproduce itself as a mode and to its ability to use non-capitalist forms to reproduce what are essentially capitalist social relations.

Therefore, within the parameters of the concepts of modes of production and articulation it is possible for the 'logic' behind capital not to necessarily call for the complete eradication of pre-existing relations of production in all productive units, but rather a gradual erosion of the reproductive capacity of the pre-existing mode as a whole. Wolpe's work is also useful in that it helps to analyse what Samir Amin (1972, pp. 503-524) has called 'Africa of the labour reserves', i.e. the Southern and Central third of the continent. Although Wolpe (1980) talks specifically about South Africa, it is clear that a great deal of his analysis applies to the regional economy that the Republic of South Africa dominates as well as the national economy. South Africa, according to Wolpe, is an amalgam of three modes of production: capitalist, labour reserve economies of the African areas, and the system of labour tenancy on white farms.

Wolpe's analysis helps us also to shed light on how racial segregation policies deepened into apartheid. The tendency of the capitalist mode is towards the disintegration of previous relations of production but that dissolution is not without concomitant changes in politics and ideology. As such he is able to offer a means of periodizing this transition in South Africa. I will look in Chapters 2 and 3 at similar states in Lesotho. The demands made by Africans in the 1940s were a response in part to the unprecedented deterioration in the reproductive capacity of the reserves. Afrikaner capital, eager to assert its strength *vis-à-vis* international capital, opted for the apartheid solution, rather than a liberalization of racial capitalism. There are for Wolpe two major contradictions within the South African social formation. The original and most fundamental contradiction is between different modes. Another is between classes within the capitalist mode. Regarding race, Wolpe rejects it as a contradiction and sees the changing forms of racist policy as the instrument through which class and 'modes' struggles are channelled and controlled. One conclusion for Wolpe is that any challenge to the racist structure challenges the capitalist one as well, and vice versa.

Extrapolating from Wolpe's South African emphasis to a regional one we find two useful generalizations can be made:

1 Capital takes advantage of the reserves system even outside South Africa because this site is where cheap migrant labour is reproduced.

2 The reproduction of that labour power is threatened by the production of any other commodities by agricultural producers and by commoditization in the reserves. This may be in turn a potential key point in helping to explain the partial and unimplemented character of the Land Act which seeks to introduce a market in land.

Of course, in extrapolating to the regional context it is important to point out that not only is there an articulation taking place between modes of production but an articulation between social formations as well. A social formation has been defined by Ray A. Kea (1982, p. 3) as 'a historically concrete society whose structure, organization and historical development were conditioned by specific systems (modes) of material production'. A social formation can be distinguished from a mode of production although the latter concept is fraught with multiple meanings. The expression is used to refer to (1) a historical epoch, (2) an economic system (Mandel 1976, pp. 12-25) and (3) a structured but interactive whole embodying a unity between economic base, social relations and superstructural institutions (Marx 1983, pp. 49-50). It is the third more expansive definition which is most useful for purposes here. Indeed the definition can be expanded to take on board the reproduction of a mode. In

12

other words, a mode of production, if it is genuinely a mode, must have the capacity to replicate its existence.

Ernesto Laclau (1979) and Hamza Alavi (1982) have shown in their separate ways how a single mode may straddle several different social formations. Indeed this seems to be the nature of peripheral capitalism. Alavi has said that 'the surplus extracted by colonial capitalism created a form of extended reproduction of capital which was generated in the colonies but accumulated in the metropolis' (Alavi 1982).

Laclau in his essay on *Feudalism and Capitalism* (1979) acknowledges the world capitalist system, but is concerned to show how this system is contradictory and how it preserves its 'logic':

> [Capitalism's] regulating principle is the average rate of profit [which] is produced by the interaction between different enterprises and includes, at the level of its definition, various modes of production ... The growth of the system depends on the accumulation of capital, the rhythm of this accumulation depends on the average rate of profit, and the level of this rate depends in turn on the consolidation and expansion of pre-capitalist relationships in the peripheral areas. (Laclau 1979, p. 40)

Alavi, for his part, has in characterizing what he terms a 'colonial mode of production' discussed the state's role in preserving elements of pre-capitalist modes:

> The destruction of conditions of reproduction of pre-capitalist society is achieved by peripheral capitalism in a variety of ways, including and especially state action ... (Alavi 1982, p.189)

Taxes of various kinds, state-imposed changes in access and administration of land, are two such state-derived actions that have been repeated all over what is now called the underdeveloped world, no less in Lesotho. Who are on the other side of this capitalist articulation? Are they workers or peasants or both? Does it matter how they are categorized? The debate on this issue is deep and wide, and I will not attempt its resolution here. Rather three points are relevant to our upcoming discussion:

1   The overwhelming number of households in Lesotho are dependent for their livelihood on both wage labour and subsistence agricultural production (Van der Wiel 1977, p. 79, Spiegal 1979, Van Apeldoorn and Turner 1984).

2   Subsistence agricultural production in Lesotho is characterized still by its predominantly non-capitalist relations of production (Phororo 1979, Mashinini 1982 and 1983, Quinlan 1983, Robertson 1987).

13

3   Other scholars on Lesotho (Murray 1980a, 1980b, 1980c, 1981, Bardill and Cobbe 1985, Winai-Strom 1978, 1986, Santho *et al.* 1984) have variously labelled those social groups that are still partially 'tied to the land' in non-capitalist relations as 'rural-based proletariat', 'semi-proletariat'.

These terms are useful in that they evoke a transitional situation with all the consequences for complex class struggle and class alliances that such a transition implies. At the same time though I would not want to argue that there is necessarily a linear progression from peasantry to proletariat which is simply taking time to play out. Likewise I do not wish to argue that non-capitalist relations of production in particular, or social relations in general, are necessarily pre-capitalist. The articulation in Lesotho is characterized I believe with non-capitalist modes, some of which are residues from a pre-capitalist past, and some of which have been and are today contingent on the ability of Sotho society to, in the words of Belinda Bozzoli writing on *Marxism and Feminism and Southern African Studies* (1983, pp. 139-171), 'resist full proletarianization', not least because of its ability to 'subordinate women's labour' and the forms that this resistance takes.

Other critiques of articulationism

At this point I am concerned to broach the issue of the persistence of non-capitalist relations in a slightly different way. Articulationism has been under attack in the development of underdevelopment literature for introducing a new dualism in characterizing developing societies. In addition, the concept had a tendency to push a kind of inevitability in the transition of peasantry to proletariat. But some critics of the concept point out that not every rural producer becomes proletarianized. Furthermore, how does one explain the production of commodities in non-agricultural sectors? But those questions are not immediately germane to understanding land management in Lesotho.

However, Bozzoli's main point about full proletarianization being resisted by the ability of some African societies to subordinate women's labour is crucial to a framework for characterizing the non-capitalist relations on the land in Lesotho.

Women, domestic labour and production

First it was not inevitable, according to Bozzoli, and I agree, that only men would become migrant workers on the mines, in agriculture or in industry. Some of the heaviest jobs have been held by women. Indeed, Angela Davis (1981, pp. 3-29) and Bell Hooks (1981, pp. 44-5) have written on the

14

'equalization' of the sexes under the impact of American slavery. This brutal equality forced African women to be responsible for the same amount of field work as their male counterparts. In addition, enslaved African women were also responsible for the domestic sphere, producing a wide range of use values as well. The notion that women should be closest to home did not stop the earliest industrialists in Japan from seeking the labour of young women, who were among the first to be proletarianized, nor did it prevent young migrant Boer women from being among the first of that group to be proletarianized through their involvement in the garment industry.

Further, Bozzoli challenges and seeks to modify what has tended to be a rather functionalist argument on the part of Wolpe to explain in the South African context the encouragement of white families to accompany workers to towns and cities and the discouragement of Black families to do the same. The idea was that it was functional in both cases to capital. While it is true that Black families being quarantined on the land did save the costs of reproduction, and that such savings may be seen to be of short and medium term benefit, nonetheless Bozzoli argues that both scenarios cannot be said to be functional.

Bozzoli is also keen to depart from articulationism and the *cul de sac* of trying to prove or disprove pre-capitalist relations of production. She does however identify non-capitalist social relations as crucial to an explanation of Southern African societies. The site she is most concerned to study is what she terms the domestic sphere. Struggle (as opposed to articulation) around this sphere has two dimensions, internal and external. The internal dimension deals with such issues as labour, income and property relations. The conflicts and compromises which take place in this dimension relate in many ways to the wider capitalist society. That inter-relationship is the external dimension of the domestic sphere.

Bozzoli argues that the outcome of these domestic struggles may in fact condition and shape the very form taken by capitalism in that society, and that it is this conflict which must be specified, rather than seeking out what is functional or dysfunctional to capitalism. In addition, she says:

> To understand who benefits from the penetration of exchange relations into the domestic sphere, or who gets proletarianized first, is to throw us immediately back to the question of household relationships and the form taken by their interaction with the wider system. (Bozzoli 1983, p. 147)

With regard to southern Africa, Bozzoli states her case thus:

> It was not simply the men's absence that placed the burden of domestic and agricultural labour on the women; nor is it just that male tasks had been undermined by the destruction of the African states; it was also that

these societies possessed a capacity to subordinate women's labour and that it is this capacity that the resilience of these systems to full proletarianization may have resisted. (Ibid., p. 151)

Despite the various and well-founded critiques of the concepts of modes of production and articulation I think it is still a valuable starting point (with modifications) in conceptualizing the transitional situation in Lesotho wherein agrarian social relations still partake of non-capitalist forms, some of which bear similarities to pre-capitalist relations.

Two aspects of this discussion of non-capitalist relations that are central to the book require further elaboration: women as a social category, which I will look at first, and secondly, property and how this concept has changed historically in relation to the dominant mode of production.

Women, law and production

In conceptualizing women as a topic for research there are several macro-level theories of the nineteenth century. Anthropologists of the time like Bachofen (1967), Morgan (1963), Briffault (1952) and Engels (1978) addressed themselves to understanding the origin and development of sex roles. They sought to explain how sex roles were related to patterns and levels of cultural development. These writers argued that 'primitive' cultural and economic levels of development were associated with matriarchal and matrilineal forms of social organization. Patriarchy, in their view, arrived with higher levels of social development. In contrast, patriarchy theorists like Maine and Westermarck opposed this view, holding instead the opinion that human society has always been organized along patriarchal lines. Both writers attempted to show that women's position in relation to men improved as society became more economically and socially developed.

Theories of twentieth century anthropology have departed in many ways from their predecessors. The unilinear theories of the previous century have been for the most part discounted by anthropologists of the present century, e.g. Boserup (1970), Sacks (1979), Coontz and Henderson (1986). The focus has shifted away from a concern with macro-level stage theories of women's status in society and concerns instead individual 'cultures' and 'social formations'. The body of data that has accumulated points to relationships between culture and sex roles. Environment, colonialism, modes of production and post-colonial state policy are representative of just a few of the factors which are recognized now as shaping and conditioning patterns of sex roles and affect directly or indirectly the balance of power between the sexes in societies. The contemporary sociological debate is cautious about the analytical categorization of women as a social group. Janet M. Bujra, in her introduction to *Women United, Women Divided* (1978) provide us with several lessons concerning the definition of women as a social category for analysis. First they acknowledge that here are three ways in which women cannot stand adequately as an analytical category:

1   In a society where women are often divided against themselves because of 'their differential relation to class and status hierarchies as well as factors such as age and kinship affiliation' (Caplan and Bujra 1978, p. 19).

2   Comparative studies of women's status are limited, for example while one society may demand that only women are allowed to make pots, in another society women may be forbidden to do so. As a result it is very difficult to say anything universal about sex roles or the sexual division of labour.

3   And finally it must be said that there are social contexts 'where the fact of sexual difference is irrelevant to the problem at issue' (Caplan and Bujra 1978, p. 19).

The task of the social scientist then would be to indicate not only the nature of social contexts where sexual difference is relevant but also reveal those cases where it is relevant and not popularly revealed as such.

Caplan and Bujra also recognize that there is among much recent writing some analytical confusion about women. Women as an immutable biological fact should not be conflated with women as a social category — a situationally varied category. The authors point out that it is in this context that Eleanor Leacock rejects analysis of the so-called status of women. She suggests that the idea of a separate women's role in society conceals the reality of the family as an economic unit. Bujra also quotes Audrey Richards' comments on cross-cultural comparisons of the position of women; she argues that 'women cease to be a separate problem and become part of the system of child production, child rearing and domestic economics' (Caplan and Bujra 1978, p. 19). Richards' inclusion of domestic economics provides a starting point in building a conceptual link between woman as a biological category and the infinitely varied forms of women's existence. The concept of domestic labour, defined by Bujra as 'the socially reproductive labour expended in the context of a domestic unit' (ibid., p. 20), seems at first glance to provide such a link. The concept of domestic labour has gained currency among writers interested in a Marxist feminist alliance of perspective and politics. Marx recognized that the capitalist process of production produces not only surplus values but also produces capitalist relations, including the conditions for their reproduction, which are required in order to replicate the capitalist relation. The first and last order of that is the renewal of the 'capacity to labour' once labour has been spent in production. This renewal problem is connected with the family in general and with women particularly. In other words, the family can be understood as the site of renewal of the capacity to labour. The needs of the family or more accurately the needs of capital confine women to the home performing unpaid but crucial socially reproductive activity. In general there are three dimensions of reproduction:

1   day-to-day regeneration of labour power, i.e. cooking, servicing the domestic area;

2   the biological reproduction of the next generation;

3   the caring for and the socialization of children including the transmission of ideas related to society and the groups that comprise it.

The debate as sketched so far, while applicable to the European and North American social context, leaves many questions unanswered if the focus switches to the 'Third World'. Is agricultural production of the subsistence variety a part of domestic labour? Further, what makes some activities and not others socially reproductive. Is an activity socially reproductive because of its location, its function or its character? Michael Burawoy (1980), building on the work Wolpe (op.cit.) carried out on South Africa and the development of apartheid, contributed to the debate on social reproduction using the three categories of reproduction in analysis of the labour reserve system. According to Burawoy what is unique to the Southern African region is the fact that there are different and legally separate geographical sites for production and reproduction of African labour. Women are for the most part confined to the homelands and other labour reserve areas where they engage in subsistence agriculture. In addition women are the source of safety net assistance in that it is they who care for the sick, elderly and unemployed. Up until recently the fact that women were left behind on the land was assumed to be unproblematic. It was thought to be because:

1   It was assumed that women could not or should not perform the heavy work associated with the mines.

2   It was assumed that the work women performed in African pre-colonial societies was and is complementary to that of men, even with their absence for much of the time. One of the main justifications on the part of mine owners for paying African workers low wages was the fact of African household production. This household production included crop cultivation; most of the chores associated with cultivation were/are perceived as women's responsibilities.

18

3   It was also assumed that familial obligations and emotional ties kept the African family together and acted as social security in times of illness, old age and unemployment.

Belinda Bozzoli has challenged these assumptions as well as other writers and, as noted above, embraces the term 'domestic sphere' as a site of struggle which should be seen as analytically prior to questions of who gets proletarianized first.   One difficulty at the abstract level concerns the exact definition of the word 'domestic', which in some senses has become very elastic, becoming a residual category for all pre-and non-capitalist production. Domestic labour can refer to unpaid work performed in the household of a nuclear family in an advanced capitalist social formation or it can refer to pre-state subsistence economies.   There is also a dualistic danger inherent in the term, echoing in some ways the feminist notions of public and private spheres, with women's energies being 'confined' to the latter.   Edholm, Harris and Young (1977, pp. 101-130) seek to disaggregate the overly conflated terms 'domestic labour' and 'reproduction'.   For Edholm, Harris and Young there are three levels of reproduction, each with their own objects of analysis: biological reproduction, labour, and social reproduction.   These insights are crucial for illustrating the role women play in Lesotho's agrarian system, as rural producers, and as unpaid caretakers of a social security system of the last resort for Lesotho's ill, aged and unemployed.

In explaining the persistence of non-capitalist social relations, I have set out to illuminate the major points I have found most useful in the literature around the debate on articulation of modes of production and the nature of capitalism. While the concepts of 'articulation' and 'modes' have been important in helping those concerned with the development of underdevelopment to recognize the contradictory interrelationship capitalism has outside 'core' areas, nonetheless such an approach tended to on the one hand conflate articulationism with an inevitable linear progression of peasantry to proletariat (which has not been the case given the continual replication of petty commodity production).   On the other hand, articulationism has also tended to conflate non-capitalist modes of production, i.e. Bozzoli's 'domestic sphere' with pre-capitalist social relations.   The term 'domestic' has also been shown to be somewhat elastic, almost a residual category for what is not clearly a capitalist social relation and all too easily confused with 'reproduction'. Nonetheless, both of these concepts may be useful in helping to define in some sense the range of roles women occupy.

One crucial role Basotho women play is that of caretaker of cropland in the absence of the male household head.   This significant group of women, *de facto* heads of over one third of Lesotho's rural households, are responsible for

19

managing/performing the activities associated with crop production (Gay 1980, p. 136, Safilios-Rothschild 1985, pp. 299-318). They do so frequently with only the most minimal economic and legal support. As jural minors for instance, they are limited in the kinds of contracts they can negotiate with regard to the land which they work and are responsible for. This point deserves emphasis because, as is shown in the book, unregulated transactions on land frequently involve female heads of households as party to unofficial contracts transferring their rights of access to 'their' fields to commercial farmers (Chapter 6). Women are generally unable to contract a lease in most instances because they are as a general rule not *de jure* holders of arable fields, neither are they considered *de jure* majors in law (Seeiso 1986, pp. 44-57). The inability to contract, to engage in lawfully protected and regulated transactions is significant given that the overall intent of the Land Act 1979 has been to introduce a market in land. It would appear to be a market in which many women cannot fully operate.

In the west the conflation of property with private property is central to the ideology which protects and justifies capitalism. The idea of property as being private forms a central part of our common sense. But such a common sense around property is not universal, nor has it always existed in the west. Prior to the 17th century both private and common forms of property were equally recognized and practised. Debates occurred over the relative merits of one or another type of property for the development of society and/or the human personality. According to C.B. MacPherson (1978), major controversies around private property centred on land as well as other goods. That our common sense of property as being private exists, reflects 'a change in social facts'. As MacPherson says,

> From the 16th and 17th centuries on, more and more of the land and resources in settled countries was becoming private property, and private property was becoming an individual right unlimited in amount, unconditional on the performance of social functions and freely transferable. (MacPherson 1978, p. 10)

In spite of the few limitations on the uses of modern private property, i.e. prohibitions against one's private property creating a nuisance or threatening others' lives, private property has become more of an absolute right in the capitalist epoch than in the previous feudal epoch. It is an absolute right in that it allows the 'right to dispose of, or alienate as well as to use; and it is a right which is not conditional on the owner's performance of any social function' (MacPherson 1978, p. 10). Such conditions were optimal for the development of a capitalist market economy.

If the market was to operate fully and freely, if it was to do the whole job

20

of allocating labour and resources among possible uses, then all labour and resources had to become, or be convertible into, this kind of property. (Ibid., p. 10, also K. Renner 1969, pp. 33-45)

However, as capitalism has changed, and as its representative class has become more tied to states which regulate their economies, so too has property changed. As the state has begun to 'do more of the work of allocation ...[p]roperty as exclusive, alienable, "absolute" individual or corporate rights in things becomes less necessary ...' to the work of allocation of 'resources', or in Marxist terms, the means of production (MacPherson 1978, p. 10). The Marxist concern with property is over the ownership of the means of production. I will outline the position briefly. Marx distinguished between different forms of property in that he associated various historical modes of production with their own dominant forms of property. Hence the dominant form of property associated with the capitalist epoch he termed bourgeois. Of non-dominant forms of property found within the capitalist mode of production, i.e. 'the property of the petty artisan and of the small peasant, forms of property that preceded the bourgeois form ...' Marx said in *The Communist Manifesto* (1981, p. 61):

> There is no need to abolish that, the development of industry has to a great extent already destroyed it, and is still destroying it daily. (Marx 1981, p. 61)

What needs abolishing, according to Marx, for the development of humankind is the bourgeois property form, the private property of contemporary society which 'is based on the antagonism of capital and wage-labour' (Marx 1981, p. 62). For Marx, capital is 'a collective product' and is therefore not a personal but a 'social power'. The private ownership of the means of production is a central contradiction of the capitalist mode of production. A contradiction which Marx claims will bring about its own negation in the form of class struggle between the owners of the means of production and those in possession of the capacity to labour.

The significance of Marx's argument for our own work lies in what he says about the capitalist mode's tendency to bring with it its own dominant form of property, destroying all preceding forms. I suggest that this tendency can be seen in the Lesotho case at the level of governmental policy since 1973, of which the Land Act 1979 is a part; wherein more individualized, exclusive social relations on land are being legislated. At the same time I would argue that this tendency also sees its expression at the level of practice in the form of actual land transactions, but some of which take place outside of the scope of 'custom' and 'law'. By outside of the scope of custom and law I mean to point to those transactions which involve the new type of sharecropping by private

21

contract with entrepreneurial farmers which depart from custom in significant ways, and which as I will show in subsequent chapters avoid involvement with the leasehold provisions of the Land Act 1979. Furthermore other land transactions outside the scope of law and custom include land sales which are prohibited by both custom and law.

Looking at the pre-capitalist forms of property in Lesotho, it is thought that both private and common forms of property are found. Schapera (1943), Sheddick (1954) and Ashton (1952) all note that, while chiefs are custodians of communal land, cattle and other domestic animals are recognized as private property over which chiefs have no claims except when such cattle are spoils of war. Limited private rights (rights of usufruct) are recognized with respect to land for residence and cultivation. However, these private rights of land use differ from the private rights of post-17th century western private property rights in that these rights do not include the absolute right to 'dispose of or alienate', nor is it a right which is 'unconditional on the performance of social functions', as he must recognize the authority of the local chief and up until 1938 had to provide tribute labour to fields under chiefs' jurisdiction. In contrast, cattle seem to be governed by private rights which are in some ways more similar to the absolute rights of the post-17th century. Cattle can be given away outright, sold or slaughtered, in short disposed of or alienated in a variety of ways. Cattle ownership is not contingent on tribal membership as the case is with land. Nevertheless, even with regard to the more 'absolute' rights associated with cattle, those rights are still circumscribed by the rights owners' relatives can claim on the cattle. For example married men must set aside some cattle for the house of each wife. In general no house has any claim to cattle belonging to another. So even though the cattle may belong to one man, i.e. the household-head, members of each of his wives' houses can assert claims over cattle which the owner has set aside for each particular house. Moreover, meat from slaughtered domestic animals is shared by all members of the household. Special portions are allotted to the wives, older sons and older daughters. It may also be distributed to other relatives. Wives have very strong rights over the produce from crops cultivated on 'their' fields, i.e. the field(s) allocated to the husband by virtue of his marriage to her (Ashton 1952, Gay 1982).

From this overview on property and its relationship to the capitalist and pre-capitalist modes of production, it is suggested that there are some elements which might be applicable in understanding how the 1979 Land Act could contribute to the transformation of ideas and practices about property in Sotho society. Prior to 1979 land could arguably and crudely be described as common property, held in trust by the King on behalf of the Basotho nation. Land currently is state property, held in trust by the King as head of State. The leasing mechanism of the Land Act 1979 allows for a greater amount of exclusivity with regard to cropland than previously known in Sotho society, but stops short of freehold and thereby implies some limitations and/or conditions attached to the use and/or transfer of such property. It also allows for the introduction of absentee ownership on the part of the state and sub-lessors, both groups of which will possess claims to revenue.

In the Lesotho situation the introduction of claims to revenue is justified by the Act's proponents as necessary to development, specifically in the case of the state for the provision of services and infrastructure. Sub-lessors' claim on revenue is justified in the Lesotho case by proponents of the Land Act on the understanding that development, i.e. increased GNP, trade, diversification of capital base, will occur with the formation of an indigenous landlord base.

It seems that there is a convergence in the Land Act 1979 between two different tendencies. One tendency is for the capitalist mode of production to bring with itself the dominance of the bourgeois property form, the ownership of the means of production and the continual destruction of all other preceding forms of property in its wake. Another tendency identified is the modification of the capitalist mode of production and with that a concomitant modification in the character of bourgeois property. Because the market no longer allocates all resources, leaving more and more of such allocation to the state, then actual ownership of resources *per se* becomes less important in comparison with rights to revenue from the employment of resources. The consequence for land in Lesotho and in other parts of the developing world without a long history of freehold could be the formation of a compromise arriving from the convergence of these two tendencies. Nevertheless, as is argued throughout the book, although the Land Act 1979 may seem like such a compromise, the provisions of the legislation remain uneven in their implementation and politically controversial.

1.2   Law and custom in underdeveloped societies

On the operability and inoperability of law

In the last section of the chapter the focus was on property, its various forms as determined by the dominant mode of production. There was in addition a brief look at Sotho property relations, circa 1937, which suggested that a mixture of common and private rights were evident in Lesotho (or Basutoland as it was known then), although the nature of private rights with regard to land were vastly different from those more absolute rights associated with cattle. Nevertheless, relatives by blood and marriage could at that time exert claims over some of the cattle owned and wives could exert claims over some portion of produce cultivated on land allocated to husbands. Legislation has sought in Lesotho as elsewhere to adjust, sometimes even to transform, social relations on the land. Time and again legislation has proved inoperable, with rural producers reverting to previous customary practices (Cliffe and Lawrence 1988).

The vexed question of what extent the same kinds of claims still in practice obtain in the rural areas of Lesotho, is a major concern of later chapters. Part of that concern will be to see how far the changed situation is a result of legislative changes. It is therefore useful to turn now to that part of the theoretical dilemma which concerns the relationship between law and practice. How does one explain law? Marxist concepts of law's relationship to society generally posit law as part of an ideological and/or repressive superstructure which reflects and protects the social relationships of the economic base (Pashukanis 1987, pp. 43-46). As the economic base transforms itself with changes in production methods, so, it is argued, that law too changes, is transformed (or not) but nevertheless is bounded in a dynamic way to serving in the final instance the dominant mode of production. This conception comes close to seeing law as functional for emerging and/or existing dominant interests. Implicit in this view is that law is usually operable in terms of serving those interests. More recently, some Marxists have departed from the over-determining 'base-reflects-superstructure-argument' and see law as an important arena for struggle (competing class or factional interests may conflict) in which concessions can be won from the dominant class by subordinate groups. In exploring these two Marxian views one implication for the book is that which specifically surrounds the question of the operability or inoperability of law.

Issa Shivji's work *Law, State and the Working Class in Tanzania* (1986) makes use of both perspectives in his discussion of the development of labour laws in Tanzania. The first view he identifies as 'instrumentalist'. The Hut and Poll Tax of 1922 that Shivji makes reference to could for instance be termed instrumental, not only in the crude sense of raising revenue, but more importantly in the indirect sense of creating a steady supply of labour (Shivji 1986, p. 12). The law as an arena for struggle argument is represented by what Shivji calls 'law's political character'. 'By political characteristic we refer to that aspect of law which encapsulates or embodies either the results of class struggle or is meant to control class struggle.' Here too, it is ultimately the interests of the ruling/dominating class that are served. Nevertheless, Shivji continues, 'they are mediated through and do embody partial successes and gains made by the ruled/dominated classes' (Shivji 1986, p. 3). This may prove of special significance in the Lesotho case in not only trying to explain

24

the hybrid nature of the tenure reform on land, but also the partial nature of its *de facto* implementation. To what extent can these two observations of the Lesotho case be explained as political concessions to subordinate classes? Examples of laws which he identifies as primarily political include those on Trade Unions and Trade Unions dispute settlement. Shivji also recognizes a third characteristic to law, which he terms ideological, i.e. a form of 'social consciousness which mystifies and disguises real relations of life'. For Shivji, ideology can only reflect partially the real relations of life. This is due to the class-based character of ideology. Nevertheless law, Shivji tells us, permeates everyone's daily lives and is not as abstracted from the real relations of society as is philosophy or religion. This, Shivji argues, is because law 'has to regulate real relations on earth, albeit relations as perceived by and in the interest of the ruling class' (ibid., p. 3).

Shivji's categorizations are useful for this study, in particular because, as he says, '...[w]hich particular aspect or characteristic of law is dominant would differ from society and with different types of legislation and within the same society in different historical periods' (ibid., p. 3). He does imply that the relative operability or inoperability of a particular piece of legislation may very well be related to the particular type of law. Although Shivji does not systematically address the vexed issue of operability, which for the purpose of the book is defined as the effectiveness of law on the ground, there is the distinct impression that laws of an instrumental character are operable as a general rule. Laws of a political character, some of which may embody the partial gains and concessions of the oppressed classes, on the other hand, could be 'continuously eroded by non-enforcement and biases of the administrators ...' (ibid., p. 150). There are no hints with regard to the effectiveness on the ground of legislation with a predominantly ideological character, because such laws dictate the terms of what is essentially an unequal contest between capital and labour.

> Such notions as conciliation between capital and labour when capital-labour relation is inherently contradictory, or setting up of tripartite arbitration tribunals which assume equality between capital and labour on the one hand and neutrality of the state on the other, are eminently ideological in character. (Ibid., p. 173)

Robert Seidman in *State, Law and Development*, (1978) provides another model which may prove useful in helping to assess the conditions under which a law is practised or not 'on the ground'. Distinguishing between real development, i.e. 'The processes by which the state acting through the legal order seeks to solve the problems of the poor, poverty and oppression', and 'soft' development, i.e. laws and practices which do nothing or exacerbate the problems, Seidman (1978, p. 468) addresses the role of law in the perpetuation (or not) of development policies and practices which have contributed to a stagnation in the development of appropriate political and economic institutions in most of the 'Third World'. Concentrating on evidence from Anglophone Africa, Seidman says that 'Soft development results inevitably from the contradictions between an authoritative legal order and the participative imperatives of development' (1978, p. 468). The contradictions themselves are a product of the colonial legacy and class conflict. Seidman builds into his model the notion that 'the legal order advantages particular strata' (ibid., p. 463) and that the various strata 'constantly contend to control the state to introduce or maintain a legal order to their own advantage' (ibid., p. 463). Further, Seidman outlines three devices used to maintain the advantage:

> By [making] laws, policies and official activity that directly benefit some strata and deprive others; by [making] laws, policies and official activity that delegate to some strata and not to others authority to make particular decisions; and ... by endowing officials with discretionary power which they ineluctably use to advantage some strata and to disadvantage others. (Ibid., pp. 463-464)

Colonial rule brought with it a legal order that 'created and reinforced the economic advantage of foreign firms and their managers and owners, mass poverty, political rule by a small elite, national dependency on the metropolitan countries, and the hinterlands' dependency on the export enclave' (ibid., p.464). Seidman's main thesis in his book is that that colonial creation has not been destroyed and replaced by a legal order more amenable to the needs of the majority in Africa. Instead colonial rule ended in most of Anglophone Africa with a 'handing over' of the state apparatus, including the legal order to a political elite who 'largely retained input and feedback circuits between themselves, other members of the political elite, and the economic ruling class and did not create new input and feedback circuits between themselves and the mass' (ibid., p. 464). Further, the political elites in retaining the colonial legal order were able to create opportunities for themselves to 'enter the private sector as entrepreneurs and rentiers ...' (ibid., p. 464).

Besides Seidman's clear and useful way of tying together class and the legacy of colonialism within the context of state, law and development, he also recognizes the extent to which law is used to encourage the development of a classical market economy. One important equation for capitalist development is thus: The market economy is a free society and its legal analogue is the law of contract (ibid., pp. 80-81). Laws of contract are what Seidman calls

Facilitative Law. These laws facilitate contracts between parties and assist in parties fulfilling their contractual obligations to one another. Within the classical free-market perspective facilitative laws are an expression of social co-operation within the state as 'neutral' institution guaranteeing voluntariness and freedom and the market as 'an invisible hand' which privileges no-one above another. However, Seidman reminds us from an anti-classical or alternative perspective that

> Parties to bargains seldom bargain from equal strength. To the extent of this inequality the contract process is inherently coercive ... A law to give two unequals equal legal rights against each other ensures dominance by the stronger. (Ibid., p. 81)

In short Seidman sees facilitative law 'in a society of unequals' as a way of transferring social '... power to make and enforce law to the economically strong. In this view facilitative law may be as authoritarian as any other law' (ibid., p. 81). In this way 'Facilitative' law echoes the more draconian features and intention behind 'instrumental' laws.

Seidman's model advances Shivji's argument then on two main counts, for showing how the basis of the colonial legal system survived political independence and for providing an explanation as to why some law does not work, or more precisely the conditions under which law is operable. These hypotheses are at the centre of my argument about the Land Act 1979, its origins and the extent of its operability, especially with regard to the introduction of the leasehold mechanism. Nonetheless, questions remain; neither Seidman nor Shivji explain why some law is inoperable. Is the Land Act 1979 a concession won by class struggle? Is it an ideological law, or is its very 'inoperability' in the interests of the dominant/governing class?

Customary law and civil law

Another theoretical area of major concern to do with law deals with issues around law and custom and whether there is a 'dual' system of law attempting to operate in underdeveloped countries. Such questions are important; it may be that a major factor in explaining the operability or inoperability of legislation is the resilience and effectiveness of the practices that existed prior to the legislation. And this may in some sense help to explain the persistence of some aspects of traditional forms of social practices. There is at the same time a concern with how notions of legal dualism parallel the economic dualism of modernization theories.

Articulating modes of production would stress not the static 'independent' character of the earlier law, which is the tendency of some dualists. Instead an articulationist approach would tend to focus on the relationship between two systems of law, both changing, but more importantly one system inferior to the other. Sotho law and custom constantly change in conjunction with new economic and social conditions, and like other law reinforce the political economy of which it is a part as well as providing an arena for struggle between conflicting social strata.

Conventional analysis of law in Southern Africa presupposes a duality, even a plurality (owing to Roman-Dutch influence) of laws. Such a dual legal system refers to customary and 'received' law. The latter being that body of European law which has been imposed/adopted by the colonial and post-colonial state. But what has come to be called 'Modern' law in the Anglophone colonies, was according to Seidman 'a truncated, limited version of English law — and a version not merely old-fashioned, but skewed in a particular direction' (Seidman 1968-69, p. 114). The bias Seidman refers to are the interests of the capitalist class (which can include political, ideological and facilitative/instrumentalist measures to the economy) prior to the latter part of the 19th century. This bias was entrenched in African law because, at the technical level, many of the reception statutes were dated prior to the beginning of what later became the Welfare State.

As a result much of received law in East and West Africa in particular is devoid of regulatory laws to protect workers, the aged and infirm. In their words some of the laws which could be interpreted as partial concessions to the working classes were not imported to Africa. In Central and Southern Africa the situation was slightly different; because the reception date is later, it is not a technical factor which prevented welfare-type legislation from being imported, but rather the motivations of the colonial state. Some welfare-oriented protection was put into place in Central and Southern Africa, although of a different character and with different consequences than that put into effect in England. Seidman claims that the political motivation was not to alleviate the poor and dispossessed, neither was it brought into effect as a response to class struggle.

> Rather, [colonial welfare legislation] ... has been merely to ensure that African labour was maintained at a level at which it might reproduce itself. State power was not used to bring about a significant redistribution of wealth, but rather to make possible the continued exploitation of Africans. (Seidman 1968-69, p. 116)

These points are significant for an analysis of the Lesotho case. In later chapters the role of land as a source of social security becomes more developed. In the absence of protective regulations on land transfers, there is a danger that that source of 'welfare' will be eroded.

Having looked at the origins of received law in Africa, I want to do the same with regard to customary law. Customary law is supposedly that body or doctrine of norms of conflict resolution said to be indigenous to the colonized society. During the colonial era it was applied with respect to disputes between Africans. Customary law understood within this approach refers to what A. Allott (1970) called 'indigenous law' and serves in many ways to reinforce the notion of British 'indirect' rule and the supposedly benign and *laissez-faire* character of the 'indirect' method of British colonization. Lloyd Fallers (1969) injects into the debate the question of power when he defines customary law 'as a legal situation wherein ... a dominant legal system supports and reinforces the local law of a politically subordinated community' (p.101).

Other writers, e.g. Francis Snyder (1982) and Martin Chanock (1982), have rejected the legal dualism thesis altogether, arguing instead that customary law is itself a colonial construct, and that customary law is no more reflective of pre-colonial custom and conflict resolution than a labour reserve is reflective of a pre-capitalist social formation. Snyder, for example, has shown in work on peasant land disputes in Senegal how what is recognized by many in society as customary law is the creature of on the one hand the colonial state, and on the other hand, in the Senegalese case, '... of rural conflicts involving fluid alliances ... frequently expressed within and mediated by the local institutions of the colonial state.' For Snyder the formation of customary law, like any other kind of law, is intimately bound up with class formation (Snyder 1982, p. 108).

Martin Chanock's work on Malawi and Zambia (1978, 1982) is also interesting, not only in that it follows Snyder's concern with the colonial construction of customary law along lines that created and empowered some classes of society over others (to the benefit of the colonialist project) through the codification of 'custom'. In addition Chanock is concerned with how the colonial construction of customary law contributed not only to the 'management' of the colonial state by colonizers in unequal partnership with so-called 'traditional' authorities but he does this by looking at the transformation of social relations between men and women. According to Chanock, African law in Southern and Central African societies represents the

> ... reaction of older men to a loss of control [over their societies] ... this reaction grew in strength over the first 30 to 40 years of the colonial period. Then in accordance with the policy of indirect rule a large portion of the administration of justice was turned over to precisely those people who had reason to define and more importantly to administer the law in a restrictive and authoritarian way. These definitions form the basis of current African law. (Chanock 1978, p. 80)

29

Chiefs in particular translated their values into colonial legal forms in order to compensate for a loss of authority. The destruction of old systems of social organization set off an imbalance of power mechanisms in African societies. This imbalance 'threw into flux the ways by which men controlled women and women were quick to take advantage of this.' Western contact with its strains on relationships at all levels, including those between men and women, were further exacerbated by demands of the colonial state and economy and increasingly so by the especially damaging effects of the migrant labour system. The language of customary law was used to legitimate new claims, as conflicts 'over the uses and effects of money, and over the control of the labour of others, required solution.' Similar forces were at work in Basutoland and led to the codification of what was at least according to some members of the Sotho ruling group, custom, i.e. The Laws of Lerotholi. The Laws of Lerotholi is an important source of law, and also carries with it much ideological clout, especially for the chieftaincy — as a symbol of nationhood, tradition and independence. Procedures for land allocation, administration and revocation are in the Laws of Lerotholi. The land legislation of the post-colonial state attempts to replace some of the features of custom. Part of the intention behind the book is to assess to what extent on-the-ground reality matches law. Along the way we shall gauge the extent to which practice departs from those rules laid down at the beginning of the century.

Still another question surrounds the reasons why the colonial state did not introduce a law of contract regarding land. Commoditization of labour was introduced by instrumentalist law to create a plentiful supply of labour. Why not introduce capitalist social relations on land as well? While not wanting to pre-empt the discussion in later chapters, the hypothesis is offered that while the colonial project in Lesotho was to supply the mines and farms of South Africa with labour, it was politically pressed to do so in such a way that the expense would be as minimal as possible; hence the costs of the reproduction of labour power would be deferred on to African areas.

One author who has made inroads into the disparity between new land and the persistence of the residual forms of customary practice is Sally Falk Moore (1986). In particular her work on the Chagga of Tanzania proves very useful on this question. For Moore two related issues are paramount. One issue deals with 'the question of the formation of class strata' and how that process involves 'sorting out relative advantage' (Moore 1986, p. 11). Another broader issue is the 'tension that can exist between activities in the domain of individual strategy and activities in the domain of law and formal organization' (Moore 1986, p. 11). Moore claims that social change cannot be understood outside of these issues, and moreover that what is considered 'legal' and 'illegal' 'must be approached analytically as parts of a single system' if we are to understand why some laws fail 'on the ground' (ibid.). Chapter 6 on cropland transactions will deal with this question in more detail.

Finally in this section I introduce the alternative theoretical perspective of Boaventura de Sousa Santos (1985, pp. 299-336) which arises out of a concern to analyse in a dynamic way several levels of analysis, i.e. 'the household place, the workplace, the citizenplace and the worldplace' and relate these various levels with different kinds of law (Santos 1985, p. 307). Santos writes of the articulation of the above four 'primary clusters of social relations' and their related 'mode of production of law'. Within each mode of production of law there is a form of law, a set of social practices, an institutional form, a mechanism of social power, and a mode of rationality associated with each system.

> The social relations clustered around the household place are constitutive of the mutual obligations imposed on family members and consist mainly of the relations between husband and wife and between either and the children and more generally of kinship relations. The social relations clustered around the workplace [under capitalism] are constitutive of the labour process and consist of both the relations of production at the level of the enterprise (between direct producers and appropriators of surplus value) and the relations in production (between workers and management and among workers). (Santos 1985, p. 307)

Those relations associated with the citizenplace likewise are made up of elements around the 'so-called public sphere and consist of relations between the citizen and state' (ibid.), ... 'those around the worldplace are the relations among the nation-states as they integrate into the world economy' (ibid., pp. 307-8). The modes of production concept is not used to refer necessarily to non-capitalist, or pre-capitalist articulation with the capitalist system, rather Santos is concerned to get to grips with two conceptual problems associated with the school of observers who recognize 'the plurality of law in society'. Those problems as identified by Santos are

> Firstly, the conception of a plurality of legal systems within the same political space could lead to a relative neglect of the state law as a central form of law in our societies ...; secondly, once the concept of law was disengaged from the concept of the state, the identification of a plurality of laws would know no limit with the result that, if law is everywhere it is nowhere. (Ibid., p. 299)

Santos' own solution to the problem is to construct a model through which the relationships between different kinds of law, i.e. Domestic, Production, Profit Maximizing, Territorial and Systematic law, including the official and the unofficial (the latter of which Santos (1987) found in operation in the Brazilian *favela* of Pasargada) can be mapped. Santos' model is useful as another perspective to add to those outlines, firstly because it represents an attempt to analytically combine several levels of analysis, household, workplace, nation-state and international community. Secondly the model furnished embraces the legal and extra-legal, official and unofficial kinds of law, and as such it provides a perspective through which the systematic 'gaps' between law and reality can be analysed.

In using this model to look specifically at property, law and land, it is important to recognize that it is a matter for the nation-state in that it involves issues of contract law, but more crucially it has a bearing on relations in and between households. It is appropriate therefore that perspectives on households are isolated, especially as it is a site of continued production and intra-household relations, and especially as this affects the position of women (featured in previous sections).

In conclusion, there are two main theoretical/conceptual areas which I will refer to throughout the book in order to help unravel the significance of the Land Act 1979 and assess its place within the context of previous land legislation, agrarian policy and other more underlying social trends in Lesotho. The concept in and around articulation of modes of production, despite its myriad of drawbacks, still promises to be analytically useful for describing the partially preserved, partially destroyed existence of non-capitalist forms of social relations from the level of production, well into and throughout the superstructure, which includes issues of property and law. The literature on property is vast. The brief overview outlined did however provide a perspective on how conceptions of property have changed not just from epoch to epoch but within the capitalist epoch as well, the rights and obligations around private property have changed as the nature of the relationship between the state and capitalism has altered. In contemporary society property is less of a right to things, and more and more often coming to be associated as a right to revenue. I believe such an insight might be of some use in helping to explain the introduction of *leasehold*, (i.e. revenue-collecting aspect of the 1979 Land Act) rather than *freehold* in land policy in Lesotho. Finally in the area of law and custom I will be concerned throughout the book with the issues which have been debated, i.e. what is the relationship between law and custom? Is there a duality of law, a plurality? What are the limitations of law for affecting social change? What is the nature of the 'gap' between law in lawbooks, and everyday practice?

2 Chiefs and land in the political economy of Lesotho (1820-1930)

Introduction

In this chapter we are concerned with outlining two separate but interrelated processes in the early political economy of Lesotho. The first process centres on the development of the material base of the social formation, in relation to land use and administration. The second process centres on the formation of the state and the role of chiefs therein. Towards this end the chapter focuses on the period 1820-1930. We use 1820 as a starting point for our discussion inasmuch as it is held significant by the Basotho themselves as symbolizing the beginning of the nation and it gives 48 years of pre-colonial experience to contrast with the post-1868 period. We close this chapter at 1930 because the year marks the beginning of the end of Lesotho's days as a grain exporting country, witnesses the institutionalization of restrictions on the import of Lesotho agricultural produce to South Africa, and presages colonial reforms to the chieftaincy with the publication of the Pim Report in 1935. But more importantly, from our point of view, the period between 1820 and 1930 sees the rise and consolidation of new kinds of chiefly powers with regard especially to the use of arable land. The chapter is composed of three sections. The first section discusses the circumstances around the creation of the Sotho nation with emphasis on issues related to chiefs' administrative powers over land. Following the establishment of the origins of Lesotho, we then turn to a discussion of the early Sotho state and the chiefs' role during the first half of the colonial period. The third section looks at the codification of so-called 'traditional' law and land tenure in Lesotho.

2.1   Creation of the Nation

The Basotho nation is a product of the *lifaqane* or period of calamities that accompanied the rise of Shaka and the Zulu Empire. The Sotho and Nguni peoples who had migrated over the previous one thousand years from Central and East Africa into Southern Africa suffered tremendous social upheaval, war, famine as a result of Zulu expansion (Casalis 1971, Ellenberger 1969, Lye 1969).

In explaining the rise and the historical tenacity of the Basotho nation, most commentators focus on the diplomatic and political attributes of Moshoeshoe, generally thought of as 'Father of the Basotho' (Thompson 1975, Sanders 1975). Born in 1786, Lepoqo the first son of a minor chief earned his initial fame among his people as an excellent cattle raider. He gave himself the name Moshoeshoe to celebrate his skill at shaving his victim's beard metaphorically, by stealing his enemies' cattle. 'Moshoeshoe' is an onomatopoeic rendering of the sound made by a razor shaving.

Having proven himself as a potential leader with his cattle raiding successes, Moshoeshoe set himself up as village headman and moved to Butha-Buthe. Meanwhile in the east Shaka was beginning the process of expansion which led to the rise of the Zulu Empire. Other linguistic groups fought Zulu hegemony and some perished in the attempt. It was Moshoeshoe's handling of the crisis which earned him the title 'Morena oa Basotho' (Father of the Basotho).   Instead of launching attacks against the Zulu, Moshoeshoe consolidated his own position in the area by paying tribute (in cattle and grain) to some Southern African groups, e.g. the Zulu, while offering refuge and protection to other groups in exchange for tribute. He also moved south to Thaba Bosiu, a flat-topped summit rising 380 feet from the fertile valley of the South Phutiatsana River (see Appendix). The area was easily defensible against military attack and offered plentiful springs and good pasturage.

In the late 1820s, with a population of approximately 3,000 people, Lesotho was comprised of various Sotho clans, Tswanas, Koras, and Griquas (Palmer and Parsons 1977, p. 21). Several mechanisms were used by Moshoeshoe to ensure the allegiance of his subjects and to accumulate wealth and power (Kimble 1985, pp. 33-35). One was through the use of *mafisa* cattle, whereby cattle are loaned to loyal retainers, i.e. politically favoured men. Although the royal cattle (i.e. the cattle owned and accumulated by chiefs) remained the property of the chief, dairy products and some of the offspring became the property of the retainer. Not all cattle were owned by chiefs, but grazing rights were determined by chiefs, and chiefs did exercise strong controls over the main means of production, i.e. land and cattle. This control would be strengthened under the colonial state. Tribute labour or *matsema* was also a very important device for securing wealth. Under this system each adult subject had to supply labour to the chief's fields during certain times in the agricultural year. Still another device for acquiring wealth and influence was through marriage with royal women from subordinate groups. It is reported that Moshoeshoe had 400 wives. For the other members of Moshoeshoe's lineage cross-cousin marriage became an important way of safeguarding the family's accumulated wealth. Finally, Moshoeshoe also instituted the unique practice of 'placing' his sons as chiefs over portions of the country. All of these practices led to the accumulation of wealth by Moshoeshoe and the senior members of his lineage. In turn this ruling group engaged in their extensive mercantilist network in the region; exchanging Basotho grains, wheat, sorghum, and maize for cattle, ploughs and later horses and guns (Kimble 1985).

In contrast to those commentators on the history of Lesotho who emphasize the charismatic appeal of Moshoeshoe, other writers find the significant causes of the nation's growth and tenacity in internal and external social forces and political policies which allowed some sections of the Basotho to prosper. Colin Murray (1980, 1981), Colin Bundy (1979) and the team of Neil Parsons and Robin Palmer (1977) have documented the 'Granary to Labour Reserve' transition undergone by most Black societies of Southern Africa, including the Batswana, Swazis, as well as the Basotho. As a granary, Lesotho traded with Griquas and the trek Boers of the Orange River area from the last 1820s if not earlier. The Basotho traded sorghum and maize for sheep and wheat. Structural efficiency in the economy was evidenced by the subsequent production of these goods as well as other popular imports by the Basotho.

Several reasons have been put forward to explain the rise of Lesotho as the granary of South Africa. Of most relevance to this book are those factors associated with land.

Firstly Lesotho in the 1820s and 1830s covered much more geographical area than it does today (see Appendix). Land west of the Caledon River was particularly fertile and was characterized by 'a hilly patchwork of "sweet" and "sour" pastures with high stock-carrying capacity and soils virtually self-fertilized by the action of the rains on phosphate-bearing rocks and able to carry ten to fifteen crops in rotation' (Palmer and Parsons 1977, p. 21). It was recorded in 1833 that the land between the river and the foot of the mountain was covered with sorghum and maize. Stored reserves of some grains were found by missionaries to be four to eight years old. The Basotho had quickly adopted the use of the plough and the increased productivity which resulted allowed them to diversify into producing wheat and raising sheep for export. In the mid-1850s the Basotho began to plough the lowlands extensively as well as buy wagons for use in transporting goods to market.

In the meantime the Boers had begun their trek in search of more land and greater political autonomy. It was perhaps inevitable that land would become a source of tension between African and Boer inasmuch as 6,000 acres was the size of the ideal Afrikaner farm (Bardill and Cobbe 1985, p. 12). The Boers began to occupy the western area of the Caledon in the 1850s. In the next decade the Basotho attempted to reclaim the area by herding cattle there and expelling the Afrikaners. In 1868 the Afrikaners retaliated by destroying Basotho crops east of the Caledon river.

As early as 1841 Moshoeshoe made diplomatic overtures to the British whom he saw as the only group powerful enough to restrain the Boers, to help the Basotho keep their land. Moshoeshoe entered into a treaty with Sir George Napier, British Commissioner in 1843 which recognized a considerable portion of Basotho territorial claims. The Boers too were pressing on the British, as indeed was the issue of policing costs to fulfil British promises to secure the border. At any rate the treaty Moshoeshoe signed with Sir Peregrine Maitland in 1848 was less beneficial to the Basotho than the one recognized earlier. A reduction of territory in the southeast was made to appease Afrikaner claims, in return for a British guarantee to control further Afrikaner encroachment.

By 1869 the Basotho had lost to the Afrikaners most of the land they had occupied on the west of the Caledon. This territory 'contained half of the total arable area in all Basutoland' (Bardill and Cobbe 1985, p. 16). Lesotho was annexed through the Proclamation of March 12, 1868 which extended British protection to the Basotho. Because this act was 'clearly induced by the need for securing peace on the frontiers of the Cape Colony and Natal, it seemed logical that one of these colonies should assume responsibility for administration.'

It was later decided that Basutoland would come under the administration of the Cape Colony. This period of Cape administration was to last from 1871 to 1883 (Burman 1976, 1981).

This initial phase of colonial domination coincided with the discovery of diamonds in South Africa (1870). The new economic conditions fostered a rapid development of markets. The opening of the Kimberley mines in the early years of the decade was not only an opportunity to maximize agricultural production for the external market, but also provided an opportunity to release some of the pressure on land through wage labour (Murray 1980, pp. 5-6).

The expropriation of Basotho land deprived the Basotho of some of their most fertile valleys, and this in turn affected the ability of some Basotho to produce enough for their subsistence needs. Migrant labour at this point would supplement household production, and enable households to purchase

36

goods increasingly available on the market: western type clothing, horses, cattle, and especially ploughs to intensify production on land currently available to them or promised to them in future (Palmer and Parsons 1977, p. 21). The Basotho have however never lost sight of the fact that the western lands were theirs. Hopes to regain the 'Conquered Territory' have lasted through the years and have at times conditioned the post-colonial state's dealings with RSA.

Accounts of the so-called Basotho 'penchant' for adopting Western ways during the last part of the nineteenth century has been used by Sandra Burman and others to show the ease with which the Basotho adapted to new economic forces in the region. Burman (1976, p. 1) has said: 'Of all Southern African tribes ...[the Basotho] were thought to be the most willing and able to adopt foreign laws and values.' For an instance of such conduct Parsons and Palmer cites an 1875 census as providing several indices to gauge the prosperity enjoyed by the Basotho nation. The population of 128,000 owned some 2,700 ploughs, 300 wagons and nearly 224,000 cattle and 300,000 sheep. While in 1872 there were thirty trading stores in Lesotho and the nation imported goods worth 150,000 and exported 100,000 *muids* (84kg each) of grain, there were also signs of increased stratification in the nation (Palmer and Parsons 1977, pp. 21-22).

Already on the eve of colonial rule the seeds had been sown which would yield less land and greater competition over its use and control. Population pressure and land shortage led to an increase in the number of land disputes. First and most obviously the Basotho lost half of all the arable land they had held prior to Boer encroachment. Secondly, the population, (80,000 in 1847, 125,000 by 1869) was growing quite steadily, not only or especially through natural increase but through the continued influx of refugees, like many of the former followers of Manthatisi and Sekonyela to name the most important of these later groups arriving from the Cape Colony (Bardill and Cobbe 1985, p. 14). The congested conditions appear not to have adversely affected aggregate figures on agricultural production. What is interesting is that young Basotho men were at this early stage in their national history more likely to engage in migrant work than most other groups in the region at this time (Murray 1980, p. 5). They were however in a position to be very selective about when and under what circumstances and conditions they would migrate to the mines. Still another factor to affect Lesotho's agricultural capacity was the erection of trade barriers by the South Africans against Basotho produce and the importation of Australian and American wheat into South Africa. Labour migration could have been what Allan Low (1986, p. 49) would describe in *Agricultural Development in Southern Africa: Farm Household Economics and the Food Crisis* as a 'vent for surplus' path for under-employed labour but it is equally possible that less available land also meant that intensive forms of agriculture were being applied more vigorously requiring more hoes and cattle, both of which could be purchased with wage earnings. We can see here perhaps the beginnings of a cycle of over-cultivation, over-grazing and the subsequent soil erosion which characterizes the Lesotho landscape today (Chakela 1981). Nevertheless, this view should be tempered with an analysis of the history of the relationship between the colonial and post-colonial states' attempts at soil conservation on the one hand and the political economy of the migrant labour system on the other hand. Kay Showers (1981) argues that the widespread belief about Lesotho's soil erosion being a product of backward farming practices simply does not fit the historical record of the period between the 1830s and 1950s. Interpreting a broad range of sources in order to locate *when* acceleration of erosion began, *where* severe erosion took place and *what* responses were offered by the British colonial adminstration, Showers concludes:

1   '... Soil erosion was relatively rare in Lesotho before the arrival of the Europeans in the 1830s and only began to be noticeable in the late nineteenth century.' (Showers 1981, p. 272)

2   Most late nineteenth and early twentieth century Europeans travelled on paths between mission stations and government camps and regularly encountered some of the most seriously eroded land in the country ... 'the busy roads themselves were the site of most erosion and thus were not representative of most of the land. Nevertheless European travellers, most of whom did not venture too far past the road, possessed a very limited knowledge of Lesotho landscape.' (Ibid., p. 273)

3   'Much of the response of the British administration came in the form of reclamation projects with an emphasis on terracing. However, inadequate engineering works resulted in the uncontrolled movement of channelled water across the landscape after major storm events.' (Ibid., p. 286)

In effect Showers argues that ill-informed soil conservation techniques practiced by the colonial states caused much of Lesotho's chronic erosion problems.

2.2   State formation

Moshoeshoe is credited by some writers (e.g. Thompson 1975, Sanders 1975) with great political savvy in being able to secure protectorate status for the people under his rule. It was to a great extent the fact of British protection that kept South African claims to the territory at bay until the advent of political sovereignty in 1966. But while Moshoeshoe had succeeded in securing the borders, he still had to continue the process of consolidation within the country.

To a large extent the very fact of hostile neighbours forced a certain amount of unity on the 22 tribal and clan fragments that came together under Moshoeshoe's leadership. In addition to the necessity for cohesiveness borne out of the *lifaqane*, and out of the military campaigns against the Boers and the British (Breytenbach 1975), Moshoeshoe also set up political institutions that served both to assimilate the many groups into a nation while at the same time promoting his own lineage as the dominant cultural and political group in society.

The concept of the chieftaincy and its relationship to the monarchy is itself very important and the institution has undergone enormous changes over the past century. The social and cultural groups in Southern Africa prior to western intervention were divided into clans, families who traced their descent from a common ancestor. Clan differentiation is distinguished in many ways including identification with a common totem. Moshoeshoe's clan is Koena and their totem is the crocodile. Clans are frequently made up of lineages, where descent is traced to a less distant ancestor. Although the composition of a chiefdom is largely related there are frequently non-related members as well. Chiefly succession among the Sotho, like most groups in the region, is patrilineal with the office bestowed generally on the first son of the chief's senior wife. The pre-colonial situation saw Sotho chiefdoms as relatively small groupings of 300-400 people. This was possible given the enormous amount of land that was available. At that time it was not unusual for an individual, generally a junior son of a chief, to recruit some followers and settle elsewhere.

The institution of *pitso* provided a forum for adult male subjects to air their views on matters of concern to the chiefdom, especially boundary and military disputes. The *pitso* itself is a pre-colonial form of rulemaking common to most Sotho societies. The first national *pitso* in Lesotho was called by Moshoeshoe's father Mokgatjhane to address the issue of the rapid spread of Christianity. Moshoeshoe began to consult the adult men on a regular basis in 1864. National *pitsos* were called by the king; senior chiefs and headmen led the discussions and decisions were reached by consensus. After 1884 national *pitsos* became more of a ceremonial occasion than a decision-making one since by that time many of the functions of the national *pitso* had been taken over by other institutions (Breytenbach 1975).

A far more durable practice set in motion by Moshoeshoe was the 'placing system', a political institution which unlike the *pitso* was not a part of Sotho pre-colonial political practice. As early as 1835 Moshoeshoe began the process of 'placing' by dividing territorial authority among his kinsmen and loyal supporters. Moshoeshoe also kept those groups who he thought were less than loyal to his wardship on the fringes of the country occupying some of the harsher lands. The idea of placing appointed representatives in control of different areas of the country allows a direct and accountable link between central and regional authorities. The practice kept political power concentrated within the Koena group. To some extent it also guarded against intra-Koena rivalry since all sons and not just the eldest were entitled to a placing. Over the years the practice of placing became the prerogative of not only the Paramount Chief, but has been used by Principal Chiefs, ward chiefs, and at times even more junior authorities until the practice was ended with colonial reforms in 1938 (Weisfelder 1977, p. 165).

According to R.F. Weisfelder (1977, p. 165), writing on the Basotho Monarchy, there was at this time also a 'rudimentary bureaucracy' — commanders of a chief's personal regiment, an official responsible for 'security and ... a chief's village also included messengers (including *baabi* who actually did the work of demarcating boundaries of land holdings), counsellors — These functionaries served the monarch exclusively.'

With respect to land allocation and use, the institution of placing has had important and far-reaching consequences. The rights and obligations of a chief include allocating arable land, managing pasturage and extracting tribute labour (*matsema*). Chiefs had their own fields as well as those which were supposed to be for public use (Edgar undated, pp. 10-11 & 137-139). Chiefs were able to call on their subjects to work on these public fields prior to them working on their own (commoners') plots. Under the extremes of the placing system the number of these public fields called for a great deal of labour, especially during very crucial times in the agricultural calendar (Sheddick 1954, pp. 82-83). Controversy around public fields included problems around the distribution of the product. There is some evidence that the product was used originally for public festivals, but that the institution degenerated into one where the product was used mostly by Moshoeshoe and his family. Also, commoners complained that they were seldom left with enough time to work on their own fields (Edgar, pp. 137-139). Another complaint often made accused the chiefs of taking the best lands for themselves.

The British colonial authorities played an important role in the restructuring of the social and political landscape of Basotho. During the brief Cape Colony rule, the authorities attempted to radically alter the basis of chiefly power in Sotho society by limiting their powers over land and judicial matters. However in 1884 when the British assumed direct responsibility over

40

Basutoland a more subtle colonial approach was employed, although the anticipated transfer of Basutoland to South Africa was still palpable. Colonial authorities hereafter tended to support the position of the monarchy and to aid the royal line in the maintenance of its acceptability and political legitimacy (Weisfelder 1977, p. 169). For their part the ruling monarchs and senior chiefs, assumed a direct relationship between national survival and expansion of their own 'customary powers'. By supporting, indeed strengthening the monarchy and chieftancy, colonial authorities could avoid direct confrontation and 'keep the peace'. Such a peace would continue to serve the interests of the colonizers by ensuring (most importantly) that the costs of conquest and colonial administration would be borne by the colonized through taxation and migrant labour.

One way in which colonial authorities embellished the powers of chiefs was through the formation of the Basutoland National Council. Although this consultative body was not a legislature it was responsible for the codification of Basotho law and custom in *The Laws of Lerotholi* (1903) which is conventionally recognized as the definitive source for Basotho law (Duncan 1960, Poulter 1981, 1976, Hamnett 1975). Correspondingly, as was mentioned earlier, the political and administrative function of national *pitsos* declined after 1884. Several reasons have been given for this decline: according to W.J. Breytenbach (1975) the increase in the secular duties assigned to the king and senior chiefs called for a forum different from that of the *pitso*. Consultation generally had become a more specialized affair confined to the senior chiefs and exclusive of commoners. Finally it was the British administrator who proposed new consultation and communication processes in dealing with the population (Breytenbach 1975). To this end the National Council was formed in 1903 by Sir Marshall Clarke the first Resident Commissioner. The council was made up of 100 members, five of whom were nominated by the Resident Commissioner, the remainder appointed by the Paramount Chief. All of the senior chiefs were included, i.e. the Sons of Moshoeshoe. Breytenbach observes that

> ... it was not the intention of the British to substitute the National Council for indigenous chiefs but only to establish an additional avenue for the expression by the Basotho of opinions which might differ from those held by the senior chiefs. (Breytenbach 1975, p. 15)

The National Council had four sessions before it was replaced in 1910 by the Basutoland Council. The main difference between the former and the latter was that the Basutoland Council was recognized by the British as an official formalized institution authorized to discuss any proposed laws, suggest amendments, and 'to take note of collected revenue', as well as to discuss other domestic matters (Breytenbach 1975, p. 17).

Non 'chief based' institutions

Another important set of institutions rose up to counter the chieftaincy and its increasing hold on the society. These were the Basutoland Progressive Association (BPA) and Lekgotla la Bafo (LLB). In order to fully comprehend the nature of these organizations it is necessary to keep in mind not only the exclusive composition of the Basutoland Council with its strong paramountcy at the apex but also to look at the rise of a small educated middle class precipitated by missionary education.

The organization began in 1907 and attracted 'teachers, interpreters, and clerical officers for the government and missions' (Bardill and Cobbe 1985, p. 31). Historically the Paris Evangelical Mission (PEMS) held sway in Christianizing the Basotho, but the Catholic Church began to dominate in religious influence from the 1940s (Bardill and Cobbe 1985, p. 30). While the Protestants were associated with the urban lowland areas, the Catholics' best infiltration efforts were in the mountains. There were other differences in strategy as well. The Protestants were known for their disdain of the chieftaincy and their campaigns to get rid of aspects of traditional life not to their liking. The Catholics on the other hand turned their attention to converting the chiefs, confident that loyal commoners would follow suit. The Catholics practised a more lenient attitude to Basotho social practices like polygyny and *bohali*, allowing members to continue these 'traditions' while belonging also to the Catholic faith. Bardill and Cobbe sum up the situation briefly when they say,

> Over time, therefore, the Catholic missionaries came to be associated with the defence of the customary status quo and with strenuous resistance to changes that seemed to threaten it. The resulting conflict with the more radical Protestant churches had a lasting and divisive impact on Basotho society. (Bardill and Cobbe 1985, p. 31)

At the level of political organization, further schisms occurred in Sotho society. Differing social attitudes to and political strategies towards colonialism were reflected in the BPA and the LLB. The Basutoland Progressive Association was essentially reformist and anti-'traditional'. It did not challenge colonial rule although it levied harsh criticisms on the chieftaincy.

The BPA's stance was in marked contrast to that of the LLB which was founded in 1919 (Edgar undated, Introduction). The latter's commoner base made it much more the voice of those without a vested interest in the chieftaincy or in colonial officialdom. Although it did not attack the institution of the chieftaincy directly, the organization did focus on the malpractices of chiefs including the paramountcy. It was also much more anti-colonial than the BPA and vigorously attacked the Basutoland Council for its collaboration with British rule. Very early on in its career, the LLB under the leadership of Josiel Lefela established contacts with the African National Congress in South Africa and, owing to the fact that the LLB's access to other publications had been withdrawn in the 1920s, published its attacks in the South African Communist Party paper, *The Worker*. Although the LLB was not popular with the colonial state and has been portrayed as a marginal extremist element in the struggle for self-determination, Bardill and Cobbe recognize the organization as having contributed far more than is conventionally accepted (Bardill and Cobbe 1985, p. 32). It was the LLB that realized that Lesotho's fate was inextricably bound up with that of South Africa, and as a result they saw the need for a strong alliance between the forces there of nationalism and self-reliance and their own aspirations for Lesotho. In the end the LLB was not able to amass strong support and further undermined its chances of leadership in the run-up to political independence by refusing '... rightly or wrongly, to enter into discussions of any kind with the British [colonial state]...' (Bardill and Cobbe 1985, p. 32). Such abdication created a vacuum that was to be filled by the political parties of the post-war nationalist movements, which will be discussed in Chapter 3.

2.3   The codification and construction of customary law and land tenure rules

The National Council set the legal tone of the nation with its codification of customary law (cf. Ranger 1983, pp. 20-41, Snyder 1982, op.cit., Chanock 1978, p. 198 op.cit.). Ian Hamnett (1975) and other authors (Poulter 1976, 1981, Burman 1981) have been concerned with the artificial nature of this codification process. The council, dominated at this time by the senior chiefs, set out in the Laws of Lerotholi (so named after Lerotholi, Moshoeshoe's heir after his death in March 1870) their view as to the duties and obligations of the chieftaincy and most importantly cemented the pre-eminent position of the paramount chief as dynastic heir of Moshoeshoe and hence the most senior chief in the nation. Although the Paramountcy is a symbol of Sotho nationhood it is equally a convenient institution in colonial terms. As Ian Hamnett has pointed out,

> The British authorities nearly always tended to support the Paramount Chiefs, no doubt for reasons of common political prudence; and the territory could be administered with less trouble if the Resident

Commissioner had one centralized ruler to deal with at national level. (Hamnett 1975, p. 35)

At independence the Paramount Chief was recognized as king.

In essence we can see then that condification of customary law was politically beneficial to the colonial state. In the following discussion it will be suggested that 'codification of customary law' was also crucial for the 'smooth' operation of the migrant labour system, itself subsidized by the ability of Sotho society to subordinate women's labour on the one hand and the tenacity of chiefly administration of land on the other hand. This guaranteed no complex proletarianization, nor social control, even of migrants.

With reference to land allocation the Laws of Lerotholi state that every married male Mosotho is entitled to the use of three fields of approximately two to three acres each. There have been several editions of the Laws, with some editions seeming to erode the rights of some groups at the expense of others. For example, while in the earlier (i.e. pre-1922) renderings, the rights of every Mosotho to have access to cropland and pasturage were emphasized, subsequently it was the rights of chiefs to allocate the use of land that were highlighted (*Laws of Lerotholi 1919, 1922, 1930, 1946*, Part I). Along with the right to allocate land came the right to administer rules and regulations regarding its use. Under this customary law it is possible for a household to lose access to some of its holdings if the household fails to cultivate the land over a specified period of time, usually two years (*Laws of Lerotholi*, Part I 7[3]). The chief also can take away some of a household's holdings if it is deemed that the household has more than enough for its subsistence (*Laws of Lerotholi* Part I 7[2]).

From the period of 1820 through to the late 1930s there was seemingly an increase in the power of chiefs over the administration of land among the Basotho. Some indication of this can be inferred from the constructed nature of the major source of law in the land, *The Laws of Lerotholi*, from the introduction of the placing system with its multiplication of courts and public fields, all of which enhanced chiefly claims to the best lands etc. and in turn led to crisis in the institution of the chieftancy in the late 1930s. At a time when there were 800,000 people in Lesotho there were 1,100 chiefs (Hamnett 1975, p. 86). Still another aspect of the chieftaincy adversely affecting commoners' claims to land involved the chiefs' role as tax collectors on behalf of the colonial state and their role as labour procurers for the gold and diamond mines in South Africa during the early part of the century.

Lesotho is part of what Samir Amin has called 'Africa of the Labour reserves', which is to say that Lesotho as part of the Southern Africa region was integrated into the world capitalist network through the particular nexus of migrant labour (Amin 1972). As mentioned previously the discovery of diamonds in 1867 brought about the beginnings of the systematic exodus of labour power from Lesotho. But in order to understand the migrant labour system it is necessary to provide an overview of the agricultural conditions that had come to prevail between 1870 and 1930.

In 1870 Lesotho became 'Basutoland' and was administered by the Cape colony for the period between 1871 and 1884. By 1870 the Basotho were still struggling to regain their production levels in crops and animal husbandry following the decimating war with the Free State over territorial boundaries (1865-1868).

> In 1873 it was reported that Basutoland exported 100,000 bags of grain and 2,000 bags of wool. Basutoland in the same year imported £150,000 of British and other foreign manufactured goods. (Murray 1980, p. 5)

It was during this peak in economic prosperity that some Basotho began to migrate to the mines. Prior to mining some Basotho did migrate to the farms of the Free State to work on short-term contracts during the years when both groups were not at war with one another. However the population census of 1875 shows evidence of a new level of migration, with 15,000 out of a total population of 127,325 obtaining passes to work outside of Basutoland (Ashton 1952, p. 162). Moreover by 1884 the number had doubled.

It is clear that social differentiation was intensified with the increase in migration and with the coming of colonial rule. Senior chiefs for instance profited from these events in at least two direct ways. Firstly, chiefs received a percentage of the annual hut tax introduced by the British colonial authorities to pay for the colonial administration of Basutoland and secondly senior chiefs were also entitled to some of every migrant's earnings, amounting to £1 or more annually (average wage for Basotho £2 10s monthly).

While some Basotho were able to make a comfortable living by staying at home and selling grain, and certainly the sale of grain was the most important source of income in the 1870s (Kimble 1979), nonetheless increasing numbers of migrants worked outside of Basutoland in order to obtain guns, horses, livestock, ploughs and manufactures. In other words, some men (and women) migrated so that they could more profitably farm, by investing some portion of their income as migrants into more modern implements and other commodities. Judy Kimble (1985, p. 41) says of labour migration in the period between 1890 and 1900 that '... although Basotho sold their labour power on a greater scale than they had done in the previous twenty years, they did so to some extent "on their own terms"', rejecting for instance six-month contract lengths on gold mines, choosing instead one-month contracts. Kimble's view rejects Van Onselen's (1978) interpretation of Basotho behaviour as indicative of 'worker consciousness', but rather as a reflection of economic viability of Sotho homesteads.

The next decade was characterized by more stringent economic policies from outside Basutoland as well as harsh agricultural conditions internally. There was drought in this period, famine and economic depression. Basutoland was unable to take advantage of the gold boom which took place in Witswatersrand between 1882-1886 because of the prohibition on imports imposed by the Transvaal. Further Basutoland's cattle were all but wiped out during the rinderpest epidemic in 1896. Although the Basotho responded to the lack of cattle for ploughing by substituting horses, the next year's crop was ruined by drought (R. Leys 1979).

The early years of the 20th century continued to be hard for agricultural production in Basutoland; 1899-1902 the Boer War saw the usual markets for Basotho produce closed, 1905 drought, 1908-1909 pestilence and drought. In 1911 with a population of 427,549 there were 24,630 absentees. Not until the First World War was Lesotho able to produce with its old vigour. Exports reached a peak in 1928. It was the last year that Basutoland was able to export 100,000 bags of maize. By this time wool and mohair had become the most important income earners for the country. By 1930 some 50% of adult Basotho males were absent from the country at any one time. This suggests that most households in the rural areas had come to depend on the income from migrant workers (Murray 1980, p. 9).

From the above evidence it is apparent that a number of internal and external factors combined to undermine the ability of Basutoland to maintain its production of surpluses of grains. Drought, disease, protective tariffs, all played their part. There was in addition the exodus of labour. From 1896 the Chamber of Mines had determined a uniform wage and recruitment policy (Murray 1980, p. 12, Magubane 1979, pp. 102-118). Competition for labour between companies was limited. This had the effect of keeping miners' wages artificially low. Secondly, in a move to protect white farmers' interests, the 1913 Land Act was passed in South Africa which prohibited Africans from owning all but 13% of the country's land. Basutoland was affected by this law in that many Sotho-speaking sharecroppers in Orange Free State were forced to leave; many came to Basutoland and added to the population pressure. Also with the law's strict limitations on squatters and sharecroppers (who were perceived by many white landowners as growing too rich with their independent activities) wages for agricultural workers were lowered. Many such agricultural workers were from Basutoland. These factors helped push men and to a lesser extent women into migrancy. The oscillating pattern was enforced on the South African side of the border with the Natives (Urban Areas) Act of 1923 which introduced the pass law for migrant men, in the words of the 1922 Report of the Transvaal Local Government Commission, '...

46

to minister to the needs of the white man...' and leave 'the urban areas, the white man's creation ... when he ceases to minister' (Magubane 1979, p. 84). In this way families were barred from joining migrants. Women, as wives and mothers, became responsible for the day-to-day maintenance of the homestead in many cases and were compelled to answer the needs of their dependents as well as themselves. Having outlined the origins and main features of the migrant labour system we can now look more closely at the codification of 'traditional' Sotho land tenure.

Codification of customary law

In our examination of the land tenure system in Lesotho, we must unpack the conventional rubrics of 'traditional' and 'modern' systems of law by looking at how these distinctions are made and showing how the notion of 'traditional' law as especially indigenous law can be challenged historically (1978, 1982).

Martin Chanock (1982 and 1985) has written convincingly of the constructed nature of 'traditional' or 'customary' law in Southern and Central Africa. He has shown how colonial officials' accounts of customary practices were distorted and/or abbreviated. Such editings and additions frequently worked to the advantage of the indigenous dominant or ruling group as well as the colonizing power. This was due to the fact that more often than not it was members of the ruling group who were the source of the testimony used in the codification of African law. Chanock has observed that codification of African legal practices led to the artificial 'freezing' of what had previously been dynamic systems.

We believe that his observations are germane in the case of Lesotho. Ian Hamnett, an important author on the *Chieftaincy and Executive Law in Lesotho,* has said that '... the fundamental norms of customary law tend to take the form of general but at at the same time concrete principles' (Hamnett 1975, p. 14). Again, Hamnett says,

> Analytically considered, the norms of customary law often seem mutually inconsistent. This inconsistency arises from the fact that legal rules are not considered in the abstract but in the context of different social situations. (Hamnett 1975, p. 15)

Chanock would argue and we would agree, that customary law as codified by the colonial state is unable to reflect the full texture of the changing social context. Nevertheless, 'the recognition of "custom" was virtually the only way in which [many] Africans could impose their social aims upon the colonial order' (Chanock 1982, pp. 66-67).

Sebastian Poulter (1981), another authority on Sotho law, comes close to

47

Chanock's view of a 'constructed' customary law in Lesotho when he says,

> Modern Lesotho law draws its inspiration from an ancient African culture. However while its origins are indigenous many of the modifications that have taken place during the past century are the product of British Administration. (Poulter 1981, p. 3)

Indeed it was British Administration which defined what African practices were considered codable. Likewise sources of testimony were chosen either by British colonial officials or by senior chiefs. Finally British colonial officials criminalized some African practices through its 'repugnancy clause' in Lesotho as elsewhere on the continent (Sumner 1982, pp. 1-39).

In the case of Lesotho, where the colonial state made two attempts to codify Sotho law and customs, Koena practices, rather than those of other Sotho clans were codified. Other linguistic groups such as the Xhosa were culturally marginalized (Hamnett 1975, p. 25). Owing to British and Southern African patriarchal norms of behaviour concerning women speaking in public forums, we can infer that women too were marginalized in the codification process (Chanock 1982, pp. 66-67). Basotho women 'traditionally' were not in the nineteenth century allowed to to speak at *pitso* whether at national or local level, although they were allowed to attend such events (albeit seated in an outer circle, and away from the men). There is some evidence that Basotho women would on occasion speak out at *pitso* but generally it seems that some related male would speak on behalf of a woman if she wished to adddress *pitso.*

Finally, the main sources of testimony were from the senior ranks of the chieftaincy, effectively silencing the voice of commoners.

As we have discussed in Chapter 1, capitalist production benefits from non-capitalist modes of production in the Southern African region by stripping the latter of labour and by levying the costs of reproduction and labour power upon it. Thus Claude Meillassoux (1981, Part Two) in *Maidens, Meal and Money* argues that migrant labour is cheap precisely because of the maintenance of non-capitalist forms of production.

He argues that the 'obsolete' organization of agriculture is propped up by the export of so-called surplus labour or through the sale of agricultural products at prices below those necessary to insure the 'full costs of reproduction'. Meillassoux argues that imperialism developed its strength and maintains its hold because of its special linkages with non-capitalist modes, what he terms the 'domestic community'. Capitalism preserves this domestic sector which produces subsistence (use value) goods.

'Articulation' between modes of production is not simply an economic phenomenon but finds its expression in political and legal structures as well.

Kimble (1985) in particular uses such a perspective in her work on the Colonial State in Basutoland.

In Lesotho as elsewhere in the region, ruling groups of indigenous Southern African societies clashed head on with British administrators initially in an often violent struggle to preserve their autonomy. Nonetheless as the capitalist mode asserted its dominance, the ruling groups were more or less co-opted into undermining the viability and autonomy of pre-existing modes while simultaneously seeking to preserve their material and ideological advantage (Kimble 1985, pp. 44-47).

Although the 'logic' of South African capital in Lesotho has not called for the complete eradication of pre-existing relations of production (including property relations on land), it has unleashed a trend towards the gradual erosion of the reproductive capacity of the pre-existing mode as a whole.

Where does this lead us in our examination of 'traditional' land tenure in Lesotho? First we suggest that the British process of codification pre-empted the pre-existing processes of African law-making. British intervention, in creating 'traditional' law, made some indigenous practices 'repugnant' and introduced into the canon practices which were alien. British intervention in law privileged in the first instance British colonial officials and secondly Lesotho's dominant social group — he chieftaincy under the leadership of Moshoeshoe and Lerotholi, the first two Paramount Chiefs.

The brief earlier discussion of Dualism and Articulation of Modes of Production theories also suggests that what is important is the nature of the relationship between so-called traditional and modern forms, whether at the level of economics or at the level of politics and law. Our perspective in this book attempts to show how so-called 'traditional' or pre-existing land tenure practices help to underwrite the effects of uneven capitalist penetration in the region.

Sotho land tenure 1820-1930

By virtue of Lesotho's origins as a nation of refugees exiled by the events of the *lifaqane*, the eventual form of social relations on the land are of relatively recent origin (Eckert 1980, p. 92). Vernon Sheddick (1954) is the main source of information on this topic although what is known about the Sotho system has been supplemented over the years by Ian Hamnett (1975), D.K. Kowet (1978), Vusi Mashinini (1983), D.R. Phororo (1979), and most recently T.K.C. Quinlan (1983) and A.F. Robertson (1987). The first and most important tenet of the system is that 'land belongs to the nation'. It was held in trust by the chief in pre-colonial times, held in trust by the Paramount Chief and the British Crown during the era of the colonial state, and during the first fifteen years of political sovereignty land again was said to be held in trust by the Paramount Chief. Between 1966 and 1979 the powers of civil servants increased and those of chiefs decreased regarding land. It is one of the primary tasks of this book to build upon the work of D.K. Kowet (1978) in this aspect in succeeding chapters.

By far the most important feature of pre-colonial Sotho social relations with regard to land is its so-called 'communal' character. The term describes a state of affairs whereby land is not privately owned, but it oversimplifies the complex and several relationships involved. It is useful to echo Sheddick's distinction between usufructory titles and administrative titles (Sheddick 1954, p. 4).

Administrative rights to land strictly speaking are the province of the chieftaincy. This is manifested in law in that land in Lesotho is said to be held in trust by the king, (in the language of the colonial state, the Paramount Chief). In practice the king has administrative title to the whole of Lesotho. However the king delegates land allocation to those chiefs who are junior to him. Hamnett (1975, p. 63) phrases it well again:

> The hierarchy of chiefly jurisdiction .... allots to every chief the specific responsibility for land allocation within the territorial area of his ward ... the proper land issuing authority is the chief or headman with immediate jurisdiction over the land in question; a superior chief cannot allocate land within the ward of his subordinates, though he can decide appeals arising from the decisions of lower chiefs and he can request, and in some cases require, a subordinate to allocate land in a particular way.

It is adult Basotho men who are married who receive allocations of arable land. Though strictly speaking women are not given allocations, allocations do reflect the presence or absence of women as wives and mothers in a household. For instance the 'traditionally' allocated three fields is a package said to be appropriate for a household comprising one wife and her offspring. If the husband sets up another household, he is entitled to more land in respect of his junior wife and her offspring.

In addition to rights of use with regard to arable land, rights of use to pasturage are especially important. The distinction between cropland and pasturage is important because Grazing Rights are vested in the Chieftaincy and are of two kinds. First there are rights to 'open grazing' which are in the mountains and are controlled by senior chiefs, and secondly there are rights to 'reserved grazing' which are controlled by local chiefs. In order to exercise one's rights to pasturage, it is necessary to own cattle and have the labour power available for herding. There is a situation of extreme competition between cropland and pasturage. Not only do the Basotho typically both farm

50

and rear livestock but also because the Lesotho terrain and density is such that arable land and pasturage overlap. At the end of the harvest arable fields in Lesotho are opened up for public use (i.e. reserved grazing) by cattle. Under the Sotho system then we can see that while individual rights to cropland are enjoyed by members of the community, these rights are restricted on the one hand by a household's need and on the other hand by communal rights to grazing land.

There are other conditions as well; the allotee must be, as we have said before, a married male. He must be a *bona fide* Mosotho (Mashinini, p. 26) recognizing the authority of the king. More concretely the allotee must be a subject of a Principal or Ward Chief and needs to be recognized as such. It is also expected that the allotee must remain a member of his community in good standing. 'No foreigners are granted land for agricultural purposes', according to author Vusi Mashinini, 'because it is feared that to do so might result in alienation of the Lesotho's limited land resource' (Mashinini 1983, p. 9).

This injunction stems from Moshoeshoe's Law of Trade which barred European claims to ownership of Basotho land (Sheddick 1954, p. 131). Although it provided the basis for the institution of 50-year leases to missionaries and traders, such action was rooted in the chieftaincy.

Gender and property rights

A woman's access to land and cattle in Southern Africa was generally mediated through her husband or eldest son (Schapera 1943, Ashton 1952, Gay 1980, Gay 1982, cf. Kuper 1982). An unmarried woman had no rights to residential or productive property at her natal homestead. By contrast a married woman had rights of access in her marital home. The amount of *bohali* paid for her marriage reflected the degree to which she was guaranteed the means of livelihood, and the male head's desire to maintain legal rights over her offspring. In practical terms, if a husband failed to provide the basic requirements for a wife's livelihood, she could appeal to her family to withhold *bohali* payments and/or prevent the husband's family from claiming her offspring.

Labour within the lineage mode of production was organized mainly around the homestead and was dependent on the mobilization of kin. A strict gender division of labour exists (Gay 1980), its salient feature being that women were barred from handling cattle. Women were responsible for most of the chores relevant to day-to-day agricultural production, as well as cleaning, cooking, childcare, and tasks associated with food storage. Some aspects of crop cultivation involved labour performed by men, especially ploughing. The women of any one homestead developed a division of labour among themselves based on age and kin status. Another important feature of the lineage mode in Southern Africa is the minor status of women in law (Gay 1980, Muller and Khabele 1985, Seeiso 1986). This means that women were dependent on men (father, husband, brother or eldest son) for representing their legal and political interests. In the lineage mode they were barred from direct participation in public forums (*pitsos*).

Men too within the lineage mode were subject to patrilineal control as young adults dependent on their fathers, uncles and on elder brothers. However the difference between men and women's relationship to patriarchy is more than simply one of degree of control. The qualitative difference is illustrated by the fact that sons had rights to property within their own lineages, although the amount of property was in direct relation to seniority. Sons were able to act on these rights after initiation when they were entitled to residential property and upon marriage when they were entitled to crop land and pasturage rights.

Adult men were also bonded in a political relationship with their chiefs. Such a relationship was an important condition for land allocation. In addition, these allegiances formed the bases of male organizations such as the military, hunting parties, and work parties.

As J. Kimble (1983) has pointed out in her essay on Basotho women, *Runaway Wives: Basotho women, chiefs, and the Colonial State c. 1890-1920*, women were not organized in this way. Nevertheless, she maintains, women did have room to manoeuvre. Some women did enjoy 'powerful positions within lineages, especially if her household was close to the chieftaincy' (Kimble 1983, p. 10).

Kimble's main argument in her essay is that the shift from lineage mode of production to tributary mode (which was sparked by the nation building process led by Moshoeshoe and his cohorts) caused certain changes in the balance of power between men and women in Sotho society. As we have seen in a previous section Moshoeshoe's power was due to his consolidation of various groups through tribute labour, *mafisa*, and marriage. Secondly the system of placing ensured the culture of the Koena clan remained the dominant one. But more importantly the placing system made one's access to land contingent not only on one's relationship to a headman, but more importantly contingent on one's relationships with a centralized political authority. This trend marks a newly inflated role of chiefs in the administration of land.

Conclusion

Picking out elements from our discussions on origins of the 'Creation of the Nation' and state formation, as well as what we have said about production and social relations on land, we can build up a picture of how chiefs' administrative powers over land grew between 1820 and 1930.

Prior to British intervention Sotho groups were characterized by fission. Which is to say that new settlements or city states would form as new leaders emerged and with their own following left to occupy other land and refused to recognize the previous chief. Fission and a plentiful supply of land allowed for less authoritarian and centralized relationships between chiefs as administrators of land and 'commoners'. With the imposition of colonial rule and the reduction and fixing of territorial boundaries, these flexible conditions changed and there developed a political system with elements from 'tradition' and elements from colonial authorities. After the failure of the Cape Administration, British colonial authorities implemeted policies which protected and increased the powers of chiefs. One consequence of the British stance was that the 'placing system' radically increased the numbers of chiefs. The repercussions for land tenure included the multiplication of *lira* ('public') fields, courts, and led to an increase in land shortage. Chiefs were allowed a better position from which to increase exploitation through exacting taxes and tribute labour.

In our introductory discussion of land tenure we rejected the simple dichotomy of 'traditional' and 'modern'. Sotho tenure has undergone external and internal changes and is not the static set of practices implied by the adjective 'traditional'. At the same time we suggest that some elements of African social practices on land have been conserved under the rubrics 'traditional' or 'customary' to the material and ideological benefit of the chieftaincy. Equally important, the conservation of some residual elements of African social practices contributes to capitalist profit by deferring the full costs of social reproduction on to those remnants of pre-colonial modes of production. Use of the terms residual and remnants are justified, we argue, because pre-colonial modes of production are not able to reproduce themselves independently. In other words, despite pre-colonial forms of production, their laws of motion are thoroughly capitalist.

3 Chiefs and land in the political economy of Basutoland (1930-1966)

In this chapter we are concerned once again to trace the relationship between the chieftaincy and land administration within a political economy framework. However in this case we examine the years between 1930 and 1966. Specifically we want to emphasize three points in this chapter:

1   It is between these years that the legal and symbolic authority of chiefs begins to be challenged, especially with regard to their ability to accumulate private revenue through court fines, and through tribute labour.

2   The function of land within the political economy also shifts as the country loses its self-sufficiency in basic grains and farming comes to be perceived as riskier and less remunerative than migrant labour in terms of income.

3   Early on in the run-up to independence, a weakened chieftaincy becomes the focus for political debate. Political parties develop and issues around land are given new forums for public expression.

In Chapter 2 we made use of the 'Granary to Labour Reserve' thesis to help periodize the discussion on the increase of chiefly authority on land issues. It is, we suggest no mere coincidence that steady agricultural decline and colonial reform to reduce the power of the chieftaincy occurred within the same decade of the 1930s. 'Reform' of the chieftaincy led to a breakdown in the agrarian social and productive system.

3.1 The 'granary' era ends

A chronicle of the major factors leading to the decline in food production has been dealt with in Chapter 2, pp.45-46. It shows that the Basotho were no strangers to the problems agricultural production presented in environmentally 'unsuitable' conditions, nor those presented by a portion of its labour displaced through migrancy, nor the problems associated with commodity production in the context of unreliable markets. Nonetheless, their production system was able to weather these problems to some extent.

However, the Basotho economy did cross a threshold in the 1930s which prevented its recovery — up to and including the present day.

Another related aspect that contributed to the decline of 'Basotho granary' focuses on the internal and external politics that led to a breakdown in the Basotho agricultural production system and productivity.

G. Winai-Strom (1986) cites evidence of two political decisions which she sees as important factors in Basutoland's agricultural decline.

First, Winai-Strom suggests that political pressure on the part of South African farmers during the recession for restrictions on wheat farming had been successful after two attempts. The second attempt was successful owing to South Africa threatening Britain with restrictions on the amount of 'Basotho labour allowed to work on British-owned mines', and threats to incorporate Basutoland, Swaziland and Botswana. Winai-Strom says that Britain capitulated to these demands as evidenced by a memo promising the South African Ministry of Native Affairs 'improved co-operation between the Union and High Commission Territories'. This memo was subsequently followed by restrictions on export of agriculture produce introduced by the Basutoland colonial government. Furthermore, 'South African subsidies to the white farmers in Orange Free State had already been given'. The result of this state investment was capital-intensive farming and the distribution of bore holes (Winai-Strom 1986, p. 27), all of which led to a decline in production in Lesotho, given that the market was restricted.

3.2 Indirect rule and the degazetting of chiefs

The second decision, that is, to change the nature of the Basutoland colonial government, is more directly pertinent to our book. Winai-Strom suggests that the Pim Report in 1935 and its subsequent recommendations enacted in 1938 irrevocably changed the agricultural productive capacity of Basutoland,

> The drainage and irrigation system, for example, depended largely upon the organizational work carried out by the chiefs and their advisors.

(Winai-Strom 1986, p. 27)

The Report, alleging that there was the complete absence of any government in Basutoland, was a harbinger of a new, more orchestrated, controlled colonial system of government, a shift to something closer to the type of Indirect Rule practised by colonial governments in Tanganyika, to name an example.

'Indirect Rule' was based on, to quote Winai-Strom, 'the misapprehension that the previous system was one of "laissez-faire" character' wherein 'according to some sources, this gave the people room to manoeuvre'. Not, of course, all the people — as Winai-Strom quickly points out, but perhaps the indigenous ruling group, and a select few others. 'Chiefs, traders, missionaries, wheat producers, gun smiths and ox wagon owners', all enjoyed, Winai-Strom says, 'a high degree of autonomy in their relationship with London' until World War II (Winai-Strom 1986, p. 32).

This (restricted) 'autonomy' was possible because it served British interests, in keeping the costs of colonial administration low, and in keeping an ample supply of cheap labour to British owned mines.

But in 1935 Sir Alan Pim suggested measures to develop a bureaucracy to replace some of the duties of the chiefs. Apparently, the high degree of autonomy given to some groups had begun not to serve British interests as it had in the past. The 'failure' of the chieftaincy to serve British interests has several aspects. One aspect was British reluctance to continue to ignore growing protest about large-scale abuse of chiefly powers, of which the proliferation of chiefs was a part. It was becoming politically untenable for the colonial state to be seen to be doing nothing about these abuses in the face of petitions from commoners. Another aspect was the potential loss of labour to the mines of South Africa presented by the chiefly abuse of the system of tribute labour. Such tribute labour owed to every 'chief' by every household within his jurisdiction began to compete with wage-labour demands (and homestead rural production demands) as the number of chiefs multiplied via the 'placing' system. The reforms, in limiting the number of chiefs and ending tribute labour, attempted in one gesture to deal with chiefs' abuse of powers and to free labour from 'traditional' obligations.

The colonial reforms also included additional measures for tax collection, in South Africa as well as Basutoland. The Basotho were also integrated into the pass law system of the Republic, thus controlling workers' mobility more strictly (Winai-Strom 1986, pp. 32-33).

And in a radical move, chiefly office 'was put on a statutory basis'. Their numbers were reduced from about 1,340 to 120. Many of their judicial functions were usurped by magistrates. Tax collection became the preserve of appointed Basotho and British civil servants (Winai-Strom 1986, p. 33).

Nevertheless those chiefs who remained 'gazetted' were still the largest landholders, still maintained powerful contacts and influence and were paid a regular salary by the colonial state.

From 1938 to 1946 lower chiefs were degazetted, which is to say they were stripped of their judicial and administrative powers as well as their sources of revenue. According to R.F. Weisfelder (1977) this slow eight-year move in executing the Proclamations of 1938 was deliberate:

> Confronted with this sudden determination to impose reform from above, Paramount Chief Griffith attempted to soften the blow by giving his consent to the proposed measures only when he had secured concessions delaying their implementation. (Weisfelder 1977, p. 171)

This suggests that Paramount Chief Griffith feared the political repercussions of immediate and full implementation of reforms, i.e. degazetting the majority of chiefs. Although the monarchy and some other senior chiefs were politically stronger with this move, nonetheless the position of the chieftaincy as a whole was compromised. This was because they had had a say in who was to stay and who was to go from the ranks of the chieftaincy. They also had input in deciding how much those staying including themselves were to be paid by the newly formed National Treasury. In other words, the upper echelons of the chieftaincy were implicated in the destruction of its lower echelons, thus weakening its 'base'. As a result, 'top' chiefs became even more dependent on colonial government. As it was, the first year of implementation saw the issuing of 'warrants' (statutory permission to act as a chief) to all 1,340 chiefs. In subsequent years fewer and fewer warrants were issued so that by 1946 there were only 112 warrants sent out. The political repercussions of the mass de-powering of 1,240 chiefs were felt also in the highest ranks of the chieftaincy where intrigue and murder threatened to topple the Moshoeshoe Dynasty in the aftermath of the untimely death of Griffith (Jones 1966, pp. 57-81).

With regard to our own concerns with land administration, evidence from this time is patchy but suggestive. G.W. Winai-Strom claims that many degazetted chiefs were financially squeezed by on the one hand, the new excise tax on agriculture and on the other hand, discontinuation of former income from court revenue, i.e. fines etc. (Winai-Strom 1986, p. 33). J.A.G. Perry (1983) says that degazetted chiefs began to rent surplus land in the aftermath of the reforms.

R.F. Weisfelder tells us that there was also a difference between what was in theory legal and what was practised:

> ...[A] host of unrecognized and uncompensated chiefs continued to perform judicial roles and were expected [by the colonial state] to carry out such crucial functions as the allocation of land. (Weisfelder 1977, p. 173)

This state of affairs no doubt left commoners confused:

> Ordinary citizens were caught between the conflicting demands of legally constituted chiefs and *de facto* authorities tolerated by superiors unwilling to disrupt the status quo. (Weisfelder 1977, p. 173)

Many disempowered chiefs sought political redress through the Basutoland National Council which by the early 1950s constituted various elements from the chieftaincy, gazetted and degazetted — senior ranks down to minor headmen as well as some commoners — all of which found a common enemy in the monarchy and colonial government.

The ruling monarch at this time, Queen MaNtsebo, Regent for the infant heir, also contributed according to Weisfelder to the decline of the chieftaincy, and furthered the rise of secularly based groups in what had previously been chiefly domains.

Weisfelder has pointed to four decisions MaNtsebo made which limited her own powers — and by extension, those of the chieftaincy in general. We outline them briefly:

1   MaNtsebo agreed to consult the National Council prior to issuing orders or regulations;

2   The Regent agreed to allow 42 indirectly elected representatives in the previously aristocratic Council — effectively weakening royal influence over membership;

3   The Regent also allowed the control and financing of the new National Treasury bureaucracy to be devolved upon the National Council.

4   Finally, the Regent also accepted advisers who were nominated by the National Council, thus relegating the monarchy, in the long run, to playing a limited role in state political affairs.

These decisions weakened the chieftaincy in that national politics and key decision-makers within the state would no longer be determined solely by the upper ranks of the chieftaincy. Moreover, as populist demands for political independence grew, secular gains (made even stronger once fuelled by de-gazetted chiefs' interests) carried over into the post-colonial state where they have gained further ground.

The Regent's decisions taken together spelled the end of an era which saw Lesotho ruled by colonial officials and the Sotho monarchy. The key to understanding why these decisions weakened the monarchy lies in looking at the constitution of the National Council, a heterogeneous mix of royal and non-royal elements, and seeing how the monarch is obligated to consult this increasingly hostile group. The principle of the monarch having to work with and negotiate with powers other than the British state was a new one. The Regent also lost legitimacy through her involvement in the Medicine Murders Scandal. To be (almost) caught at participating in traditional supernatural practices in an attempt at boosting her own power over political rivals had the effect of revealing her insecurity and incompetence. We will explore this issue more in Chapter 5.

To summarize thus far the Pim Reforms were far-reaching for political economy in Basutoland. In Chapter 2 in the section on state formation, we discussed the 'placing' system and the evolution of the chieftaincy. Bluntly stated the Pim Reforms restructured the Basotho state by ending this system. Another restructuring comes with the advent of the post-colonial state and we will discuss in Chapter 5 the limitations of the post-colonial state around the usurpation of the chieftaincy and its administration of rural areas.

But for now the Pim Reforms can be seen to be furthering British mining interests in South Africa and colonial interests in Basutoland. The reforms increased the control and mobility of labour by freeing potential labour from providing tribute labour. It may also have increased the potential supply of labour by upsetting the complex agrarian system and its maintenance by local chiefs, which included the setting of planting and harvesting times and irrigation works, by the degazetting of just those authorities. It may, also, at the national level have contributed to the inability of Basutoland to recover from the blows suffered to its agricultural productivity during the 1929 Depression.

But the Pim Reforms also provided regulations around land tenure and use as well. These regulations were geared towards conservation and reflect, I believe, British concerns to maintain Basutoland as a somewhat viable geographic site of labour 'reproduction' and 'retirement'. Proclamation 61/38 paragraphs include these provisions:

'e) re: preventing the pollution of the water;

f) prohibiting, restricting or regulating the cutting or destruction of trees;

i) prohibiting the cultivation, use or possession of dagga; provisions for the destruction of wild dagga;

j) provisions for destruction of noxious weeds;

k) regulating grazing, and setting aside reserved areas;

l) prohibiting the restriction of the burning of grass or bush;

q) requiring any native to cultivate land to such an extent and with such crops as will secure an adequate supply of food for the support of such native and of those dependent on him;

r)   preventing soil erosion and for the protection of anti-erosion works.'
(Sheddick 1954, p. 30)

As can be seen, they all reflect the growing concern of British colonization throughout Africa with conservation (Beinart 1984, pp. 52-63).

As discussed more thoroughly in Chapter 2 Section 2.2, it is far from clear that soil erosion was caused by poor farming methods. In fact evidence suggests that reforms carried out may have worsened the landscape in two ways:

1   by disempowering those whose responsibility it was to oversee land management; and

2   by introducing projects and practices which were inappropriate to Lesotho conditions.

The above Proclamations on land use and control taken with the other Pim Reforms suggest that there was a colonial interest in preserving the capacity of the Basotho to reproduce themselves to provide for their own social security through agricultural production but with less chiefly manpower and no state compensation. The money-making functions, e.g. holding court and tax collection, was to be controlled instead by a small educated bureaucracy. All of this was to take place with the Basotho continuing to play a part in South Africa's underpaid Black mining, manufacturing and farming workforce.

Embedded within the preceding discussion are contradictions between the aims and effects of the Pim Reforms. Made explicit they include:

1   The reforms disempowered those who had been responsible for land management, including techniques around conservation. The Pim Reforms intended to improve land management, especially with regard to conservation.

2   The reforms left in place and increased the protection of those chiefs who were the biggest individual landholders, contrary to the objectives of Pim.

3   The reforms led to poorer degazetted chiefs potentially *increasing* the abuse of their powers in the absence of the income they had previously received as state recognized (and supported) chiefs.

3.3   The effects of the Pim reforms

In this section we are concerned with on the one hand parallel developments in the ranks of the civil service, and on the other hand, events in the countryside concerning land allocation.

We have already seen how degazetted chiefs were implicated in the renting of surplus land, that many were also continuing to act as *de facto* land authorities without compensation or state recognition, and that agricultural production may have suffered owing to the breakdown of chiefly authority — and as a result there may have been a subsequent vacuum in organizing certain forms of production.

How can these trends around the chieftaincy and land be explained? One way is through recourse to the nature and structure of the Pim Reforms (i.e. the System of Indirect Rule).

The Reforms, according to Winai-Strom (1986) and Weisfelder (1977), did protect British interests in South Africa. But if we look at the structure of Indirect Rule then we find areas ripe for potential confusion around the issues of land administration and dispute settlement.

Under Indirect Rule, it is 'the Resident Commissioner under the direction of the High Commissioner who alone possesses full legislative authority' (Sheddick 1954, p. 26). The Basutoland National Council could only act as an advisory body to the Residential Commissioner who possessed full executive power along with his supporting officers. 'The legal status of the Paramount Chief derived exclusively from the Crown' (Sheddick 1954, p. 26).

According to Sheddick 'the Judiciary consists of two systems with a single High Court to which all appeals from both systems lie' (Sheddick 1954, p. 26). Native Courts were those which under Proclamation 62/38 tried civil and criminal cases which were considered under their lawful jurisdiction. Those cases outside of the scope of Native Courts were dealt with by Subordinate Courts. These were handled by British Administration. These formal courtly structures were only loosely connected with the handling of land disputes, which in any event were taking new forms. Sheddick (1954) found in his study on *Land Tenure in Basutoland* that sharecropping had become a very important part of the agricultural scene. The assistance of neighbours and extended kin was crucial for many producers since at that time he found that 37% did not have enough labour within their households and had to go outside their immediate family for assistance. He also found that access to farming equipment including oxen was a problem and that 42% had to go outside the immediate family for assistance (Sheddick 1954, p. 84).

At the local level land allocation was becoming increasingly problematic:

The actual work of demarcating fields and of allocating them to entitled applicants is delegated to officials who are commoners. (Mashinini 1983, p. 9-11)

Hamnett says that these commoners, or *baabi* 'satisfy the need for publicity in land transactions', but because these posts were customarily filled at the chief's discretion, the individuals chosen were therefore vulnerable to pressure from all sides of the community, which could result in corruption. Further areas of confusion at the local level included new measures introduced by the Pim reforms which were supposed to 'rationalize' the tax collecting and judicial functions of the chieftaincy.

The National Treasury and the Judiciary were intended to have separate functions, nonetheless confusion arose in the popular mind and these ostensibly separate functions merged in people's everyday consciousness.

> It happens this way; each area usually has one Court which now serves the whole area. The Court officials are paid by the Treasury, the local representatives of which have an office next door to the Court. At the same time the Chiefs and other local authorities [i.e. magistrates and members of new bureaucracy created by Indirect Rule] receive their salaries and allowances from local Treasury offices... People have been quick to notice this intimate relation between Treasury and Court — they speak of National Treasury Courts [sic] — and further the relation existing between National Treasury Courts and the local authority. (Sheddick 1954, pp. 31-32)

Indirect Rule also allowed for a Chief's order to be appealed against locally. This meant, that, 'on the ground' Sheddick observed during the early 1950s a three-way competition for local authority control. There were the local chief, the new Court President and the National Treasury sub-accountant, all vying for supremacy in legal decision-making.

To clarify, within the Judiciary at that time were the Courts of Arbitration. These courts replaced the Chiefs Courts which have proliferated during the era of 'placing' when every Chief and headman could hold court and demand fines and punishment. Such courts were allowed to continue operating but without a chiefly warrant they could not fine or punish. They were left to 'dealing with ordinary domestic disputes or with trivial matters which are normally settled by arbitration by the head of the family or village' (Sheddick 1954, p. 26).

Another feature of Indirect Rule was the formation of a National Treasury which, as we have mentioned, figured prominently in the politics of weakening the Queen Regent MaNtsebo. The treasury was also crucial in making chiefs superfluous to the colonial administration. With the National Treasury, the responsibility for collecting tax revenue now devolved upon a bureaucracy which was not responsible or obligated in any way to the chieftaincy (Sheddick 1954, p. 26-27).

Previously fines paid at court remained with the chieftaincy, specifically the Chief's Courts. Under Indirect Rule, fines went to the National Treasury, whose staff were paid regular salaries by the Government, i.e. the National Treasury. Sheddick describes a situation at local level which he speaks of as an important consequence of the establishment of the Treasury.

The third leg of the triangle was the National Treasury sub-accountant, 'invariably a commoner with a standard of European education which gives him a considerable advantage in cases where both Chief and Court President may lack his training and may even be illiterate' (Sheddick 1954, p. 32).

Under Indirect Rule, the Basotho also had access to British District Administration, providing their case fell outside the scope of the Native Courts and the BDA's Subordinate Courts. Sheddick calculated that:

> The net result of this wholly unexpected development of the operation of Indirect Rule is to restrict constantly the authority of all except the most forceful local chiefs and headmen. (Sheddick 1954, p. 32)

Sheddick then seems to say that in this clash of roles, it is the man with the greatest personal power, even charisma, who wins out. However, for the purpose of this book the clash of personalities as an unforeseen consequence of Indirect Rule is not as important as the clash between social roles or power bases and the rise of a secular civil service, a bureaucracy independent of the chieftaincy. Elements of this bureaucracy were created by the institution of Indirect Rule, a consequence in Lesotho of the Pim Report (Bardill and Cobbe 1985, p. 23).

Let us now turn our attention to land tenure and use, particularly crop production. We find that during 1930-1966 chiefs provided 'the main chronological framework in which agricultural activities take place by regulating grazing activities'. There were five types of grazing areas. Sheddick outlined them as follows:

1   Village commonage, which is not associated with any one production role, used by cattle at the beginning of winter before other areas become available.

2   Grazing plots, used specifically for grazing; are closed only to allow pasturage to recuperate from use.

3   Grazing plots, used for other productive purposes when closed to grazing;

4   Arable fields, wherein rights to cultivate have been temporarily suspended. 'Arable land that has ceased to carry crops becomes a grazing

area. The moment of transition from arable to grazing rights is decided by the local authority [i.e. chief or headman]. It is the entire community which benefits from the "opening up" of cropland for pasturage. Stock can be driven over fields regardless of landholders' boundaries.' (Sheddick 1954, pp. 110-111)

5   Lowland summer grazing: these areas are 'associated with definite control and are protected' like (2) for recuperation. They are a *substitute* for summer open grazing and remain under control of provincial chief.

Chiefs also orchestrated the move of cattle to Highland areas when arable areas were in cultivation. Chiefs also were responsible for surrounding arable areas with strips of reserved grazing to minimize the danger of cattle trespassing on cropland, and for establishing the main chronological framework in which agricultural activities take place in relation to grazing activities.

'These functions', said Sheddick, 'depend on the degree of co-operation between the chief and the villagers. Where there is no co-operation the villagers may be left to fend for themselves' (Sheddick 1954, p. 80). Given what has been discussed about the Pim Reforms and the massive reduction in the number of chiefs, as well as the colonial state's 'expectation' that degazetted chiefs would somehow carry on performing such functions, it can be inferred that some of these systems began to deteriorate. After all, these functions also depended on the chiefs being able to receive a livelihood as well. The Pim Reforms ended this ability for most chiefs, who then had to find other sources of revenue — perhaps renting 'surplus' land. Since this was an activity outside of the scope of custom and law, then renting so-called surplus land must be seen as a corruption of the 'traditional' system, although 'understandable'.

Another long-term effect of the changes was to restrict chief-managed collective/communal production.

Up until April 1950, the Chieftainship could call upon *matsema* (tribute) labour to work *lira* (public) fields. Failure to attend was an offence in the Chief Courts, although such a crime did not exist pre-colonially. The main complaint with *lira* fields among commoners was that while once upon a time *matsema* was reserved for major chiefs, *subsequently* less important chiefs and headmen had claimed the privilege as well. Such a state of affairs left commoners with less and less time for their own fields, work and enterprises.

The *lira* fields and chieftainship go hand in hand. But the chiefs *now* do as they like with these *lira* lands. The *lira* lands are no longer national lands. They are only benefiting the chiefs ... the chiefs should feed us, and have only one *lira* land. We should remember that it is one kaffir corn land, one maize land, and the chiefs now use grain from these *lira* lands for their own requirements... (Edgar undated, p. 129)

Kimble suggests that the early decades of colonialism saw an increase in 'Tribute Labour' as one way to extract more surplus and consolidate their control over land. Another effect it had was to challenge an 'infant' middle class:

> ... a native miller is required to close his mill and go to the chief's *letsema* to plough, five or six days a year, according to the number of the chief's *masimo*. Another five or six days for scoffing, and there is reaping, the gathering in of the *mabele* and the mealies and *hopola*. In addition ... the chief can send him wherever and whenever he likes, it matters not to the chief whether the poor miller is away a month or two or six from his business. So that really the poor man has not time to devote to his business. (Edgar undated, ibid.)

Tribute labour was replaced in 1950 by the payment of a one-shilling tax per household (Sheddick 1954, p. 83).

Sheddick claims that the practice was abolished not so much for ideological reasons but because of the pressure on those people who remained for work. In other words *matsema* was seen to threaten the ability of households to produce for their own subsistence.

Lira fields had long since stopped being 'public', the produce from *lira* was disposed of by chiefs, mostly in the market. By these means the minor degazetted chiefs deprived of salary sought nevertheless to develop ways of accumulating simply by taking advantage of 'traditional' rights over labour and land (Sheddick 1954, p. 151).

The end of *matsema* then was a blow to all but the most senior level chiefs. Those with the most acreage suffered most, because they felt the end of 'tribute' labour more keenly. Again the link with 'renting surplus land' comes to mind, as well as the *de facto* opportunities for 'corruption'. Ian Hamnett talks for instance of the opportunities for corruption presented in the post of *baabi:*.

> There is no way of determining what they choose to remember, misremember or forget ... This is one of the ways in which chiefs can manipulate land allocation and render their subjects' tenure less well protected than the rules make it appear ... One of the easiest ways to deprive a man of his land is to declare that it had never been allocated to him in the first place. (Hamnett 1975, p. 69)

3.4 The succession crisis and the development of political parties

Exploration of the development of the political parties is important to understanding land issues in Lesotho. First, political parties developed at least partially as a consequence of the perceived failures of the monarchy and colonialism. Second, political parties in their attempt to secure a power base devised competing platforms for Lesotho's development. A major part of those platforms were land issues. Questions about the distribution of land, its management by village committees and/or chiefs, the kind of crops grown on it, its use for industry as opposed to agriculture, for Basotho as opposed to non-Basotho — all these issues figured prominently in the development of political parties and their bases. The following discussion is necessary to show the development of a political base concerned to preserve the custodial powers of the chieftaincy, which included the distribution and management of agricultural land. Another base that was being developed was one which supported the greater empowerment of secular and civil forces in Sotho society. This base wanted social mobility based on education and occupation. For this group land was to be managed by those trained and educated to do so. The final base being developed stressed the importance of equity and basic needs and recognized the importance of land as social security for the Basotho, most of whom were dependent on income from RSA.

In the 1950s the public focus in Basutoland shifted from concerns over the monarchy to concerns over Basutoland's relationship with South Africa, which was laying into place the legal structures of apartheid, i.e. 'separate development'.

The reforms to the chieftaincy and their effects as perceived by different groups plus the situation which was unfolding in South Africa played a major part in the development of political parties, their respective ideologies and the pressure for political independence.

Weisfelder says that some groups critical of the reforms like the Basutoland African Congress (BAC) formed by Ntsu Mokhele in 1952 'interpreted the ... reforms as a deliberate attempt to introduce the South African pattern of native administration in preparation for the ultimate transfer of the Basotho to the Union Government' (Weisfelder 1977, p. 174).

Another concern during this time of constitutional deliberations was over the fate of the senior ranks of the chieftaincy, in particular the monarchy. The Queen Regent had already proved weak in the way she capitulated her powers to the new bureaucracy created by the colonial reforms, the National Treasury and the newly revamped National Council. Secondly, she had been implicated in the 'Medicine Murders' Scandal and although the Queen Regent was exonerated the incident served to mortally discredit her and undermined her authority further.

Chief S.S. Matete was among the first to call for the Regent's retirement in favour of Constantine Bereng Seeiso. The Queen Regent was opposed to retirement at that time and insisted that the heir should be allowed to pursue his studies at Oxford and marry first before assuming the duties of a monarch (Weisfelder 1977, pp. 174-5).

Matete formed the Marematlou Party in 1957 in order to bring Bereng Seeiso to the throne as quickly as possible (Weisfelder 1977, pp. 174-5, Khaketla 1971).

There could be no doubt that Bereng Seeiso would be king. However, for the parties involved, timing was the important issue. While the Marematlou Party wanted Bereng Seeiso to ascend the throne quickly in order to make critical appointments and decisions that would have a crucial bearing on the political make-up of the newly reconstituted National Council, the Regent and her advisors opposed the Marematlou Party and argued a king should be well-educated and married, so that the decisive appointments etc. would remain with the Queen. Chief Leabua Jonathan, one of the Queen's staunchest allies, led the formation of the Basutoland National Party to defend the Queen Regent. They sought support, not so much as opponents of the Marematlou Party but as opponents of another group, the BAC (now called the Basutoland Congress Party [BCP]), on the basis that the BCP ideology was considered threatening to 'traditional patterns of life and basic Christian values' in that they were seen to be 'communistic' (Bardill and Cobbe 1985, pp. 32-33).

The social basis of the three factions is not clear cut, although Weisfelder tells us that the BAC was known to have politically radical roots and connections. The BAC took up politically where the LLB had left off, championing anti-imperialist struggles with strong links with Communists and the African National Congress in South Africa. The BNP and the Marematlou Party seemed to have been founded specifically around the succession debate, although some of the BNP platform was reminiscent of the Progressive Association, in that both groups were at best cautious towards a strong chieftaincy. Both organizations tended to represent the interests of an incipient petty bourgeoisie tied to the colonial bureaucracy. To clarify, both the BNP and the BCP represented an opposition to the Marematlou Party, which represented the interests of the monarchy primarily and secondarily other chiefs. Not all chiefs supported the Marematlou party though, owing to the fact that most chiefs had been 'degazetted' by the colonial officials with the help and implementation of the monarchy, and other senior-level (and still gazetted) chiefs. Some of these chiefs joined the BNP, others the BCP, each group 'cautious' of the chieftaincy/monarchy but for different reasons. As a general rule, the BNP represented the would-be 'secular' holders of power, who did not query British influence, while the BCP was anti-colonial and saw the chieftaincy/monarchy issue as secondary to imperialism in Southern Africa. The Marematlou Party, although it was the first political party to be formed, has remained one of the most marginal. It is the *chief's party*, the party of 'tradition' and 'kingship'.

The Basutoland Congress Party were silent on the succession debate, working instead to win the 1960 District Area elections.

Bereng Seeiso himself resolved the Succession issue when in September 1959 he requested 'the Regent to arrange his accession without delay'. According to Weisfelder, 'MaNtsebo was forced to capitulate when the immediate family and the Sons of Moshoeshoe [other Principal Chiefs descended from Moshoeshoe's sons and brothers] supported his demand' (Weisfelder 1977, p. 170). Bereng Seeiso ascended the throne and took the name Moshoeshoe II in recognition of Basotho national rebirth as the country moved toward regaining political sovereignty.

However, the Basutoland Constitution of 1959 further weakened the chieftaincy.

Although the new monarch, Moshoeshoe II, was able to exert some influence on major appointments and maintain a supervisory role on land allocation, in that the land is held in Trust for the nation by his office, nonetheless he lost the power 'to delay or force reconsideration of legal and executive decisions' (Weisfelder 1977, p. 176). He also lost direct access to the new bureaucratic structures whose functions were devalued to the district levels.

Further constitutional re-structuring occurred before Basutoland became independent in 1966, and Moshoeshoe II failed to win back any of the powers lost by the previous monarch. According to Weisfelder:

> The overwhelming weight of public testimony supporting a 'constitutional' Head of State or not wanting to be the cause of delayed national sovereignty, Moshoeshoe II signed the Constitutional Conference Report and pinned his hopes on a massive Marematlou party electoral victory. (Weisfelder 1977, p. 177)

It was however the National Party which won the first national elections.

It is said by many observers (e.g. Bardill and Cobbe 1985, Khaketla 1971) that the BNP had a predominantly Catholic support base which included high-level civil servants, sub-chiefs, headmen and white traders. Chiefs who supported and/or led the BNP were resentful of the reforms which cut their hereditary powers.

Other BNP supporters had benefited from the colonial state and saw the best way forward for the nation being to continue the 'alliance' with the British and maintain a 'benign' relationship with South Africa. As we have discussed previously, the BNP was born in an immediate sense from its leaders' concerns with forestalling the accession of Bereng Seeiso to the throne. The BNP went on to lose the initial 1960 District Council elections. Moreover, B.M. Khaketla in his work *Lesotho 1970* detailing the events leading up to the coup in 1970 tells us that Chief Jonathan, BNP founder, failed to secure a seat in the 1960 elections and was indeed brought in from the 'political wilderness' by Moshoeshoe II, his arch rival who appointed him to the new Legislative Council.

The Basutoland Congress Party has its origins in the Basutoland African Congress which in its turn contains ideological elements from the African National Congress of South Africa. Its political base was strongest among educated commoners. It was anti-colonial and anti-apartheid. Precursors of the BCP include the Basutoland Progressive Association (BPA) but more especially Lekhotla La Bafo (LLB). The BCP won the initial District Council elections.

We have discussed the origins of the Marematlou Party. A split within the BCP led to the Marematlou Freedom Party which started in 1964. It had its roots in the Basutoland Progressive Association as well. It was a party perceived to be royalist and sought to protect the higher ranks of the chieftaincy with an ideology that stressed the monarch's role, in the first instance, as crucial to national identity and also as an important check on the powers of the Prime Minister: Khaketla has said that,

> There were genuine fears that Jonathan might rule arbitrarily and betray Basotho interests to South Africa unless the monarch gained viable options to check his power. (Khaketla 1971, p. 25)

While the King refused to condone the new constitution and the BCP leader walked out in protest from deliberations, the British unilaterally inserted a fresh paragraph to the constitution which further empowered the Prime Minister to act on behalf of the king if the monarch refused to perform the duties required of him. These duties dealt with implementing the Emergency Powers Act, the Internal Security Act, the Societies Act and the Printing and Publishing Act. These powers would soon be used by Prime Minister Jonathan to silence opposition forces, especially the BCP (Khaketla 1971, Bardill and Cobbe 1985, p. 39).

Under BNP leadership, Lesotho's labour reserve relationship remained unquestioned and there was an increase in South African influence in the country. Jonathan's position in the Legislative Council, courtesy, as we have said, of an appointment made by Moshoeshoe II, provides us with clues to his

(Jonathan's) behaviour during his first term as Prime Minister.

Jonathan introduced a motion in the Council 'calling upon the British Administration ... to relax restrictions on the importation of livestock from the Republic of South Africa... regardless of overgrazing consequences ...' (Khaketla 1971, p. 27). He also opposed the construction of various tarred roads in order to protect arable land. He also opposed employment of Europeans in the civil service in favour of Basotho.

As Prime Minister Jonathan reversed his position, according to Khaketla (1971), on all these issues and acted in accordance with his new views.

The BNP constitution also gives us some clues as to the nature of BNP plans for Lesotho. It contrasts with the BCP document which commits itself to 'fight oppression, exploitation and discrimination in all its manifestations, to fight colonialism and imperialism and in particular against incorporation of any part of Lesotho into South Africa.' The BCP's methods include 'strengthening trade unions and ... striving for democratically elected government whereas the BNP ... believes in freedom from discrimination, freedom from religion' (Winai-Strom 1986, pp. 45-56); models its rhetoric from the United Nations Charter on human rights and emphasizes its firm opposition to Communist ideology.

According to G. Winai-Strom the BNP's Anti-Communist stance 'has resulted in co-operation with movements and governments which fear communism and seek to form anti-communist international alliances' like the German Christian Democrats and the Taiwanese government (Winai-Strom 1986, p. 44).

Jonathan himself was also seen as South Africa's favourite Basotho leader. At a time when BCP and MFP leaders were being barred from speaking in South Africa, Jonathan could boast of being the only Basotho leader who could have tea with Dr. H.F. Verwoerd (Khaketla 1971, p. 31).

Conclusion

In conclusion to this section of the Chapter, we suggest that during 1930-1966 the system of Indirect Rule created confusion for the ordinary commoner, and also created opportunities for corruption in land allocation by gazetted and degazetted chiefs. The government expected that degazetted chiefs would continue to deal with 'on the ground' disputes, and land allocation without compensation. Many other chiefly functions (and virtually all official sources of revenue) were transferred to a new bureaucracy whose base was in the colonial government. The new system also contributed to a breakdown of chief-managed social relations on the land — with regard to those forms of production and conservation initiated by the chief. With the mass degazetting of chiefs the potential for such a breakdown is clear.

The main objectives of the Pim Report and the subsequent reforms were to check the proliferation of chiefs (and thereby check the reported widespread abuse of chiefs' powers) and to secularize taxation and land management, introducing in particular new techniques in conservation.

However, the Pim Reforms led, in fact, to poorer land management, increased soil erosion and the creation of a class of poorer degazetted chiefs. This group in possession of some land and popular authority were in a position to engage in greater abuse of their 'power' than previously; thus causing a new level of social breakdown in relations in rural areas.

Certainly S. Jingoes (1975), author of *A Chief is A Chief of The People*, believed that a social breakdown did occur with the Pim Reforms and that it coloured land transactions afterwards:

> In those days [the past] the Chiefs were not paid salaries .. [they were] not civil servants. They lived on what the people gave them. If today a chief accepts a gift for giving someone land, he is taking a bribe, because he is being paid a salary by the Government for his work. (Sheddick 1954, p. 151)

Nonetheless, Sheddick observed that some degazetted chiefs did continue to administer land and law, and that this was expected by the colonial state. Corruption did result, but it was not until 1966 that legislation regarding the allocation of land was set out in procedural form other than 'customary' practice. Chapter 5 explores the debate that led to legislation which adjusted, and in some important ways attempts to transform, social relations on land.

4   The land tenure debate

Communal tenure has long been seen by one set of writers and advisors as a principal cause for stagnant and/or low agricultural production in Southern (and other regions of) Africa, a view that is challenged by others.

The purpose of this chapter is to explore some of these debates around communal tenure in Africa generally and to link what has been a widely contested debate with the discussion as to the desirability or otherwise of changes in communal tenure in Lesotho, in particular.

We believe both levels of this debate are important to our general argument on Land and Law in Lesotho, in particular the 1979 Land Act inasmuch as the main justifications for legal change were couched in terms of this debate.

4.1   Communal tenure in Africa

In an overall sense, land tenure studies that followed World War II have given way to land use studies. This reflects the general concern with economic growth in Africa. As a consequence developmentalists of the modernization school ignored the anthropological concern with how individuals and groups in Africa expressed relationships between one another through a system of mutual rights and obligations with regard to land (Middleton 1980, p. i).

Over the past 30 years the economics of land use has glossed over complex social and historical processes which characterized the work of I. Schapera (1943), A.I. Richard (1939) and M. Gluckman (1945). Issues around land distribution and social inequality also have been ignored, with the result that, according to some observers (Picard 1980, Werbner 1980, Markowitz 1977, p. 210), government personnel have been the principal beneficiaries of the few land tenure reforms carried out. According to John Middleton, writing in the Foreword to *Land and Society in Contemporary Africa,*

...[A] government composed of those with power to control the lives of others all too often allows that power to be abused ... (Middleton 1988, p. ix)

Despite what may very well be the best of intentions,

> What so frequently happens is that the abuse of centrally held power not only weakens or destroys the tight sewn structures of rural communities but also destroys their ability and will to produce food, since their long tried and effective methods of production are intimately tied to their own relations between one another as expressed in traditional rights to land. (Middleton 1988, p. x)

What are these 'traditional' or 'communal' rights to land?   Although generalizations about Africa can be spurious, 'communal tenure' is widespread in the African context and can be roughly characterized by four main features (Dorner 1972, p. 40). First land is considered to be part of the communal heritage of the users of the land, and as such does not belong and can not belong to any one individual. Rather land is held in trust by chiefs on behalf of the community. Secondly, land is allocated for use, for the allottee and his family contingent on continued use and political allegiance. Land cannot be bought, sold, transferred or exchanged. Third, rights to allocation are traced from one's membership in the community, although, fourthly — outsiders have on some occasions been conceded rights to use.

Some developmentalists, especially those who see development as solely concerned with economic growth, were concerned with the economics of land use and embraced a narrow definition of land tenure limited to an understanding of the varied kind of legal rights that can be held on land. On the whole, they have defined 'communal' tenure as a whole, inimical to high levels of agricultural production (Williams 1972, pp. 6-12, Lowe 1986).

Developmentalists tend to share a common orthodoxy on such issues with the international financial institutions like the World Bank, the International Monetary Fund, powerful bi-lateral donor organizations, i.e. United States Assistance For International Development (USAID), U.K. Overseas Development Assistance (ODA) etc., and with decision-making powers in developing countries. Aid and loans are frequently 'tied' (or perceived as such) to policy changes sometimes including land tenure changes, although as yet very rarely. They seem as though they would like to tie aid to private tenure, but often hesitate to pursue.

Colonial states for much of their time worked to preserve so-called traditional tenure though often in moderated form, but often made some limited moves in the late colonial period towards introducing more exclusive individual tenures that allowed for a market in land. Colonialism thus left in

73

many areas of Africa a legacy of plurality in tenure systems and left a political 'elite' with 'command over regulations affecting the whole society but exercisable *de facto* in their own interest' (Seidman 1978). This is an important starting point for looking at the debate on communal tenure and what has been seen to be its 'constraints' on agricultural growth, because in addition to querying the validity of such criticisms to 'communal' forms of tenure, it is important to also bear in mind that legislation to remove 'constraints' (like all legislation) benefits certain strata of society, frequently to the detriment of other strata.

In brief communal tenure is said to carry with it the following obstacles to higher productivity (within a capitalist framework). First and considered most important by those identifying such obstacles, 'communal tenure does not provide enough security to the farmer'. Secondly communal tenure that recognizes everyone's right of access to land ultimately, encourages fragmentation and parcellization, which leads to poor economies of scale, particularly when employing capital-intensive methods of production. Thirdly, communal tenure inhibits farmers' ability to obtain credit from financial institutions. Fourthly communal tenure inhibits innovation in choice of crops grown and in soil management.

These concerns have been elaborated as recently as 1975 in the World Bank's Publications *Assault on World Poverty* (1975) pp.189-234 and *Sub-Saharan Africa: From Crisis to Sustainable Growth* (1989). In the latter text the World Bank has singled out the agricultural sector as the key to reversing the decline in living conditions in Sub-Saharan Africa. The challenge for this part of the world is to 'transform its agriculture and expand its productive capacity' to feed a rapidly growing population. The growth in food crops needs to be enough to not only maintain 'output per person but also to reduce food calories' deficits and reduce food imports. In the process this sector must become 'a major employer of an increasing labour force' and 'compete on world markets to earn the foreign exchange that Africa needs to fuel its economic growth'. Further, '...[a]nd it must do that while reversing the degradation of natural resources that threatens long term production' (World Bank, 1989, p. 89).

There are several assumptions in this line of argument that need to be made explicit. First, there is the assumption that agriculture *can* and *must* be the 'engine' of development.

Secondly, there is an assumption that with increased food production, food imports *will* go down.

Thirdly, there is the idea that increased food production will stem mass undernourishment.

Fourthly, the World Bank assumes that agriculture can generate sufficient

74

employment.

Fifthly, the World Bank assumes that foreign exchange is *required* for development to take place and that Sub-Saharan Africa will be able to successfully meet the terms and conditions of competition on the world market.

It is interesting (and alarming) to note that in the midst of an agrarian 'crisis' on the continent the development 'logic' of the Work Bank remains unchanged.

The 1975 publication lays out a similar formula for development. With regard to land reform it specifically gauges the effectiveness of land reform by examining the effects of farm size on productivity, equity, employment savings and market surplus.

The World Bank devotes some space to what it perceives as equity issues.

Over the past 20 years the Bank has grown concerned over 'the extent and gravity of the employment problem and income disparities in developing countries ... from an equity as well as productivity standpoint' (World Bank 1975, pp. 198-199).

However, the World Bank's land reform policies seem to be much more heavily weighted for increasing output and expanding employment rather than improving the living conditions of the poorest in society.

In an 'over-crowded' country, for instance where the population clearly outstrips the amount of landowners and where land held in common is subjected to multiple cultivation by industry, the solution to poverty is not to be found in land.

> In these situations, it might be wise to give land only to the minimum number of farmers and to attack the poverty problem of the landless by means of a massive rural works programme. The settlement of landless on new land wherever available and their migration to urban areas, when possible, are other obvious alternatives. (World Bank 1975, p.219)

The World Bank claims that 'the most successful land reforms include those whereby tenants become owners of the land they operate' (World Bank 1975, p. 222). Once security of tenure is insured through land reform (specifically registration, titling and an end to parcellization), incomes for farmers increase, leading to an increase in savings — and an increase in farm investment leading to, supposedly, higher output.

The history of these concerns with land tenure in Africa go back to the East Africa Royal Commission [EARC] which was the first U.K. official body to discuss the issue of customary tenure and its relationship to a 'modern' national economy in the African context. E. Jacoby, writing in *Man and Land*, says that the findings of this commission encouraged the prioritization of 'land use' over 'land needs' as a way of achieving 'a degree of mobility in the transfer and disposition of land, which without ignoring existing property rights, enable access to land for its economic use.' While the EARC recommends the individualization of land holding, '... it [does] not identify individualization of land tenure with private ownership and [the report] states explicitly that modern African societies should be based on property owned individually as well as by agencies for communal action such as co-operatives' (Jacoby 1971, p. 346).

Another report on land tenure in Africa from around this time comes from the Conference on African Land Tenure in East and Central Africa at Arusha, Tanzania, in 1956. This report takes an opposing view to the aforementioned EARC recommendation and comes down firmly on the side of individual, exclusive rights to holdings as the best way forward to economic growth. And this pattern was in fact implemented thereafter in Kenya — where the containing of a rebellion made it possible politically. It was also tried and then reversed in Zimbabwe and remained merely an aspiration elsewhere.

The literature on African tenure over the past 30 years (e.g. Lowe 1986, Williams 1972, Cowen 1967, East Africa Royal Commission 1956, World Bank 1975, 1989) repeat these views over and over again. Simultaneously but slowly some modifications to indigenous land tenure systems have attempted to overcome the aforementioned constraints. At one time it was thought conventionally that these constraints could only be overcome with the imposition of freehold tenure. Freehold has been introduced to some degree in South Africa, Malawi and Kenya. But freehold has not been successful in reaching the goals, especially economic growth and eradication of fragmentation, stipulated by policy in, for example, Kenya.

The colonial state had in Kenya created two systems of tenure, one African, the other European. Ostensibly the African system operated according to the laws and customs of the indigenous groups and emphasized subsistence agriculture. The European side was made up of plantation style ranches and 'mixed' (i.e. plantation and subsistence) farming. Lucrative markets in coffee and other cash crops were reserved exclusively for Europeans.

A more detailed look at the Kenyan case is necessary in order to understand the challenges and opportunities presented by land reforms in Africa. The Kenyan example of individual land titling and registration is approximately 30 years old and has been held up as a success by the World Bank (World Bank *Assault on World Poverty* 1975, pp. 189-234). In this necessarily brief discussion of the Kenyan experience we will explore the origins of the reform, its implementation, its effects on the political economy of Kenya, and finally the relevance of the Kenyan case to Lesotho.

M.P.K. Sorrenson in his book *Land Reform in the Kikuyu Country: A Study in Government Policy* (1967) promotes the view that senior level colonial officials resisted pressure from more junior officials and from some African groups to introduce individual tenure in African areas. This view was maintained although it was evident that in some African areas there was clearly a predisposition toward individual tenure. For some groups certain kinds of individualized tenure pre-dated colonialism. Other groups very quickly adapted to the dominant mode during colonialism and practised *de facto* individualized tenure. Indeed the official line in Kenya associated economic development with European settlement, Africans as a necessary labour force, and the reservation of separate African and European farming areas. African peasant agriculture was not seen as potentially progressive. Agricultural credit and markets were denied Africans. In response to calls for individualized tenure in the African areas the government expressed concern that the African community should retain control over the disposition of land in reserved areas. There was a call for more 'traditional' control by the government and for African land users 'to reorient themselves on clan lines' (ibid., p. 56). Instead of giving real consideration to Kikuyu demands for secure titles, the government sought ways to politically contain the demands by reviving elders' powers. Not until after April 1948 did the official view change.

This change was signalled with the discussion of extending long-term leases to African farmers with 'well-run farms' in Kiambu. Although four years were spent in developing the experiment, leasehold was never put into effect under this programme. Nonetheless another idea was floated this time coming from the Registrar of Co-operative Societies, E.J.A. Leslie, who sought support for a special title which would allow African farmers to obtain credit. Such a title, he argued, would encourage Africans to invest capital in improvements and would prevent further fragmentation. Further, implementation of the policy would involve government scrutiny of claims to title and the consolidation of holdings into economic units. This was a policy clearly aimed at encouraging the progressive African farmer who was also most likely to be a chief or government civil servant (ibid., p. 66). Despite this class bias it was clear that government could no longer ignore African farmers *en masse*.

Indeed, the political crisis triggered by the rebellion of the Mau Mau made it impossible for the government to ignore African demands. In the aftermath of what has been termed the Emergency, settlement schemes grew up thick and fast in an attempt to absorb some of the growing landlessness. Nevertheless the class element continued to dominate government thinking as evidenced by the Swynnerton Report and the subsequent adoption of its recommendations. The Swynnerton Report (1955) called for the consolidation of fragmented holdings, requiring of landholders that they unify their acreage, thus enabling them to obtain individual title and thereby qualify for loans to improve agricultural productivity. It also called for extension services to be made more readily available to African farmers and the removal of the ban on Africans growing coffee. The Swynnerton Report said:

> Former government policy will be reversed and able energetic or rich Africans will be able to acquire more land and bad or poor farmers less, creating a landless and a landed class. This is a normal step in the evolution of a country. (Swynnerton 1955, p. 10)

The Report was written in 1953. By 1956 it was official policy and was beginning to be applied to the Kikuyu. By 1960 most Kikuyu land had been registered. Finally, according to the Lawrance Report (1966), commissioned in 1965 to assess the programme in consolidation and registration, progress in reform had been made in all provinces of the country to date and there was no doubt that the programme was in a general way very beneficial to individuals and the government.

However, the report remained cautious in connecting the possibility of land registration as an important factor in improving productivity. The Lawrance Report did say that individual titling exacerbated landlessness and called for an acceleration of the programme. The logic behind this thinking was that improving prospects for 'progressive' farmers would generate employment prospects for the landless. It is important to note that the Lawrance Report was written in part in order to persuade external agencies (UNDP, USAID, SIDA and the West German government) of the necessity for aid in order to carry out a broad programme of agricultural development.

Certainly the implementation of the Swynnerton recommendations changed the face of agriculture in Kenya. Gone was the state emphasis on subsidizing the increasingly expensive white highland agriculture, denial of agricultural credit and the most lucrative cash crop markets to Africans. All of this occurred in the context of more and better land becoming available to the African population. The output of African farmers, according to Colin Leys (*Underdevelopment in Kenya: The Political Economy of Neo-colonialism 1964-1971*) increased from £5.2 million in 1955 to £14 million in 1964 with coffee alone from Central Province contributing to 55% of the increase (Leys 1976, p. 49).

In looking at the long-term effects of the reform J. Heyer (1976, p. 81) expresses the view that government and external intervention in agriculture led to the improvement in living conditions for the majority of the population. But in explaining how this came about she emphasizes that there was in the Kenyan instance at that time a coincidence of interests among external agencies, the national government and African (potential) smallholders. For Heyer, though, the key factor lay not so much in tenurial reform as in the opening of long-denied markets to African producers. Although living conditions improved generally, reform did not hasten the generation of employment opportunities for those left landless as intended and while the income of the middle strata (30%) of African rural producers increased as much as that of the upper 30%, the income of the lowest 40% actually fell (Heyer 1981, p. 103). An earlier book co-edited by Heyer with J.K. Maitha and W.M. Senga in 1976 titled *Agricultural Development in Kenya* provides a similar analysis. An article by Senga, 'African Land Tenure Reform' (pp.167-183) offers the following cynical conclusions regarding state intervention in tenure:

> As it is we were simply told by colonial agronomists that tenurial reform was necessary and we believed it. The result has been at most a disruption of the social systems of many groups in the country. And at best no appreciable change at all. There is every reason to believe that even if Swynnerton was right about the ills of customary land tenure, his prescriptions did and cannot cure its ailments. (Senga, p. 183)

Under the communal system poorer families could borrow the use of someone else's fields; the new system did not allow for that kind of flexibility, its *raison d'être* being to prevent just those kinds of families from getting land. Land use was to be governed not by the needs of subsistence or of social security but rather by the demands of global commerce.

Despite the obvious differences of the lack of a white settler population in Lesotho, and a concomitant reserved areas situation in Lesotho, there are many parallels between the intention for and implementation of land reform in Kenya and Lesotho. If we take one step further and broaden our understanding of the problem by figuratively erasing the national borders between Lesotho and the Republic of South Africa then the parallels become even more plain.

In both cases the origins of reform lie in the problems of the colonial state in managing political discontent. This discontent is brought on by the expropriation of land, early colonial intervention in land use and management, especially through 'conservationism', the introduction of market barriers to make commercial African farming untenable, the creation of a migrant labour system to provide cheap African labour to white areas, the manipulation of African systems of custom and law to contain demands for more land and the devolution of powers over land. In both cases the reforms represent an about-face on previous official lines about preserving African tenure systems and not imposing European concepts on African systems of law. However there are certain difficulties in insisting on too great a parallel.

There are indeed important lessons for Lesotho in the Kenyan case. Some of these lessons become more salient as we examine some key differences between the cases:

1   In the absence of sudden land reform in South Africa and the dissolution of national boundaries, and with them the Lesotho state, there is no possibility of more land becoming available to the Basotho unlike Kenya.

2   There are no particularly lucrative cash crops grown in Lesotho unlike Kenya, renowned for its agrarian produce, especially coffee.

3   Although in the past South African tariffs helped made African commercial farming unviable, there are currently no particularly lucrative markets denied to Basotho farmers, unlike the pre-Swynnerton situation in Kenya with regard to coffee.

4   Kenyan 'success' involved the convergence of interests of external agencies, the government and the potential (landless and near-landless) beneficiaries. This is unlike Lesotho where government ministries are divided, and where the common perception of the law is that it will benefit a tiny segment of the *current* landholding population wealthy enough to buy the lease and with enough capital and/or social clout to develop the land (or *not* develop it; rumours abound of those who simply lease land for speculation purposes).

Kenya's reform left 40% of the rural population with less percentage of the overall income than before the reform. There is evidence that social relations in the rural areas are reverting to communal practices (Cliffe and Lawrence *inter alia*).

In the absence of employment and/or adequate social security for those 'freed' from their prior means of production it is no wonder that rural producers should revert to a system that entitles them to borrow, share or otherwise petition (and perhaps pay) an elder/headman/chief for the use of some land. What other choices are available to them?

Given these points it appears that the Kenyan model is in the main not replicable in Lesotho in terms of increase in agricultural production of a popular crop.

Moreover the external pressures were not the determining factors for reform in Kenya. It was the organization and politicization of Africans calling for more land (previously expropriated by white settlers). African demands for 'security of title' could be better understood in the light of the overall political situation.

80

It remains doubtful that even the increase in income of the middle strata of African farmers was due to tenure change *per se*. Agricultural credit, extension services, increased availability of land and access to markets previously denied appear to be more important factors in the equation.

Gavin Kitching's (1980) thorough work *Class and Economic Change in Kenya: The Making of an African Petite Bourgeoisie 1905-1970* reveals the relationships between land reform carried out in Kenya and the increase in class formation and division. Essentially Kitching is concerned to show how 'the process of land consolidation and enclosure on the one hand, and the adoption of new higher value crops by African cultivators on the other ...' (Kitching 1980, p. 316) led to an increase in social inequality including landlessness. More recent evidence from the Kenyan experience suggests that in some areas at least a reversion to customary practice is occurring. According to Lionel Cliffe and Peter Lawrence in *The Dynamics of Land Tenure and Agrarian Systems in Africa* (1989),

> ... customary practices still persist despite legislation. Land on settlements, and especially land-buying companies' properties, and on consolidated holdings, is sub-divided for use between heirs. This has limited but not eliminated the rise of landlessness. (Cliffe and Lawrence 1989, p. 17)

In Kenya's 30-year experience with title registration, resettlement and African access to cash crop production, there has been an increase in production and 'in the use of improved methods and seed,' but Cliffe and Lawrence query to what extent these changes have occurred, expressly '*because* of land tenure rationalization...' (Cliffe and Lawrence 1989, p. 17). The inoperativeness of some land legislation in post-colonial rural Africa has been observed in Ghana and Madagascar as well. Such observations have been echoed in a 1983 World Bank survey of land tenure in Africa. Cliffe and Lawrence quote the report as saying that 'there is often no relationship between formal legislation and what actually takes place on the ground.' Further, 'The existence of such a gap,' according to Cliffe and Lawrence, 'between formal provision and grass roots reality is in part due ... to the existence of [a] separate residual sphere where "custom" is allowed to operate and to government's reluctance and often inability to enter it' (Cliffe and Lawrence 1989, p. 16). In fact, law, it would appear, is frequently unsuccessful on its own in replacing 'custom'. Customary practices 'tend to reassert themselves in indirect ways, but in ways that are not unaltered, merely transformed more by general social forces than by planned political interventions' (Cliffe and Lawrence 1989, p. 16).

Given the problems associated with earlier attempts at conversion to freehold, i.e. increased social inequality and the general inoperativeness of land law to replace (on its own) 'custom', less drastic policies encouraging individualization of land holding have been developed, specifically leasehold, in Lesotho and other countries in the region.

What were these problems with freehold conversion? According to the FAO report, at the empirical level many 'freehold' areas have reverted to customary practices. At a deeper level freehold conversion caused problems because changing land tenure is more than changing peoples' rights to land, more to the point it changes peoples' rights towards one another.

This recognition of the interconnectedness of land tenure with other aspects of agrarian social relations forms an important part of the view that customary land tenure is not by itself an obstacle to agricultural development. In the Lesotho case, the 'defence' of customary tenure has been taken up recently by e.g. Phororo (1979), Gattinara (1984), Santho et al. (1985), Mashinini (1983).

The aforementioned writers respond to all the allegations made about the 'unsuitability' of customary tenure to agricultural development.

With regard to the 'insecurity of tenure' obstacle, for instance, Gattinara (1983, pp. 111-113) presents evidence of inter-generational continuity of holdings in the lowlands, foothills and mountain zones of the country.

Phororo (1979) and Mashinini (1983) reinforce the observation of *de facto* inheritance by their stress on chiefs' reluctance to exercise the rights to revoke arable land — without close consultation with their Council of Elders (pre-1967) or Land Allocation Committees (post-1967).

Customary tenure has also been blamed for the promotion of 'sub-optimal' land buildings, resulting in poor economies of scale with the application of mechanization on farms.

Defendants argue that there is little incidence of sub-division of holdings because land is (*de facto*) inherited on a unit basis. That unit is the 'field'. In addition customary tenure has been flexible enough to accommodate mechanization programmes such as the government-sponsored Technical Operations Unit (T.O.U.) which does enhance economies of scale.

Customary tenure has also been associated with production exclusively for subsistence, thus discouraging commercial farming. Defendants such as Santho et al. and Mashinini (1983), point to historical evidence presented by Murray (op.cit.) and Parsons and Palmer (1977 op.cit.) which indicate that Sotho tenure was not an obstacle to Lesotho in the past, when it was considered a 'granary' of the region. Farmers produced a surplus for the market because there existed attractive markets and prices for their produce, a situation which has been subsequently changed (Chapter 3), and may be of more importance, according to Mashinini (1983), than land tenure in deterring farmers from producing a marketable surplus.

'Failure to provide security for credit' is the final obstacle to agricultural growth blamed on customary tenure. Defendants of the system challenge this view by pointing out that there is no lack of finance in Lesotho for agricultural purposes, because 60% of all migrants' wages are banked in Lesotho as deferred pay. There is sufficient finance in the country (Mashinini 1983, p. 40, Gattinara 1984, p. 98); the problem is the government failure to introduce incentives for investment.

It would appear that some policy makers in Lesotho have heeded both sides of the debate and have, with the 1979 Land Act, come down somewhere short of freehold, but pointed in the definite direction of private and exclusive social relationships to land. This is reflected in the views of Abner Mosaase, Commissioner for Lands in the Ministry of Interior:

> The divergent views of the two groups [opponents and defenders of custom] has invariably affected the direction of land policy including the Land Act 1979. (Mosaase 1987, p. 1)

Mosaase claims that the Land Act 1979 has been influenced by arguments on both sides:

1   The main provision is for leasehold not freehold.

2   Land still cannot be sold.

3   It still belongs to the Basotho nation, and allays fears of land being alienated from Basotho to foreigners.

4   The Land Act provides for *optional* leasehold for those wishing the security and mortgageability that such a tenure implies.

5   The Act reinforces the *de facto* pattern of inheritance by providing it *de jure*.

6   The Act also includes mandatory 'automatic' leasehold in selected agricultural areas and selected development areas.

Despite these concessions to both sides, Mosaase admits that the parties are still poles apart with the Ministry of Agriculture refusing to endorse or otherwise give input for the design or implementation of the Land Act (1987, p. 8). D.R. Phororo, a leading opponent of the Act, and defender of customary tenure, was until 1989 an important figure associated with the Ministry of Agriculture and this may account for the Ministry's stance on land policy.

One of Phororo's (1987) strongest contributions to the debate on land policy has been his focus on land as the ultimate (and for the majority the only) source of social security. In a speech given to the Land Policy Seminar in

1987, Phororo said that for poor rural and urban-based people

> ... that land ... is the only asset that assures them some amount of security ... When the chips are down, Mosotho man or even Mosotho woman ... will go, will leave [his/her] employer knowing he [or she] has got that piece of land on which to fall back on. Even a man in the mines, when he has had problems with his employer, when he has been involved in tribal fights, he knows that in the final analysis his security is in the land. Whether he uses that land to the best of his abilities, that is not the question. (Phororo 1987, p. 5)

In Lesotho then, land still has important social security functions. Changing land tenure then will have a bearing on that social security aspect of agrarian social relations.

> Land tenure is not an institution which can be separated from the everyday life of the people, a 'piece' which can be changed without upsetting the whole system. (Gattinara 1984, p. 101)

The aforementioned quote by Gattinara, in an FAO Report, *Basotho Culture and Lesotho Territory,* of the late 80's is hardly original, although it signals a break in the orthodox position of some Developmentalists employed in international agencies of development. As long ago as 1935 B. Malinowski wrote in *Coral Gardens* that

> Land tenure ... controls political life, gives access to opportunities, determines territorial citizenship, influences residence and settlement and is closely related to the economic utilization of the land, and is above all the relationship of man to soil in the widest sense. (Malinowski 1935, p. 318)

Malinowski was an anthropologist, and like other anthropologists of his time, specifically those working in the Southern African context, i.e. Schapera (1943), Ellenberger (1969) and Ashton (1952), he was a practitioner of a discipline which stressed the inter-connectedness of social change. The relationship between a society and soil cannot be divorced from social relations in general, or agrarian social relations in particular, as such changes in land tenure arrangements are part of a process, 'in which political, social, demographic, ecological, agronomic and economic changes interact and in turn act upon tenure arrangements' (Cliffe and Lawrence 1989, pp. 3-4). A more interconnected approach to agrarian change has recently been put on the agenda of international agencies. Certainly part of the reason for this shift must be the failure of freehold in previous African experience. At the same time some of the new tenurial arrangements put on the agenda, in particular leasehold, which arguably retain aspects of traditional systems, still allow for agrarian change within capitalist parameters. However the question must be asked as to whether leasehold will prove easier to implement, more operable on the ground, more acceptable by the population as a replacement for custom (yet still encouraging economic growth). This book aims to shed light on the above question. Specifically upcoming chapters will examine the role proposed by leasehold in Lesotho and explore in detail the scope of its introduction and the limited extent of implementation, which I believe is related to the questions of the operability of land legislation in the face of 'customary practices'.

For now though I turn to an examination of the specific context of debate in Lesotho: some land tenure changes in Southern Africa over the past 30 years that have helped to shape thinking in Lesotho and elsewhere. Our purpose is to explore in a broad comparative way, 'What has been the significance of legally induced tenure arrangements in non-socialist countries of the region?' It will then be possible to see to what extent arguments from these experiences and other arguments were part of the debate in Lesotho.

In responding to this question we will be looking at tenure changes in the Republic of South Africa (RSA), Swaziland, and Botswana. RSA tenurial reforms are obviously important for Lesotho, Swaziland and Botswana inasmuch as historically the BLS countries have been shaped by their relationship with RSA. Certainly, in the Lesotho case, we can pinpoint three areas wherein the South African example has been influential, despite the fact that its tenure changes imposed on the African population go back further than thirty years (although these changes, I hasten to add, are not all individual tenure).

1   We have already emphasized the depth of Lesotho's historical, political, and economic links with RSA, including migrant labour, the expropriation of the Western Territory, Cape Colony rule, and the constant threat of incorporation into RSA.

2   The South African state plays a role, sometimes greater, sometimes lesser in shaping the character of the Lesotho state, although not necessarily with regard to policy on land. Chapter 5 will deal with this more systematically. Some examples include

   a   South African support of the Basutoland National Party and Leabua Jonathan through financial assistance and promise of military support (if needed) prior to Jonathan's break with the apartheid regime in 1973.

   b   Also the RSA blockade of Lesotho in November and December 1985 precipitated a January coup inaugurating a military regime headed by

General Lekhanya. 'The coup was the outcome of a decade of systematic destabilization by Pretoria', wrote Judy Kimble. 'From 1979, in the face of rising domestic resistance, South Africa began to pressure Lesotho. The two worst moments were the two military raids of December 1982 and December 1985' (Kimble 1986, p. 27), but has included economic blockades and support for the Lesotho Liberation Army, the armed wing of a movement supposedly and paradoxically headed by members of the Basotho Congress Party, whose Party was banned after the 1970 coup.

c   RSA has provided judicial and bureaucratic expertise to Lesotho. These arms of Lesotho's state to a great extent have been designed to mirror RSA's. And by more general and subtle processes, South Africa has over half a century been the source of a certain orthodoxy over many land and agricultural issues (Beinart 1989).

3   The South African experience with changing land tenure is important to the Lesotho case finally, because RSA has implemented reforms which Basotho critics of the RSA regime have identified with apartheid and with the threat of incorporation. Therefore, there is a tendency on the part of some people in Lesotho to scrutinize policies — from colonial times to the present — mindful and suspicious of policies which remind them of their powerful neighbour. At the same time the RSA pattern may also be tempting to some elements within the Lesotho government, given the RSA's claims to have improved agriculture in African areas.

4.2   South African tenure in African areas

Many writers (Rutman 1969, Swart Commission 1983, Louw 1985) have echoed the orthodoxy outlined previously regarding communal tenure in South Africa. Conventionally it is pointed out that while white South African agricultural production is high, African agricultural production is stagnant or in decline. Communal tenure in African areas was seen to be the main blockage to growth. And in this way Land Reform was justified, and the geographical foundations for apartheid were laid.

Peter G. Moll (1988) is concerned, in his article 'Transition to Freehold in the South African Reserves', with the attempt to change tenure in the South African states of Kwazulu, Ciskei and Transkei, e.g. the eastern seaboard of RSA, which according to Moll shares a common history, including land being used as 'commonage for land grazing, and the rest for homesteads and cultivation of maize and sorghum' (Moll 1988, p. 349). Land was allocated to young men on marriage for residential and arable purposes, contingent on political allegiance.

Slightly differently from the Lesotho case, inheritance rights were recognized on the eastern seaboard and a widow could bequeath what had already been her husband's allocation 'on to her youngest son, her eldest sons having already set up homesteads elsewhere' (Moll 1988, p. 349).

The Glen Grey Act in 1894 introduced individual tenure on the eastern seaboard and 'enforced primogeniture and outlawed the subdivision of holdings' (Moll 1988, p. 349). The intention was that, according to Moll,

> ... in time, more people would be driven into the labour market ... It was hoped furthermore, that this form of limited individual tenure would induce farmers to enter the commercial economy by selling their produce. (Moll 1988, p. 350)

Moll has found that in practice that changeover from 'communal' to individual tenure was uneven in its acceptance by African areas. He writes,

> In villages which accepted the changeover, married men were granted arable plots of about 4.3 ha. and a building site under 'quitrent' tenure, together with commonage grazing rights. (Moll 1988, p. 350)

Moll says that over the past 40 years quitrent tenure has spread 'patchwork fashion' throughout the eastern seaboard, 'through all of Ciskei, 9 districts of Transkei and 2 districts of Natal' (Moll 1988, p. 350).

Exactly what is quitrent tenure? If we compare quitrent with what we know about 'communal' tenure, there are as Moll points out, a number of similarities, specifically mortgaging in both is unlawful, unused land is liable to forfeiture, allocations are small holdings. Under quitrent arable allocation is limited to one plot 3-4 ha. in size. The differences are very important though.

'Communal tenure' depended on chiefs for allocations. Because quitrent bypassed chiefly authority Pondoland Chiefs fought against the imposition of a quitrent tenure. Unlike communal tenure, quitrent allowed for land to be sold, (with Native Commissioner's approval), inheritance was automatic and no new allotments would be given. In other words the land distribution under quitrent was intended to be 'frozen', in that only one heir (primogeniture) was legally recognized and subdivision prohibited.

It was thought by the authorities that quitrent would greatly improve incentives for those who had land to production. The creation of this 'limited land market would', it was anticipated, 'enable less efficient farmers to sell to the more efficient' (Moll 1988, p. 350). In addition, automatic inheritance was intended to provide incentive to farmers to invest with the next generation in mind. A very crucial part of this policy was to encourage those 'less efficient'

87

farmers to give up their land and enter wage labour.

The effects of quitrent have, however, not lived up to the expectations. 'In fact', says Moll, 'observed differences in productivity are not substantial' (Moll 1988, p. 350). Landlessness has nevertheless increased among both tenure forms, the size of average holdings has decreased and finally farming methods were not substantially different from one tenure form to another.

According to Moll, 'the hopes of colonialists that individual tenure would improve production had failed'. He claims this failure was due, 'partly to the thinness of the land market; the majority of land transfers were from owner to heir' (Moll 1988, p. 350). Moll, in an aside, also claims that the evidence shows that allottees in communal areas were no more insecure than quitrent landholders. In addition Moll also argues that individual freehold had several drawbacks. The initial costs necessitated by surveying were prohibitive for many families when compared to the costs of gifts and bribes for a chief to allocate a plot.

Moll also recognized that there were significant social effects in the wake of the introduction of quitrent. In particular the undermining of chiefly authority represented by the introduction of quitrent has presented a problem. The close relationship between reserve governments and chiefs has fostered a strong mutual dependence between a chief's subjects and chiefs. What is so often forgotten, and this we will look at more closely in later chapters — is that undermining chiefly authority through the usurpation of their land allocation powers does not by itself make everyone in a community independent of chiefs' influence. Another social effect recognized by Moll was women's lowered accessibility to land. Quitrent tenure allows husbands to sell the small holding despite wives' protests, or protests of other members of the family. Widows may lose access to land in favour of senior sons. In the context of a high level of migrancy many rural families face potential dispossession, since the loss of labour power can lead to inability to cultivate regularly. Despite these effects Moll, controversially, does not believe that freehold would lead to less access to land for the poor. The creation of a market in land and the costs of tenure conversion 'may well be equivalent to the costs of bribes required under the communal system' (Moll 1988, p. 354). He concludes though that while money is blind, chiefs can be arbitrary in their decisions at times. In short, Moll is arguing that a creation of a genuine land market open to all is preferable to the system in existence wherein chiefly decisions are made not exclusively on the basis of bribes/gifts. Nevertheless, what has been called Land Reform in RSA cannot be understood outside of the system of racial capitalism that fostered it. These points are also relevant in the *contradiction* (recognized by the state) between capital's need for individual tenure and the loss of social control by chiefs.

4.3   Swazi tenure

Swaziland is a useful case for looking at changes in land tenure because communal tenure, in the face of prevailing trends, has been on the increase. Margo Russell in her article in *Ceres* (Number 113 1988) relates the increase in communal tenure alongside the expansion in agricultural and industrial production. 'Between 1914 and 1980', she writes, 'as manufacturing rose to 25% of gross domestic product, the area under communal tenure rose from 36% to 60% of the country's land area' (Russell 1988, p. 30).

Very important for the debate on the supposed incongruence between communal tenure and agricultural growth, the Swazi case seems (at first glance) to 'challenge the bland assertion of the incompatibility of this form of tenure with capitalist development' (Russell 1988, p. 30).

Why is communal tenure increasing in Swaziland? The response to this question must take into account the Swazi's historical experience of land alienation and the concerted effort on the part of the Swazi ruling groups to win back control over Swazi land.

In the late 1800's extensive land rights were given to 'foreign, mainly white, settlers who came to look for gold, grazing for their sheep, or a cheap living' (Russell 1988, p. 30). In spite of this, the Swazi monarchy maintained the basic principle of Swazi pre-colonial social relations, i.e. the inalienability of land. Nonetheless the Swazi monarchy collected revenue for the concessions.

Swaziland became a British protectorate in 1902 and conceded areas were made freehold — thus depriving the Swazi nation of the majority of their land and the monarchy of an important source of revenue. According to Russell,

> ...[o]ne third of each of their [concessionaires'] holdings was set aside for exclusive Swazi use and possession. In this way, the Swazi lost control over two-thirds of their land. (Russell 1988, p. 30)

Furthermore,

> ... the portion of land seized by the British Crown itself was rapidly sold off as freehold to settlers to raise revenue for roads, bridges, and other services which the new settler state required. (Russell 1988, p. 30)

The Swazi's Queen Regent responded with the creation of a

> ... national fund to purchase alienated land and urged all young men into the newly opened mines of Witswatersrand with a view to contribute a percentage of the mines [sic] earnings to the nation for this purpose. (Russell 1988, p. 31)

What began as a colonial period policy of land repurchase continues up to this day well past independence (including a U.K.-funded land deal to transfer 10% of the land back as part of the de-colonization process).

Russell believes that the history of land alienation has made the Swazi people 'impassioned' defenders of communal tenure and has contributed to a 'well-articulated' resistance against further encroachment on Swazi land rights.

> And by creating a market in privately owned land alongside communal land, it gave scope to that entrepreneurial minority who might otherwise have mounted a more sustained attack on a system which is probably rightly seen as a brake on certain kinds of uneven development. (Russell 1988, p. 31)

Richard Levin (1987) has looked more closely at the land tenure system in Swaziland in *Social Relations in Swaziland* and has found 3 types of tenure, and several different categories of land use within 'communal' land.

The three types of tenure include freehold Government land and Swazi Nation Land. With the suspension of the constitution in 1973 the latter two types of land, both of which are vested in the King, one might be confused as to the distinction between Government (what used to be called Crown) land and Swazi Nation Land (SNL). According to Levin, there is at least a legal distinction; if the Ministry of Agriculture requires the land, then it is deemed Government land. If, on the other hand, the King buys land and asks others to administer it, then that land is deemed SNL, with the King in trust of it (Levin 1987, pp. 153-154).

SNL itself has four categories of land occurring: there is chieftaincy allocated 'traditional' tenure, there is leasehold land to private firms, there are Irrigation Schemes and land held by Tibiyo/Tisuka, which are state farms purchased under U.K.-funded Land Purchase Programme. Although Tibiyo/Tisuka land is considered SNL, unlike other categories of SNL, it can be 'sold, leased or alienated as if it were freehold title deed land ... Tibiyo and Tisuka have launched capitalist productive enterprises on their land both with and independently of foreign capital' (Levin 1987, p. 165).

Notwithstanding Tibiyo and Tisuka land which clearly operates under quite different social relations from those practised 'traditionally', Levin's research, 'shows that there is no technical basis for the assumption that 'traditional' land tenure in Swaziland automatically makes for low output' (Levin 1987, p. 166).

Levin suggests that this situation, i.e. 'traditional' tenure leading to low output, is 'partially due to the existence of considerable opportunities for variation in the labour process and social division of labour and innovation in the form of fencing and land consolidation which are now possible on SNL' (Levin 1987, p. 166).

For Levin, 'the question of whether or not the existing form of customary tenure provides a sound legal environment which is conducive towards intensive agricultural development by peasant producers' (Levin 1987, p. 166) is not the most significant question.   For him of greater importance is identifying the limits and obstacles of customary allocation in the context of 'democratic structures'.   Referring specifically to his work on Mangwanyane Sugar Project, Levin has found that the social relations for Swazi customary tenure conflict with elected committees to oversee land use and control. Moreover even the presence of a 'progressive chief who encourages development is in itself insufficient' to ensure the 'efficiency of peasant agricultural production schemes' (Levin 1987, p. 167).   Levin believes this is due to the tendency for democratically elected committees to be inhibited by 'the presence of a chief and the constraints of customary tenure which, *inter alia*, make it difficult [sic] to evict and penalize individuals who fail to comply with the rules of the scheme' (Levin 1987, p. 167).

4.4   Tswana tenure

The Botswana case is useful to observers of changes in tenure in Lesotho because the new tenure option introduced in Lesotho through the 1979 Land Act, i.e. leasehold, bears a very close resemblance to the leasehold conversion provisions in The Grazing Land Policy (TGLP) which was first announced in July 1975.

According to Bennett, Laury, and Riddell (1986), in *Land Tenure and Livestock Development in Sub-Saharan Africa*,

The TGLP is a complex policy and program for the development of commercial livestock production in Botswana. At the heart of the policy is the granting of exclusive, long-term leasehold rights to extensive areas of previously communal rangeland to cattle owners commanding sufficient capital resources and management expertise to engage in strictly commercial cattle ranching enterprises.

TGLP also seemed to make some concessions to other classes, besides entrepreneurs:

The grazing policy includes a strong rhetorical commitment to equity and fair income distribution, and at least initial program plans provided that rents generated by ranch leases would be invested in projects to improve the management of the remaining communal ranges, still occupied by small holders. (Bennett et al. 1986, p. 94)

But in practice there is no evidence that the grazing policy has lived up to its rhetoric. Indeed, R.P. Werbner (1980) and Louis A. Picard (1988) have examined the role of the bureaucracy in the implementation of TGLP and therefore are able to shed light on the vexed question of how and why the new land law frequently benefits the implementers themselves.

For Werbner, he has detected an 'us and them' mentality in TGLP which contributes to and exacerbates the colonial legacy of plural tenure/legal systems. He quotes a 1971 speech by Sekahoma Khama, President Khama's cousin and a 'big' farmer, as an example of this kind of thinking:

> 'For the big farmers who are keen to invest money in development, a survey of a vast grazing area should be made and liberal loans for the purchase of farms in this area should be demarcated into well-delineated farms which should be leased for long terms and developed. The rest of the country should be left as rural areas where traditional users of land should be encouraged to improve their agriculture and animal husbandry ... if they form themselves into groups they can enjoy the benefits of the large scale farmer ... locus for development, improved stock, fencing ... marketing facilities.' (Werbner 1980, p. vi)

Werbner sees the attack on the indigenous tenure system as coming from two sides, from the 'logic and rhetoric of capitalist farmers or ranchers ... and technocrats and planners' (Werbner 1980, p. vi).

However, Picard (1980) establishes a stronger connection between capitalist farming and bureaucrats. Cattle farming is made successful owing to investment and 'if we know that the bureaucracy is the only group ... with relatively high economic status', then we need to assume 'that the bureaucratic bourgeoisie or organizational bourgeoisie uses its power to influence public policy' (Picard 1980, p. 315). The only question is *how*, to what *extent* are they allowed to use the state machinery in their own economic interests.

Picard has identified two levels of policy making over the grazing land scheme, 'those who formulate and those who implement'. The former level were made up of 'less than 30 political leaders' and about 'the same number of senior bureaucrats'. At the second level were 'policy elites, who created an evaluation of support in business and government' to fend off critics of the scheme. Picard is certain that leasehold and other aspects of TGLP 'will mostly benefit the bureaucracy (senior levels) of other members of Botswana's socio-economic elite who can most readily take advantage of the move towards freehold land tenure...' (Picard 1980, p. 349).

Picard also situates the Developmentalists in his argument about 'who benefits under TGLP?' He says that 'Experts might argue that the fact that the policy serves political and administrative elites does not mean that the changes should not be undertaken' (Picard 1980, p. 350).

Werbner, however senses an ambivalent effect — he quotes Colclough and McCarthy at length,

> Many of the more redistributive policies ... have been advocated or encouraged by expatriate advisors ... However the extent to which these outside influences are an effective force for redistribution is probably small. (Werbner 1980, p. 244)

On the other hand, Colclough and McCarthy distinguish between individual expatriate experts and the policies of the agencies for which they work,

> ... Aid agencies themselves, while preaching the needs of the poor have continued to support projects which favour the wealthy ... In addition, some of the expatriates whom they supply under technical co-operative arrangements are out of sympathy with this part of the goal, and even where this is not the case such people often lack the local knowledge and cultural background to know how it might be achieved. (Werbner 1980, p. 244)

I have outlined the Botswana experience despite the fact that the reform there has been with regard to grazing, and not arable land. The situation in Lesotho is the reverse, with the Land Act 1979 attempting change on arable lands, and a TGLP-type policy has not been approved with regard to arable lands in Botswana. Nonetheless, the Botswana case is useful in that

1   Leasehold is the major mechanism being introduced into law and this formula was adopted as a compromise between capitalism and uneven development and also the concessions to poor were mainly at the rhetorical level;

2   The level of NGO interest is similar historically;

3   Botswana and Lesotho share some similar features in their political economies.

The above discussion of tenurial changes in South Africa, Swaziland and Botswana were necessarily brief and broadly sketched. Nevertheless useful comparisons with Lesotho can be made, if we bear in mind that our purpose for comparison is to understand the debate on land tenure in Lesotho.

Firstly, in all cases indigenous tenure is under attack from some officials and experts and one kind of orthodoxy for being inimical to high levels of agricultural productivity. While questionable in logic and evidence, that at least is the justification used by governments to initiate changes in the tenure system leading to greater individualization and exclusivity of land use.

Nonetheless in all the cases sketched some form of 'customary' tenure has been in evidence, if by customary we take to mean chiefly allocated plots for arable use.

Secondly, despite attacks on the chieftaincy, chiefs remain important arbiters of rural power. They are also in all the cases cited represented in the senior ranks of bureaucracies as well as in the accumulating classes and as such are able to command the status of 'traditional authority' while at the same time wielding state and class power and therefore freehold undermines that power and is resisted. The dictates of labour migrancy and political worries about landless unemployed leads to compromise.

Third, customary tenure and capitalist social relations can and do co-exist. The problem of declining agricultural productivity in African areas cannot be laid at the altar of communal tenure in South Africa nor be simply solved. Land Reform there cannot be understood without reference to segregation and apartheid and the mechanisms of labour migrancy and Bantustan control. The Swazi case also is steeped in a history of land alienation. While Tswana land has not been subject to such massive foreign intervention choice pieces of territory were incorporated into RSA, and the nation existed with the continual threat of incorporation into RSA until independence. The Botswana case is interesting in that unlike Swaziland and South Africa, leasehold has been introduced on grazing areas only, specifically to encourage commercial cattle farming. Botswana also provides us with a case wherein tenure change has been closely associated with international agencies on a large scale. In general, though, all cases feature legislation aimed at limited individualizing tenure short of freehold, new conditions for access to land, and the imposition of governmental authorities over and alongside that of chiefs. In Lesotho as well, the dictates of labour migration and need for access to land to meet some 'reproduction' requirements keeps open some access to land for *most people* if *not all*, crucial if political leaders are to avoid the problems of landless unemployed.

5 Land legislation and the post-colonial state

Introduction

Thus far in the book we have attempted to show how customary practices on land changed, specifically as a result of colonial intervention in the powers of chiefs *vis-à-vis* themselves and their subjects, or 'commoners', and *vis-à-vis* the monarchy and other subordinate branches of the chieftaincy (Chapter 2).

We have also discussed how the chieftaincy was attacked through the implementation of the Pim Reforms and how Indirect Rule was one mechanism used by the colonial state to address the changing needs of British capital in South Africa while keeping costs of administering Basutoland as low as possible. Financial costs were to be met by higher taxes, more efficiently collected. Political costs were paid by chiefs whose powers and numbers and sources of revenue were drastically cut (Chapter 3).

None of this amounted to a sudden transformation of tenure in the narrow legalistic sense of the word. But we have seen that colonial interventions at the beginning of the colonial period and later with the imposition of Indirect Rule did affect agrarian social relations in general, and in particular those relations between people as expressed through land.

In the last chapter we have discussed some of the arguments for individualizing tenure in the African context, and looked briefly at some moves toward individualized tenure in the region. We closed the last chapter with an outline of the debate on land tenure in Lesotho, and how government representatives associated with the Act perceive the legislation as a compromise between opposing sides of the debate.

We can now focus more clearly on the origins of the 1979 Land Act, discussing its provisions, the reasons for its adoption and the interests promoting it.

In the first half of this chapter we turn to the land tenure debate in Lesotho once again, this time situating it within the context of the post-colonial state and its previous land legislation. In the second half we explore the provisions of the Land Act 1979 with special attention to the introduction of leasehold and inheritance provisions on arable land, including a discussion of the *Land Policy Review Report* (1989) with its recommendations for amendments to the Land Act.

5.1   The post-colonial state

The state in Africa like the 'state' worldwide is the subject of deep and long debate with regard to its role, composition, powers and constraints on those powers. John Lonsdale (1981, and 1979 with Bruce Berman) who has written extensively on the nature of the colonial and post-colonial state in Africa says that part of the controversy lies in the fact of intellectuals' own changing political aspirations for Africa. The study of the state is also at the vortex of understanding political and economic crises in the capitalist and socialist worlds. Still another problem lies in the unresolvable contradictions between structure and action, function and agency as expressed in Marxist terms in the debate between Poulantzas and Miliband.

Lonsdale has discerned what he calls three 'paradigms' in the literature on the state in Africa. Over the past forty years there has evolved the autonomist, the instrumentalist and the process theories of the state. The autonomist model encompasses all the theories of the state which privilege the latter's independent and sovereign character; independent from external forces, hence the importance of nationalism, independent from internal forces, hence the importance of charismatic leaders as the main decision-makers, nation builders etc.

Another model takes as its starting point the notion that the state is an apparatus which can be used by a class against other classes, one ethnic group against others. Closely related to the instrumentalist model are the theoretical interventions made by Alavi (1982), Saul (1974), Shivji (1976), Von Freyhold (1977) and Leys (1976). Alavi's analysis in particular has proved of lasting importance in that he postulates a different geographical and national location of most Third World states' bourgeoisie. Because one of the legacies of colonialism was an undeveloped and suppressed indigenous capitalist class, metropolitan bourgeoisies have been the main organizers of capital in the post-colonial era. In the absence of a truly national bourgeoisie, those who govern, 'acting as the executive committee of the ruling class' (who are overseas) are drawn from another class and have been called comprador bourgeoisie, or bureaucratic bourgeoisie, the former term distinguishes a governing class which collaborates in creating conditions most amenable to capital accumulation and expansion on behalf of foreign interests. The latter term has been applied to cases where the state has behaved as a collective capitalist. The crux of the matter in understanding the varied explanations of the character of African states for Lonsdale is that both the colonial state and the post-colonial state 'were imposed according to the needs of the market rather than developing as the continuous culmination of internal social conflicts' (Lonsdale 1981, p. 144).

Lonsdale's third paradigm of the state, the process model, emphasizes 'the slow, conflict-ridden, continuous formation of the state'. In this model of the state, the one which he seems to find the most useful, the state is seen as being made up of 'successive pragmatic rules of power which become norms ...new layers of institutions to cope with new problems ... [then] partially rubbed out and written over again' (Lonsdale 1981, p. 151).

Part of the process of state formation is that 'one instrument of state clashes against another ... anomalies occur frequently'. Lonsdale says that 'managerial roles [with] their political and administrative ramifications ... can scarcely be adequately explained unless seen in some part as a continual response to the social disorders and economic crises of capitalism' (Lonsdale 1981, p. 152). Also, '... one must be more alert to the constraints on economic development which were imposed by the conflicts within and contradiction between the different forms of production, non-capitalist and capitalist, within the former colonial lands' (ibid.).

Applying this variation of the process model of the state to the Kenyan case, Lonsdale makes 'four points of general importance in understanding the role of the colonial state in Africa'. Firstly he sees the state as both a factor of cohesion and the focus of contradictions in the context of capitalist articulation with preexisting forms and/or modes of production. Secondly he sees the colonial state as providing the conditions for the reproduction of settler capitalism and its justification. Thirdly the colonial state provides a way of fragmenting African resistance. This is done by containing African political and economic forces by representing them in the state on the basis of ethnic categories. Fourthly he explains the expansion of powers on the part of the state by referring to its increasing difficulties in managing the crises of its articulated economy. Such crises stemmed from on the one hand the socially disruptive consequences of imposing capitalist laws of motion onto and alongside indigenous modes of production and on the other hand 'the restructuring of local production to meet metropolitan demand' (ibid., p. 153). All four points while generated from the Kenyan example are equally applicable in the Basutoland case. Furthermore changes within the institution of the chieftaincy were pivotal to the process of state formation.

In Lonsdale's analysis of the colonial and post-colonial states, he is arguing for an analysis of Third World states which brings their determining factors back to the society of which they are a part, rather than seeking those factors in a country's relationship with what he has termed a 'metro-bogey'.

The post-colonial state in Lesotho

Moving our discussion of states from the general to the particular, we find that there have been a few sustained studies of the state in Lesotho, Judy Kimble's work on the colonial state (e.g. 1982, 1985, 1986), John D. Holm's (1972) work on the post-Colonial state and Gabriele Winai-Strom's (1978, 1986) detailed look at state institutions, providing the key examples.

Kimble's work employs an articulationist framework for understanding the changing character of the Basutoland colonial state. Holm takes a statist approach in explaining the autonomist and expansionist behaviour of the post-colonial state in Lesotho, while Winai-Strom is more interested in assessing the degree to which the Lesotho state is dependent on South Africa. There is a rough fit between these works and the three paradigms outlined previously. Kimble's (1985, pp. 44-57) work comes closest to the process theory of the state in that she seems to appreciate the changing contingencies within which the colonial state operates. Holm's work (Bardill and Cobbe 1985, pp. 154-157) apparently fits the autonomist model and Winai-Strom's work can be said to be instrumentalist in the sense that the post-colonial state in Lesotho is seen to be an instrument of certain sectors in the South African bourgeoisie (Winai-Strom 1986, pp. 95-130).

Another view of the state in Lesotho concentrates on the ways in which the post-colonial state does not challenge the system of labour migration which has dominated the national economy since the turn of the century. D.K. Kowet (1978), author of *Land, Labour Migration and Politics in Southern Africa* puts forth a strong thesis that labour migration undermined attempts by the subordinate classes to force chiefs into greater democratization of land distribution. Kowet argues that the ruling group that assumed state power at independence did not question Lesotho's role as a labour reserve and like Winai-Strom, Kowet says that the Lesotho leadership sought to win investment from South Africa and that the post-colonial legislation on land and on other aspects of the economy sought not only to break the power base of the chieftaincy but also to win South African support. Like Bardill and Cobbe, Kowet views the governing group which assumed state power to be weak in support. In order to compensate for the lack of a strong base, the government made ruling party membership a condition for wage employment, not only in the public sector, but in the private sphere as well, with the

Republic's labour recruiting organizations following suit (Kowet 1978, pp. 208-212).

Both Holm and Winai-Strom have been criticized by Bardill and Cobbe for the excesses and/or silences inherent in their approaches. Holm for instance suggests that the state in Lesotho 'has in many ways become the dominant force in society' and far from carrying out any discernible class project (in Marxist terms) or responding to a plurality of vested interests (in liberal terms) the Lesotho state has since independence been carrying out its own project. Holm justifies this assertion by pointing to the fact that the state has been destroying the power bases of the chieftaincy, church, and that of white and Asian traders. This has been replaced by the 'self-aggrandizement of the holders of state power who through political ambition or through a desire to make their mark on posterity' have created a state which acts independently of internal and external controls (Bardill and Cobbe 1980, pp. 154-155).

Holm's basic excess lies in overstating the Lesotho state's ability to be independent of the South African controlled Customs Union and foreign aid. His overwhelming silences concern South African successes at preventing Japanese, West German and Italian investment. Bardill and Cobbe (1985, pp. 156-157) critique Holm's analysis by questioning the basis for the state's expansion. Starting from the basic Marxist premise of looking at the relationship between capitalist accumulation and the state, Bardill and Cobbe claim that the government which came to power at independence, the Basotho National Party (BNP) did not have the support of the important albeit small class of indigenous commercial interests. Instead this class supported the Basotho Congress Party (BCP), a more populist and radical party whose platform called for less South African economic dominance and greater reliance on the Basotho's own resources. The first years of the BNP government favoured closer economic relations with the Republic and this move toward even greater integration with the Republic was the linchpin of many of the government's development policies. Although the BNP won the election in 1965 and led the nation to independence in 1966, its margin of victory was slender and its support base was weak, lacked the backing of teachers, other members of the African petty bourgeoisie as well as senior chiefs. In view of this Bardill and Cobbe argue that it was essential for the state to build up its own basis for support over time by consolidating its own power and by weakening the opposition parties, especially the BCP. Some of the mechanisms used to bring about these objectives 'include the politicization and centralization of state institutions, the denial of effective constitutional mechanisms for the articulation of opposition interests and grievances, and the somewhat paradoxical combination of intimidation and co-optation of opposition leaders' (Bardill and Cobbe 1985, p. 157).

99

On the other hand the state has succeeded in broadening its basis of support by attaching political conditions to employment and offering relatively attractive salaries in state institutions. Bardill and Cobbe employ the term coined by M. Von Freyhold (1977), 'supportive classes' to describe this strata 'who do not control the state but which benefit from it' (Bardill and Cobbe 1985, p. 158). Inasmuch as education and family clout still play an important role in determining the likelihood of being employed in the civil service, for instance, it suggests that the supportive classes are 'drawn largely from sections of the ... petty bourgeoisie and from the lower ranks of the chieftainship' (Bardill and Cobbe 1985, p. 158). It would have been impossible to fund the expansion of the state without revenue from two sources, the Customs Union and foreign aid, in contrast to Holm's view that the Lesotho state has acted independently of external forces. Holm says that the state has been able to usurp the power of certain powerful groups e.g. the chiefs. However we will see in upcoming sections that the chieftaincy has been able to frustrate various attempts to totally depower them, especially in the arena of land allocation. Even Holm himself has had to admit this in his own work.

Winai-Strom has also been critiqued by Bardill in the *South African Labour Bulletin* (Vol.6, Number 4 1980). Her main excess has been seen as overstating '[Prime Minister Jonathan's] failings of the regime, important as they are; and for placing too little emphasis on the structural constraints imposed upon it by Lesotho's historically determined position in relation to metropolitan and particularly South African capital' (Bardill 1980, pp. 86-87).

In particular Bardill charges her with 'providing no real theoretical exploration of the nature and role of the post-colonial state, and specifically of its class determination' (Bardill 1980, p. 87). In other words although Winai-Strom's work is placed within a dependency framework, in the end the continuing state of dependence is placed squarely at the feet of Jonathan and 'the particular proclivities of the BNP government' (ibid.).

Bardill's reading of Winai-Strom emphasizes her tendency to cast state institutions in a neutral role which is at odds with her overall framework. Bardill as a Marxist cannot theoretically accept the neutrality of state institutions:

> ... [T]he state emerges in class societies to protect the interests of the dominant class; or perhaps more accurately to protect and reinforce a prevailing set of relations of production under which the dominant class is able, through its control of the means of production and its use of this to extract surplus from the subordinate classes, to guarantee the conditions of its own reproduction and dominance as a class. This the state does by repressing, containing and deflecting the struggles of the dominated

classes to overcome their subordinate position, and by mediating the contradictions that exist between the various sections or fractions of the dominant class itself — contradictions which left unchecked might ultimately weaken its collective supremacy in relation to the subordinate strata. (Bardill 1980, p. 89)

Having said that, it is important to keep in mind that no indigenous bourgeoisie has been allowed to emerge in Lesotho, courtesy of policies which protected British capital in South Africa during the colonial era and South African capital more recently. At the same time what is apparent is that the Lesotho state has attempted to take advantage of the fact that the dominant metropolitan class is divided into different fractions with sometimes slightly differing interests.

Although South Africa has been successful in preempting European and Japanese foreign investment in Lesotho (Bardill and Cobbe 1985, p. 157) there has been a sharp increase in the volume of aid that the Lesotho state has received since Jonathan's anti-apartheid stance and since Pretoria's policy of destabilization in Lesotho and the region in general. Holm has claimed that the increase in aid has not led to a 'commensurate increase in the amount of leverage donor agencies have been able to exert' (ibid., p. 156). Bardill and Cobbe disagree by drawing attention to key programmes in the government's development strategy, like for instance the Cooperative Crop Production Program which has failed to get donor funding. The interests of white and Asian traders continue to be protected at the expense of Basotho traders and would-be traders as evidenced by the sacking of Cabinet Minister for Commerce and Industry, Joel Moitse for, according to Cobbe and Bardill, 'his specific advocacy of a more aggressive stance toward such groups' (ibid., p. 156).

South Africa also shapes the economic character of the country not only with its ability to stop certain foreign investors from coming to Lesotho but also by its own ability to invest in Lesotho; taking advantage of its open door, *laissez-faire* policies aimed at attracting foreign investment (Winai-Strom 1986, pp. 98-105).

Since 1986 there is evidence that some South African capitalists are beginning to move their operations to Lesotho in order 'to break into the European and American markets, (*Financial Times* 4th October 1989, p. 7) from which South African-made goods are either barred or boycotted'. Moreover it is not necessary for the goods to originate in Lesotho, only that they have at least 25% valued added in Lesotho. This percentage entitled the products to carry a Lesotho certificate of national origin. In 1988 manufactured goods, primarily clothing, became the biggest single export-earner growing from 7m *maloti* in 1986 to 49m *maloti* in 1988. Since 1986 more than 20 companies, predominantly textiles, have moved to Lesotho. In addition to South African firms, there are operations from Hong Kong, Taiwan and the US. Asian investors in particular benefit from the fact that Lesotho enjoys access to the US market under the Generalized System of Preference, a status which many newly industrialized nations have recently lost. That plus the 'quota imposed on textile producing nations by the Multi-Fibre Agreement explains why Asian investors have moved their base to Lesotho' (*Financial Times* 4th October 1989, p. 7). One ceramics firm from the US has moved to Lesotho 'mostly for customers in SACU, who under the weight of the constantly depreciating South African rand can no longer import from abroad on an economic basis' (ibid.). It is interesting that while South Africa was successful in stopping foreign investment during the Jonathan regime, it is now, under the pressure of international sanctions, finding General Lekhanya's Lesotho a useful place to spread some of its capital, and moreover is willing to allow (or is unable to prevent) others sharing this base as well.

Since independence in 1966 Lesotho has been trying through its parastatal the Lesotho National Development Corporation, to attract foreign investment with a package that allows for a 15-year tax holiday, government subsidies for training, favourable terms on loans, security for investment through its membership in the Multilateral Investments Guarantee Agency (Winai-Strom 1986, p. 98). Lesotho also provides foreign investors with free access to foreign exchange and allows for the repatriation of investment capital and earnings. But it has only been in the context of a military takeover of the Lesotho government on the one hand and a climate of limited international sanctions on South Africa on the other hand that significant foreign investment has increased, and most of that from South Africa.

Pre-1979 land legislation

In this section we examine some of the government's earlier attempts at changing the way land is allocated, managed, and used among the Basotho. There were six major pieces of land legislation enacted before the 1979 Land Act. These include the Land Advisory Boards Procedure Regulations of 1965 (Reg No 15 of 1965), The Land Procedure Act of 1967 (Act 24 of 1967), The Land Husbandry Act of 1969 (Act 22 of 1969), The Administration of Lands Act of 1973 (Act 16 of 1973), The Land Act of 1973 (Act 20 of 1973), and The Land Regulations of 1974 (Legal Notice No 9 of 1974).

The legislation can be divided into two distinct categories. The first category, within which the 1965, 1967, the Land Act of 1973 and the Land Regulations of 1974 fit, attempt to democratize the decision-making process on land at the local level. These laws attempted to set down national guidelines for the election and functioning of land boards, (and in the case of the 1974 legislation, 'village development committees') rights of appeal and procedures to be followed for land allocation. Other land legislation enacted during the post-colonial pre-1979 period, i.e. The Land Husbandry Act of 1969 and the Administration of Lands Act 1973 attempted to establish greater governmental control, through the instruments of the Ministry of the Interior and/or of the Ministry of Agriculture, over land matters. Specifically the Land Husbandry Act of 1969 was intended to facilitate soil conservation, protect water resources and prevent harmful agricultural practices among rural producers, by establishing the right of the Ministry of Agriculture to lay down regulations concerning the control and regulation of grazing, the limitation of numbers of animals in a grazing area as well as the limitation of certain species of grazing animals. This law also attempted to establish traditional law as codified in the Laws of Lerotholi as being 'subsidiary to the 1969 Act'. Likewise the 1973 Administration of Lands Act also gave broad powers to the government, in this case the Ministry of Interior in particular. This legislation also introduced a system of leases and licences to be established on all but agricultural land. With respect to leases and licences, the law allows for rent to be charged with the revenue to be used for public purposes. The same legislation also introduces the concept of Selected Development Areas, where the state is able to target a specific non-agricultural geographical area for mandatory leasehold conversion and subsequent government controlled development.

As will become clear in the next section, The Land Administration Act of 1973 has many features found later in the 1979 Land Act. Indeed it has been observed by Eckert that in 'many of its provisions this Act anticipated (or provided the model for) the 1979 Land Act', and further that The Administration of Lands 1973 Act and The 1969 Land Act 'are consolidated into the Land Act 1979' (Eckert 1980, p. 28). However Eckert's observation begs the question of why it would be necessary to restate what are in essence very similar laws over and over again. If we go back for instance to our first category of land laws, i.e. those attempting to establish orderly land allocation procedures and introducing a more popular (as opposed to chiefly) voice in local land matters we find that these principles are stated in no less than four laws (as well as in Section 90 of the Constitution) and are stated as well in the Land Act 1979. The short answer is that the principles require restating because thus far the laws and their implementation have been ineffective in convincing the subjects of the law to conform to the practices being introduced. Eckert himself in his discussion of the 1979 Land Act recognizes the disparity between what is law and what is practised on Sotho land:

> There have previously been several significant attempts to effect change in Lesotho's land tenure. None have been fully successful. Some designs have been language unutilized; others have reached the state of legislation only to be incompletely implemented. (Eckert 1980, p. 45)

Although Eckert allows that the 1979 Land Act 'differs in the extent of debate and participation during its preparation ... and in the thorough and systematic preparations being made for its implementation ...'. Nevertheless he warns that because the 1979 Land Act calls for many changes, many of which will have an impact on 'the structure of society and the polity', that '[i]t remains to be seen whether, and how far, implementation can proceed' (Eckert 1980, p. 45).

Before moving on to the next section which looks at the 1979 Act in detail let us attempt to link our previous discussion of the state with the foregoing look at land legislation in post-colonial Lesotho. Establishing such a link is important for illustrating the significance of the Land Act 1979. In particular one's conception of the Lesotho state will condition one's understanding of the Act. An analysis following Holm's notion of the state in Lesotho would understand the legislation as an attempt on the part of the government to increase its control by deepening its influence even so far as to the local level of land allocation. Winai-Strom would emphasize the extent to which land legislation had been designed by and for South Africans and how many of its provisions logically follow the capitalist development strategy set in motion at independence. Following Bardill and Cobbe one would be reminded that while the state may have its own project it has nonetheless not been successful in carrying it out, hence the necessity for stating and restating the same legal principles which in one way or another remain partially implemented. A dependency type analysis like Winai-Strom's also would probably not be able to address the problem of why the same legal principles have failed to become adopted.

But such a problem becomes an important area of focus if we accept Bardill's Marxist definition of the state as the set of institutions which '... protect and reinforce a prevailing set of relations of production under which the dominant class is able, through its control of the means of production and its use of this to extract surplus from the subordinate classes, to guarantee the conditions of its own reproduction and dominance as a class' (Bardill op.cit.).

Such a definition reinforces our own view that change in land tenure is more than a new legal precept of holding land for some technical purpose but rather that tenurial changes in the broadest sense stem from or are a part of fundamental changes in social and in particular production relations to further certain interests. In other words post-colonial legislation in Lesotho has struggled to introduce a new set of production relations on land which are more conducive to the interests of the dominant class. Within such a class-orientated context, the failure of such legal projects as the establishment of Land Boards, and the introduction of leasehold in agricultural areas, can be attributed to either resistance from subordinate classes, or the government acting without sufficient support from the dominant classes.

5.2   Provisions of the 1979 Land Act

The purpose of this part of the chapter is to provide:

1   an exposition of the major provisions contained in the Land Act, including

2   an account of how and to what extent the Act has been implemented, and

3   an outline of how leases are processed;

4   major provisions of the 1979 Land Act

The Land Act 1979 as printed in Supplement No 1 to Gazette No 41 of 14th December 1979 has thirteen parts. The bulk of the legislation is best understood if we begin by looking at provisions for Agricultural and Urban land in the legislation as this is how land is distinguished in the legislation.

Agricultural land and urban land

There are broad provisions of the Act which introduce new tenure options for arable lands in the rural areas. The traditional land tenure system was based on the premise that all Basotho were entitled to arable land and for subsistence. With the expropriation of Basotho lands by the Afrikaners late in the last century, and with the increase of population, over the century (but its impact being felt particularly during the 1970s), Lesotho does not have enough arable land to accommodate new families (Mosaase, 1984, p. 2, Mashinini 1983, p. 10, Bruce 1984a, p. 1). The average size of arable land holdings is approximately 1.7 hectares (Eckert 1980, p. 8). It is argued by many proponents of the Act that the small size and generally poor quality of the holdings results in the inviability of farming. As a consequence families seek income from the so-called 'modern sector', i.e. the urban areas of Lesotho or more likely the mines and farms and manufacturing centres of South Africa. Within this context proponents argue that it is necessary to provide secure tenure 'in order to promote intensification of production through increased investment on existing land holdings' (Bruce 1984a, p. 1).

Four mechanisms

The 1979 Land Act introduces four mechanisms to achieve the basic objective of tenure security as an incentive for increased investment. First there is the modification of the rules of inheritance. Secondly there is the selective introduction of an agricultural lease, at the option of the allottee or through Government instigation under the Selected Agricultural Areas provisions of the Act. Third is the government instigated automatic conversion of agricultural land in urban areas to a new tenurial arrangement — the licence. The fourth and final mechanism is the legal provision for new institutions to implement the Land Act. These include the Land Committees, Office of the Commissioner of Lands and a Land Tribunal.

Provisions for state ownership

All land in Lesotho is owned by the state on behalf of the Basotho nation. The power to grant titles is vested in the Office of the King as Head of State. Land Administration is the responsibility of the Minister of the Interior. Titles are granted by Land Committees in rural areas. Basotho citizens requiring land must apply to the chairman of the Committee involved. The applicant must be a Basotho citizen or the holder of a permit of indefinite sojourn. In addition, there are various legal formulae for determining the nationality of companies, corporations, co-operatives etc. While these provisions are from previous legislation, they are restated in the 1979 Act (Bruce 1984a, pp. 37-41).

Types of title available in rural areas

Under the 1979 Land Act land in rural areas is held by virtue of two types of title, an 'Allocation' and a registerable Title. The latter applies to land held for use in non-agricultural pursuits, i.e. commercial, educational, residential, religious, industrial, etc. An 'Allocation' is title to land used primarily for agriculture, specifically crop land (Bruce 1984a, p. 41).

The Allocation is similar to the traditional allocation of pre-1979 in that the use rights are non-transferable and non-negotiable. The use rights are similarly for the lifetime of the individual allottee. The difference is that under the 1979 Land Act arable fields are subject to inheritance. In law the traditional allocation always reverted in theory to the custody of the chief for reallocation. Usually the practice was to reallocate the fields to the next generation of the deceased's family, specifically to the eldest son. Under the 1979 Act an allottee may through a last will and testament bequeath their

106

holdings to whomever they wish. If the landholder dies intestate the land will pass on to the eldest son. Should that course prove impossible, then the land becomes the subject of a family council for a year. At the end of that time, the family council appoints a beneficiary. In the event of a deadlock in the family's decision, the land then reverts to the local Land Committee for reallocation. The object of these provisions is to remove any grounds for fear on the part of farmers that any improvements they make to the land will not be enjoyed by their families (albeit through a *single* heir [Eckert 1980, p. 43]) after the landholder's death due to the land being reallocated outside of the family. However certain development regulations in Sesotho law have been strengthened with regard to use rights. Specifically use rights can be revoked on various grounds by the local chief and his Land Committee. The 1980 Land Regulations Act gives four major grounds for revocation; over-grazing, refusal or inability to implement governmental policy on combating soil erosion, refusal or inability to cultivate crop land for over three years, and finally, on the grounds that the allocated land is required for public purposes (Bruce 1984a, pp. 42-43).

While the inheritance provision represents a major shift in land law in Lesotho in practice it has been argued that the law merely codifies what has been generally the case in Sesotho law and custom pre-1979, i.e. landholder's offspring have the strongest rights to their father's land when the fields are being reallocated (Hamnett 1975, Gattinara 1984, p. 113, Mashinini 1983, p. 14).

The Agricultural Lease, however, marks a far more radical departure with pre-1979 tenure. The Agricultural Lease can be transferred sub-leased, mortgaged, and willed. Leased land is more secure than allocated land, it is argued, in that leased land need not be subject to customary communal practices in Sesotho tenure like the opening of cultivated fields to grazing after harvest. The exclusivity of possession offered by such an arrangement is not without its own conditions. Under section 8 of the Act, for instance, a lessee can only sell or mortgage or sublet his interest in the leased land with the consent of the Minister of Interior. As with an allocation a lease can be inherited. John W. Bruce in *A Layman's Guide to the Land Act* sets out the rather complex inheritance pattern:

A lease can be disposed of by will or other designation of an heir. Where there is no will and the lease is not governed by a written law related to succession, the matter will be handled by the Land Committee under regulations 7 and 8. If no legal heir is available to inherit the lease by a surviving spouse and/or minor children are in occupation, the Commissioner should issue a writ of occupation, notwithstanding the reversion of the lease interest of the state. (Bruce 1984a, p. 44)

Proponents of the Act claim that the introduction of the agricultural lease will provide mobility in land transactions, revenue in the form of ground rent for leased land (in excess of what is required for normal residential use) and 'can be the basis of a regularized and controlled land market', replacing 'the existing cladenstine [sic] land market which has resulted in most of the good agricultural land being lost to the peri-urban sprawl and ribbon development' (Mateka 1987, p. 7).

Agricultural leases can be obtained through an optional application to the Commissioner of Lands. Several steps must be taken in order to acquire a lease, including vetting by the Land Committee, the Ministry of Agriculture, as well as the Ministry of the Interior. In addition there are cadastral surveying costs that must be paid by the applicant, as well as public notification in the newspapers of the applicant's intention to acquire a lease on a designated plot. Government spokesmen point out very readily that the lease is not for everyone: 'unless the agricultural activity envisaged is economically viable and the land has potential the allottee could be ill-advised to secure an agricultural lease' (Mosaase 1984, p. 12, Kanel 1984, pp. 90-91).

Selected agricultural areas

Another new policy designed to circumvent the sporadic and piecemeal nature of individual optional conversion is the Selected Agricultural Area (SAA). SAAs provide for systematic conversion of an area to leasing.

> Where a special agricultural activity such as horticulture or an irrigation scheme, is envisaged and provided the majority of allottees agree to the scheme, the Minister of the Interior on the advice of the Minister of Agriculture can declare an area an SAA. (Bruce 1984a, p. 48)

Such a declaration terminates all other titles, i.e. allocations and licences after a three month grace period 'to allow flexibility to re-arrange land parcels and to provide infrastructure.' Agricultural leases are granted by the Minister of Interior. In granting leases first consideration is, according to law (i.e. S.51), given to previous allottees and licensees.

Urban land

There are 16 legally designated urban areas according to the Second Schedule to the Land Act 1979. The Land Act provided for the automatic conversion of all agricultural land in urban areas to a use right called a licence. Unlike the lease the licence is not transferable, subject to inheritance or negotiable. The object of the licence is to 'facilitate urban development through flexibility in planning by providing a relatively insecure tenure for land considered to have a transient land use'. Licences supposedly circumvent over-acquisition of urban land by a few individuals (Bruce, 1984a, p. 47).

Institutions for implementation

There are three main institutions to implement the 1979 Land Act. Prior to 1979 the Kings' Power of land allocation was delegated to the chiefs. Under the Act chiefs are now *ex-officio* members of Land Committees. Land Committees are not a new provision. As we have seen from previous chapters some form of Land Committee has been provided for under two previous Acts. The idea behind Land Committees is to introduce a democratic tone to decision making around land issues. Decisions are made by majority vote. Chiefs vote only in the event of a stalemate. It has been said that the Land Committee is a cheap, people-orientated, and decentralized way of handling land matters. Bureaucracy is minimized and it provides some leverage for co-option (Bruce 1984b, p. 77). 'Projects requiring SAAs may be more acceptable if local Land Committees are involved from [sic] some decision making in the beginning' (Bruce 1984b, pp. 82-83). In actual fact Land Committees are a very volatile issue in Lesotho. With approximately 1,084 chiefs with 'traditional' administrative rights over land in their areas, that means that in theory there should be 1,084 Land Committees all of them operating with the chiefs as chair and *ex-officio* members. The sheer number of land granting authorities makes it difficult to control or advise these authorities in their function (Land Act Administration Group, pp. 33-35). Both Mosaase (1984) and Bruce (1987), just to give two examples from the Act's proponents, have pointed out on separate occasions that there is mounting evidence of chiefs ignoring their Land Committees' decisions, or of not having them at all. Land Committee members are not paid a sitting allowance and as a result some members only come to meetings when their own interests are involved. The new Land Act tries to address these problems with the constitution of a new land committee structure by the Minister of Interior — wherein those members with a material interest should declare their interest and withdraw from the proceedings. This is seen as a politically contentious move given the strong hierarchical structure of chieftainship which exists in the country (Land Act Administration Group 1987, p. 35).

Secondly, the Land Act of 1979 calls for an office of the Commissioner of Lands. The Office is responsible for administration of all land in urban areas, selected development areas, selected agricultural areas and all land converted into leasehold (S.74). All lease and licence titles are executed by the Commissioner of Lands and such titles are registered by the Office with the

Deeds Registry. In addition the Office of the Commissioner of Lands is charged with handling 'all land transactions for and on behalf of Government' (S.75). Pre-1979 lease transactions were handled by the King or Paramount Chief. It is thought by the Act's proponents that to have an office with expertise in land administration, valuation, surveying and physical planning makes for a more suitable transition to 'modern land administration'. The problems in this institution stem from an inability to recruit and maintain properly trained staff. Resignations have been an issue, mostly over the vast amount of work, it is claimed (Maseru Development Plan undated Working Paper No. 4, pp. 25-26). Better wages and working conditions are easily found elsewhere, especially in South Africa. Chronic staff shortage in the Office of the Commissioner of the Lands coupled with lack of funds has been seen as the major reason for the failure of this institution to carry out its various roles. This is the reason given as to why tenure conversions have only taken place in urban areas. It has been said by Mosaase (1985, p. 8) that 'probably a donor funded' pilot project may be necessary in order to begin to implement the agricultural provisions of the 1979 Land Act.

Appeal provisions

The third institution provided by the Act calls for the creation of a three-member Land Tribunal comprised of a Chair, who is a judge drawn from the High Court, or a resident magistrate and two assessors (S.64). One assessor is drawn from amongst the Principal Chiefs, the other assessor is to be a lawyer or more ideally a land economist. Appeal structures also exist within the Land Committee hierarchy to settle disputes, however the rationale behind the Tribunal is seen to further insure security of tenure. It is empowered for instance to hear appeals against the governments in cases where land was taken for a public purpose and in cases where there are disputes over fair compensation for previous landholders (S.56).

Experiences with implementation (Aitken 1987)

Chris Aitken is a Senior Lands Officer in the Office of Lands, Surveys and Physical Planning. In a paper presented to the 1986 Quthing Seminar on the Land Act 1979 he outlined the Office's main successes and failures in implementing the law. Overall he cites lack of public information about the Land Act in general and lease titles in particular, money, time and staff as the main obstacles faced by the institution in implementing the Act. Nevertheless he says

... the Land Act is still with us and it is commendable that the

Government has appreciated the importance of Land and the need for sound land administration ... Since June 1980 some 5,000 lease applications have been received and 3,000 dealings processed. (Aitken 1987, p. 1)

All have been urban leases. This means that there was during the time that I was in Lesotho (January 1987) a backlog of 2,000. At the same time applications continue to be made daily. Aitken stresses other difficulties as well. He feels it is significant for instance 'that some 400 leases prepared since the implementation of the Land Act 1979 have not been returned, resulting in a loss of revenue and much abortive work' (Aitken 1987, p. 5).

Processing a lease

There are eight steps in the processing of a lease according to Aitken. While many leases have taken years to process, there have been others that have only taken two months. Delays surround steps dealing with surveying, adverse claims, title complications, and applicant's signature and payment for costs.

1   Application Every applicant completes a form giving his/her full details. This includes information on his qualifications to hold land in Lesotho, i.e. citizenship, evidence of his current title, and evidence of the applicant's intention to make use of the lease in a financial transaction; 'it is still a Ministerial instruction that only applications involving a transaction can be accepted' (ibid.).

2   Record The application is recorded. A title check is run to ensure that the applicant's evidence of his current title is correct. At this point the application is allocated a lease number. The application is acknowledged in writing to the applicant who is instructed to make note of the lease number and use it in future correspondence or inquiries.

3   Survey The Lands Office then consults with the Survey Division to 'ascertain whether or not further survey work is required or whether sufficient survey work has been done to enable the application to proceed' (ibid., p. 20). It is with this step that delays can begin. If the land in question is in one of the former urban areas then survey work may not be required since sufficient information would be readily available. In which case the Survey Division returns the application with a note of the pilot area and most importantly a plot number. However if there is not sufficient information about the plot area then delays can begin and costs can mount up. At this point the applicant is notified that survey work must be carried out before the application can proceed, the applicant is advised that work must be carried out by a Government Surveyor or by a private surveyor. According to Aitken 'there is an acute shortage of both and a delay of 12 months or more has not been uncommon in the past' (ibid., p. 9).

4   *Public notice* After the survey stage, the Land Act 1979 stipulates that applications must be advertised in a newspaper in order to allow for adverse claims to be made by persons who wish to challenge the conversion of the plot under application. Persons wishing to challenge the application are given one month from the date of the notice in the newspaper to do so.

5   *Adverse claims* 'Some 15% of the old titles are defective in one way or another' says Aitken, 'mainly because the allottees failed to comply with the provisions of previous legislation' (ibid., p. 8). One example of this is that 'allocations for commercial sites in rural areas were supposed to be registered within a three month statutory period under the Deeds Registry Act 1969 and in terms of the Land Act 1979 such unregistered titles have become null and void and the title has reverted to the Nation' (ibid., p. 26). But what has happened is that these plots have been allocated and reallocated. Aitken says that it is in such circumstances that public opportunities for adverse claims must be created and maintained.

6   *Draft* If there has been no adverse claim then the lease can be drafted. Drafting includes a great deal of preparation in that it involves rechecking the title, and calculation of ground rent. There are also statutory fees and stamp duties which must be calculated and data records to complete.

7   *Signature and payment* The Draft lease is then sent to the applicant along with a bill for the payment of costs. The applicant is supposed to sign the draft and return it along with payment.

8   *Registration* Once the draft is returned it is covered and bound, signed on behalf of the state by the Commissioner of Lands and sent to the Registrar of Deeds for registration. One copy of the lease is then sent to the lessee, one copy kept by the Commissioner of Lands, and a third copy is kept by the Registrar of Deeds.

Selected development areas

In addition to processing leases in fulfilment of the Act's optional conversion scheme just described, the Department of Lands, Surveys and Physical Planning also are responsible for automatic conversion of titles within the

Selected Development Areas scheme in urban areas. SDAs are intended under Part Five of the Land Act to allow for land tenure control in 'large-scale urban areas' (ibid., p. 12). Efficient application of the SDA mechanism has been hampered on two fronts. According to Lands Officer Aitken the Land Act is a problematic piece of legislation; not least the difficulties it presents for practical application. The Act inhibits effective and efficient land use in urban areas. Aitken claims that the law is too 'vague on the finer details of the acquisition procedures' and that as a result the Department has had to establish a policy of its own (ibid., p. 12). Briefly these guidelines stress that public support and co-operation is vital if an area is to be converted into an SDA, especially from those members of the public who will be affected by the tenurial conversion. Likewise public deliberations on the proposed change must have Ministerial and government support. Further, public notice of such proposed changes, including a map detailing current and proposed plots should be made available. With the creation of an SDA, title holders and occupiers should be notified that all previous titles have been made null, and given the opportunity to lodge any claims for compensation. Revaluation of the plots should be made as improvements are made to the plot in order to determine if any payment is due to or from the lessee. Valuation assessments and substitute rights should be published in a schedule, and finally each lessee in an SDA should have their own individual lease. Aitken emphasizes not only the necessity for establishing these guidelines but also the importance of following them in this order, otherwise 'the result has been unnecessary confusion and expense' (ibid., p. 6).

Having had to fill in policy gaps left in the law for the acquisition of land for SDAs, Aitken also criticizes the way in which the law has been applied. He begins by drawing attention to the lack of public awareness about the Land Act in general and SDAs in particular. 'Thus far' says Aitken, 'about the only assumption that many residents make is that a proposed Selected Development Area will provide many potential benefits in their personal favour' (ibid., p. 12). He continues, claiming that 'This has increased speculative activities, including illegal sub-division and sale of sites and proliferation of uncontrolled development' (ibid., pp. 14-15). Although two major intentions of the Land Act are to curb uncontrolled development in the urban areas and to curb land speculation and hoarding, in fact, according to Aitken, the Land Act has not helped in either regard. This is due he says mostly to the extent of delays encountered in the creation of an SDA.

> The time taken to collect tenurial data and valuation assessment, for example, is far too long. These delays are due to staffing shortages and to the fact that the information gathering is dependent upon adjudication, survey and tracing owners, many of whom are either out at work or are

113

absentee landlords.   The lack of speedy information-gathering and introduction of the various Land Act requirements promotes and gives opportunity for speculative development and community discontent. (Ibid., p. 20)

Another serious problem for SDAs is the issue of compensation.   Again Aitken draws attention to the lack of public information around the subject, especially the early identification of alternative sites for occupiers if necessary. In addition, he calls for a 'tenurial register and valuation register concurrent with the Declaration Notice', which he claims would be most useful 'in awarding compensation and in deterring illegal developments at the outset' (ibid.).

While the Act is clear on the possibilities of compensation for those who hold title to residential or commercial land, those with arable plots in urban areas are not entitled to compensation. However, no provision for payment has been made for those entitled to compensation.

> (W)e have seen cases where roads have been re-routed around a plot (at presumably a far greater cost) rather than paying compensation to an affected owner for the loss of some of his land. (Ibid., p. 26)

Currently most SDAs are found in the peri-urban fringe of Maseru. The problem here is not only the fact that there is resistance around the fact that agricultural land may be taken without compensation, but also that many landholders on hearing that the area is to be converted into an SDA, will promptly rush to convert their fields into a commercial or residential site and sell it.   Their purpose — to circumvent a law which explicitly refuses to compensate for the loss of fields in an SDA. Wherever possible the practice has been to give landholders alternative fields outside the SDA.   In effect, agricultural land around Maseru has been illegally sub-divided and used for purposes other than agriculture. Such uncontrolled sub-division and change of land use has meant that areas around Maseru have increased in density. All of which is significant for issues around the provision of services and other urban planning.

A final difficulty associated with SDAs are the delays in lease processing. Frustrated expectations get in the way, according to Aitken,

> ... people are given to understand that SDAs will provide a modern infrastructure which will in turn encourage them to carry out development. They are then discouraged because development capital, probably by way of a bank loan, will need a lease as collateral and they find that it takes a seemingly indefinite period to obtain that lease. (Ibid., p. 22)

114

The Thamae SDA scheme began in 1981. As of January 1987 1,508 sites had been legally established, only 47 leases had been granted. Aitken claims that, besides staff shortages it is the reluctance of individual plot holders to give out necessary information which causes much of the delay.

> Plot holders fear that if they give information they will be penalized either in terms of losing a portion or the whole of their site or that it will cost them money. (Ibid., p. 19)

Aitken admits that some of their fears are justified since landholders 'will have to pay lease preparation costs, ground rent and rates' (ibid.) Furthermore landholders in peri-urban areas especially may be sensitive to questions about how the land came into their possession. Inquiries can reveal that the land was illegally allocated.

In summary to this section on lease processing, we can see that in both optional and automatic tenure conversion there have been problems in both the 1979 Act and in its application. At some points the Act has been vague as in issues around land acquisition for SDAs. The Act also has failed to address the issue of compensation, both in actual provision of compensation for those legally entitled to it, and in dealing with the resistance of those who are not so entitled. We turn now to the other main provision of the Act, i.e. Inheritance. In addition, a brief discussion of some of the effects of the expropriation of land for the Highland Water Scheme is offered.

Inheritance

The Land Act is clear in its intention to introduce full legal rights of inheritance over arable land. Such a provision lays to rest some of the ambiguities over re-allocation of land to the next generation. Under customary law land was not an inheritance. Therefore upon the death of the landholder, arable fields became the custody of the chief who then reallocated them, in the vast majority of cases, to the eldest son of the house(s).

Part II subsection 2 of the Land Act provides for inheritance:

> [W]here an allottee of land therein dies, the Chairman of the Land Committee having jurisdiction shall record in his register the passing of the interest in the land of the deceased allottee to:-
>
> a) the first male issue of the deceased allottee (who shall share with his junior brothers in accordance with the advice of the family) unless the deceased allottee had designated otherwise;
>
> b) where paragraph a. does not apply, the person nominated as the heir of the deceased allottee by the surviving members of the deceased

allottee's family; or

c) where paragraphs a. and b. do not apply within twelve months from the date of the death of the allottee, the State.

Section 3 then goes on to outline the rights of the spouse and minor dependents:

Notwithstanding subsection 2 a surviving spouse or a minor child of the deceased allottee shall be entitled to remain in occupation of the land allocated to the deceased allottee until his own decease.

Nevertheless many aspects of the inheritance provision raise new uncertainties, or at least throw old uncertainties in bold relief. The concept of the family council for instance is crucial in many areas of conflict between family members, and the decision of a family council can carry the force of law, as suggested by the Land Act provision. However the actual details of what constitutes a family council will no doubt come under closer scrutiny. It is also not made plain in the Land Act exactly what the rights and obligations of an inheritor are with regard to the other members of the family. As long as widows remain part of the deceased allottees' families they and their minor children can occupy the land. It is probable that some female members of the family may opt for the security of their father's homestead where they may be able through occupation to win access to land for a vegetable garden (the produce can be used for subsistence, sale or barter). In this small way the Land Act could reinforce the trend toward women choosing to remain unmarried. To what extent are inheritors required to share fields? Or to share the revenue from land that has been sub-leased? These questions will be debated in the law courts for a long time to come.

Taking land for public purpose

The ability of the state to expropriate land 'in the public interest' has been strengthened by the Land Act. However for some rural people in Lesotho the loss of their lands to the Lesotho Highlands Water project may be their first direct contact with the Land Act 1979 in operation.

The Land Act, through its provisions on leasing, both optional and mandatory, transfers the bulk of administrative powers over land from (gazetted) chiefs to the state in the form of the Ministry of the Interior. This gives the state, and especially the Ministry of the Interior, tremendous powers over land use and control. The Lesotho Highlands Water Project (*Work for Justice,* Number 20, December 1988, 1,7) provides one example of how important these powers can be to the state. The Project which took 30 years to negotiate is a scheme whereby Lesotho will sell 2,000 cubic metres annually to South Africa when completed in 2019. Although the state will receive approximately 50 million *maloti* annually during the first phase of the project (1987-2003), it has been estimated that 20,000 people will directly suffer a loss of land; some 4,000 hectares of arable land and 18,700 hectares of grazing area will be flooded. The far-reaching powers of the Land Act 1979 will contribute to the process of transferring land from the rural people who currently occupy it to the state's eminent domain. Nonetheless it is important to note that the Land Act was not the only way of ensuring that the Project was done, although the Act may have made it technically easier to expropriate the land.

Work for Justice, the monthly newspaper published and edited by the ecumenical Transformation Resource Centre wrote in December 1988:

> M'e 'Malikabiso Mofolo and Ntate Thabeng Khetsi of Thaba Tseka have been directly affected by the project. Their fields have been taken for construction of residential houses for project officials. 'M'e 'Malikabiso cried out that the government had promised to compensate them for the fields, but in September (1988) she was given only 16 bags of maize. She is not sure whether the 16 bags are compensation for this year's crop or whether she will be given more maize in future. 'We are neither told anything nor given any documents that promise us something. We are stuck.' (*Work for Justice,* Number 20 1988, p. 2)

The newspaper also printed Ntate Khetsi's experience:

> ...(T)his is the second field he has lost for 'development'. The first one was taken in 1975 when the Thaba Tseka Development Programme was established. Ntate Khetsi is bitter: 'I have given up, because I know from my previous experience that the government won't help us. I won't be surprised if I don't get any more than these 10 bags that I have recently received. Maybe things might be different this time, but I doubt it, especially because we are not told anything as usual.' (*Work for Justice,* Number 20 1988, p. 2)

Land Policy Review Commission

We turn now to look at the Land Policy Review Report (1987) and its recommendations to Land Policy in Lesotho. The Report is significant on two levels. First, it reflects the level of interest on the part of government to have a comprehensive land policy. Second, the policy review can also be seen as a public relations exercise, whereby the Land Act 1979 was 'sold' (or at least canvassed) to 'the people.'

In January of 1987 a Land Policy Review Commission was formed by the government of Lesotho to systematically review the Land Act of 1979 and other land legislation from the perspective of the public. The Land Act had long been seen as controversial and a six month canvass of opinion in *pitsos* throughout the country by the Commission confirmed that fact.

Rumour and anecdote over the Act and its failures abounded, e.g. that the Land Act had caused land sales, had led to land falling into non-Basotho hands, had been drafted hurriedly so that Prime Minister Jonathan could attend a conference with representatives of the World Bank, confident that more loans would be approved for Lesotho, let alone the broader issue that the Act like the government that drafted it was illegal and anti-democratic.

The Commission also found that there was increased confusion and concern over the use and control of pasturage. In urban areas the issue of housing was a pressing concern. Complaints also were made about the centralized nature of the land administration system and the attendant problems of bureaucratic red tape, delay and corruption (Land Policy Review Commission 1987, p. viii). However, the Commission found that there was no need to radically alter or to abolish the Land Act of 1979, 'as many Basotho agree that under population pressure the traditional land tenure system is outdated, and a new approach to land use and land management is required' (Land Policy Review Commission 1987, p. ix).

Recommendations were however made in the following areas:

1 Main Principle of Land Tenure

2 Residential Sites in Urban Areas

3 Commercial and Industrial Land Use in Rural Areas

4 Uncontrolled Settlements in Agricultural Lands

5 Measures to Improve Agricultural Production

6 Regrouping of Villages

7 Land Use Plans

8 Legislation in Farming

9 Management and Protection of Rangelands

10 Urban Development Strategy

11 The Policy of Allocating Unserviced Sites in Urban Areas

12 The Need for a National Settlement Plan

Many recommended areas of reform are of immediate interest to the main topic of the book. In our discussion of these we have grouped the recommendations into categories to make discussion more meaningful. The

119

first category deals with the authority of the state as opposed to the chieftaincy, the second deals with the obligations and duties of the landholder as opposed to the state institutions, and the third category deals with the relationship between landholders and those without land. The various recommendations confirm and reinforce the authority of the state over that of the chieftaincy. The very first recommendation concerning the main principle of the Land Act confirms this authority (Land Policy Review Commission 1987, p. ix). The original law confused many Basotho by stating that land was to be held by the state. The Sesotho language does not make a distinction between government and state, many people then understood the land to be in the hands of the government of the day, which was very unpopular. In clarifying that Land is to be held by the King as Head of State, then the state is able to achieve two things, first it acquires the glamour of transcending the individual governments that created it and in particular the unpopularity of the Jonathan regime, and second it is able to claim also the legitimacy of the King while simultaneously keeping the King and through him the entire chieftaincy as servants of the state, as opposed to the much more vague term, 'nation' which was used in the past. Another crucial recommendation which strengthens the role of the state at the expense of the chiefly powers calls for the abolition of the present land committee system (which has had serious problems in day-to-day work). In order to end the present confusion and power vacuum which chiefs have simply filled, around land matters in the rural areas, the commission has recommended that chiefs work with the new Village Development Councils (VDCs). The commission recommends further that the VDCs should be strengthened 'by incorporating Agricultural Extension Officers, as ex-officio members or progressive farmers where there are no agricultural officers'. There is only one other stipulation in the report concerning the selection of prospective members, and that calls for 'candidates who can read and write'. The report recommends that gazetted chiefs be 'charged with overall responsibilities on land allocations and land use control and therefore be answerable for any malpractices against approved land policy' (ibid., p. xxiv).

Chiefs were often cautioned against making light of their responsibilities:

> Where a chief fails to undertake his duties and responsibilities as defined under the Chieftainship Act 1968 severe disciplinary action should be taken against him. (Ibid., p. xxiv)

No mention is made in the report of how members of the VDCs are to be elected: the implication is that the same formula from the 1979 Act holds true, i.e. 9 members; 4 nominated (by the Minister of Interior) members and 5 elected (at *pitso*) members (Bruce 1984a, pp. 14-15). While the inheritance provision of the Act makes redundant chiefs' powers of allocation (or more properly speaking, reallocation) with regard to arable fields, management and control of pasturage areas remain a vital part of the social fabric of Lesotho, likewise the move of old villages to new sites.

In the relationships between landholders and the state, the report recommendations centre around state encouragement of landholders to improve and develop their holdings. There are strong condemnations against accumulating land and leaving it idle: 'It appears there is a general hoarding of (unserviced sites) by the Government parastatals, and the public'. The Report calls for the end to the release of unserviced sites. The Report is not explicit in saying how to stop the release of unserviced sites (likewise it is not explicit on how to carry out any of the reforms outlined). Such sites, termed unserviced because they lack the infrastructure for water, electricity, etc., are located in urban areas and have been popular for speculative purposes. Also leased land which is then subleased has created its own set of problems:

> (U)nscrupulous businessmen take advantage of sublessors by putting in minimum investment on sub-leased sites. In order to protect sublessors and safeguard proper land development, (Land Policy Review Commission 1987, p. xxviii)

the commission recommended the stipulation of a minimum level of investment in the contract between those who wish to sublease their land to developers, and further that the material used in development should be of a standard 'which will safeguard the long term interests of the sublessor' (Land Policy Review Commission 1987, p. xxviii).

The leasehold itself is upheld by the commission predominantly for urban land, but also as a promising tenure to encourage higher levels of agricultural productivity (Land Policy Review Commission 1987, p. 9). The Report calls for a strengthening of widows' rights of 'ownership' by recommending they be given 'full title rights'. 'The land should pass to the heirs only when both spouses are deceased', moreover 'Designation by deceased allottee as incorporated in the law should be retained'. However the widow's rights to land are revoked in the event of her re-marriage. The land then 'remains in the control of the original allottee's family' (Land Policy Review Commission 1987, p. xix,27).

In conclusion to this section on recommendations from the Land Policy Review Commission, after a six month national review of land policy in Lesotho the public report of findings and recommendations is notable for its insistence that the major provisions of the 1979 Land Act suffers not so much from genuine unpopularity as it does from the public's general ignorance about the Act and the potential benefits to Basotho. Leasehold title, of the optional conversion and automatic conversion variety, have both been recommended by the Commission as beneficial to orderly and controlled land use and development. The inheritance provision too has been affirmed. Likewise reaffirmed is the narrowing of chiefs' duties regarding land administration, coupled with yet another cautionary edict targeted at chiefs to work within a representative structure of some kind at the village level. Relationships between landholders and the state are to be quite complex, with foreigners encouraged to joint ventures with the state, hoarding discouraged, revenue collected and ceilings fixed firmly in place. The Report is all but silent on the practices we found to be taking place between entrepreneurial farmers and poor households with land they are unable to cultivate on their own, (merely hinting that 'the existing informal sub-leasing [system] will need to be reviewed and legalized') but the Report does suggest that it should be made clear in the law that widows are entitled to full rights to the deceased holdings, and that only upon her death do the rights devolve to the next generation. However there was a special message to the entrepreneurial types. These farmers who wish to specialize in particular kinds of produce may have been disappointed in the Commission's findings that

> ... it is probably premature to legislate for (specialization) at this stage of Lesotho's economic development .... it is necessary and unwise to introduce legislation as it is best left to the economic forces to encourage farmers one way or other. (Land Policy Review Commission 1987, p. xii)

In brief the Report attempts a re-statement of the government's development equation for Lesotho:

> Those that hold the land must produce enough to feed the nation at large, and provide surplus which should be channelled to investment activity in the non-farm sector. The landless families must also get the share of the land resources by obtaining jobs in industries created from the surplus food and raw materials. (Ibid., p. 8).

The way forward to end 'low and stagnant agricultural productivity ...' is set out in the Report also: 'Formal subleasing (should) be encouraged from people who, through lack of resources and those that practice part-time farming, are unable to achieve potential production levels. Ideally the lease system under the Land Act 1979 would offer the best security for such subleasing; however the expense and delays would make it unpopular' (ibid., p. 9). Not only that, there remains the question of the co-operation of the Ministry of Agriculture as discussed in Chapter 4. While the reluctance of the Ministry of Agriculture is not mentioned in the Report, it is apparent that the Commission took great pains to suggest the transfer of some of the more discretionary and mundane powers of the Ministry of the Interior which 'has too many important portfolios to give land matters serious attention' down the hierarchy to the Department of Lands, Surveys and Physical Planning (ibid., p. 48). More decentralization was recommended with regional offices and Deputy Commissioners of Land being appointed.

First, there is the *state* interest in being able to quickly acquire land for public use, e.g. Highlands Water Scheme at minimum costs.

The state is also interested in being seen to be encouraging commercial farming, thereby promoting food self-sufficiency.

This 'encouragement' also happens to benefit medium to high-level personnel working within state institutions as civil servants.

The Land Act also continues to erode the administrative and patronage powers of chiefly authority, thus elevating secular (civil service) counterparts.

The Land Act also fits comfortably within the modernizing framework of the World Bank in terms of its development strategy, its secularization of powers around land, and also for the opportunities the Act might open up for *some* Basotho women. Hence, the Act (and its partial implementation) may prove to attract more revenue for agricultural development or at the very least might prevent current assistance from being slashed.

Nevertheless the Land Act stops short of an immediate and dramatic dispossession of adult male Basotho of their rights to land. Politically astute, the framers of the Act saw a way of promoting capitalist enterprise without the Basotho losing formal rights 'in perpetuity' as would be the case with freehold.

The Act also does little to change (in the short term) established practices especially with regard to *de facto* heritability of arable land.

6 The social impact of new trends in land transactions and policies

Introduction

Thus far the book has looked at how the origins and development of the Basotho nation are rooted in land administration and control. I have reviewed the various legislation on land since independence and have shown how chiefs' powers over land were being steadily eroded. These powers now reside in the state under the control of civil servants. In this chapter looking at the impact of new trends in land transactions and land policy, I intend to show that although the 1979 legislation supposedly takes away chiefs' rights of field allocation through its provisions on inheritance, nevertheless at the village level chiefly management and mediation of land issues continues. It is suggested that the state's project to divest chiefs of their powers over land is proving long and difficult to implement. Previous legislation with a similar agenda has proven unacceptable and/or unworkable. Indeed evidence from my fieldwork suggests that 'Extra-Customary' arrangements on land, i.e. renting and sales, are more significant on arable land than leasing. Moreover it appears that it is chiefs who govern much of this unconventional access. I believe, therefore, that some chiefs have responded to new and threatening trends in policy by carving out new roles for themselves which have (at least for some entrepreneurial farmers) pre-empted the leasing mechanism of the 1979 legislation.

In assessing the social impact and responses to new trends in agrarian social and production relations, I start with the premise that the impact is likely to be different from one social group to another. Gender, class and status play important roles in shaping people's interests and capacities to respond to changes in legislation.

In the following discussion I will look in turn at the position of women, various classes, and multinational companies, with regard to the Land Act.

124

6.1   Women

With the increased attention paid to the plight of Third World women during the 1970-1980 United Nations Decade for Women, literature on African women has become copious. It is now accepted as part of the conventional wisdom of international agencies that women play a vital role in a nation's development (e.g. FAO 1985, NUL 1985, Judith Gay [USAID] 1982). However, all too often the projects funded by these agencies seek to integrate women into the development process, defined as the global economy, without taking into account all the duties that some women perform, the fact that women are members of different classes in societies and occupy various statuses. Most importantly many projects are designed without taking into account that women are already involved in the market economy (Safilios-Rothschild 1985b). Therefore a great deal of energy and funds to thus tap the important resources held by women is misdirected and further double-burdens poor women.

In looking at the Lesotho case, Basotho women have been the object of close academic scrutiny for several reasons; first, the nature of the political economy of the region means that most women have been, as a matter of deliberate policy, 'left behind' as men have migrated to South Africa. Lesotho provides the most extreme example of oscillating migration in the region. Second, the absence of men has had many implications for women who are not able to work in South Africa, including increased work in the rural areas, increased responsibilities and increased familial tension (Judith Gay 1980, Judith Gay 1982). On the other hand the literacy rate among Basotho women is on average higher than that of Basotho males. Women are at par with men as university entrants and form a significant portion of civil servants (Qunta 1987, p. 230, Bardill and Cobbe 1985, pp. 105-106). Third, Basotho women have been recognized by the Lesotho government as important sources of support. Significant foreign aid has been targeted to women's groups and issues and Prime Minister Jonathan was successful in acquiring female political support to the extent that women's issues were perceived as part of the ruling party's agenda (Judith Gay 1980). As a result the Women's Bureau was started in 1979 within the Ministry of Rural Development Co-operatives, Women and Youth Affairs. After the 1985 military coup, projects targeted specifically to women have been shelved or given a smaller profile. In the legal arena women are beginning to be recognized in some areas as adult subjects rather than minor or dependent legal subjects (Seeiso 1986). As will become apparent in the following discussion and later in the Conclusion, the Land Act could potentially improve the legal status of women in general and in particular could give some women the independent legal capacity to acquire land. This is due to the fact that the Land Act allows for land to be bequeathed through a will, and that it has been recommended that widows receive full title rights to their holdings for as long as they do not remarry.

In their unpublished paper Karen Muller and Joan Khabele (1985) argue that the Act, properly executed, will allow some women access to land in their own right, without having to rely on the goodwill of husbands, fathers or brothers. Some international agencies have stipulated that the Act should be amended to further improve women's legal capacity to hold title in their own right (WCARRD 1982, Lawry 1986).

As it is now, daughters have no rights to land in intestacy and since the majority of landholders in rural areas fail to make wills, only male heirs will be able to compete for the property. Even so, the 1979 Land Act allows for the eldest son to have the strongest rights of inheritance. Widows, who are a significant minority owing to the high degree of mortality connected with the South African mining industry and the labour migration system, appear to have strong customary rights to the land they occupy after their husbands' death. Equally strong, however, are the customary practices that can deprive widows of their best fields and cattle (NUL 1985, Sheddick 1954). The logic behind the practice of taking away two out of three fields, for example, is that widows supposedly require less land. In addition, widows are less able to keep cattle owing to strong cultural prohibitions on women tending cattle. This means that unless there are other men around looking after widows' interests, their cattle may be lost or stolen. Most frequently the men present looking after widows' interests will be sons or other relations. These are precisely the men who have the strongest claims to re-allocated land (pre-1979) or inherited land (post 1979). Nonetheless the number of female-headed households is significant and increasing, ranging from the 25-35% *de jure* female-headed households in some sample populations to 60-70% *de facto* female-headed in others (Judith Gay 1982, p. 7). These households frequently have access to cropland but few or no cattle, little capital, inadequate sources of labour and few implements. As a consequence they are not always able to plant when they should. They are more vulnerable when a crop fails, and some years some of the households in this category may not plant at all. D.R. Phororo (1987) has said that no doubt this group and their dependants constitute a 'Headache' for many in the planning profession. In the aggregate a considerable amount of land could be had by those (men) with capital, expertise and incentive enough to produce 'efficiently', some planners may argue, if only female-headed households would get off the land, turning it over to those who could make 'effective' use of it.

Evidence from the field suggests that in some sense this transfer of land from resource-poor female-headed households to capital and input-rich 'entrepreneurs' is already beginning to happen. Emerging entrepreneurial types in agriculture are acquiring access to cropland from predominantly *de jure* female-headed households who rent their land in exchange for cash, food, payment of children's school fees, shelter, or funeral expenses. Women I spoke with said that allowing others to use their land was a way of getting the land cultivated and thus ensuring that the land would not be taken from them on those grounds, and also providing for themselves and their dependants with a guaranteed income of some sort, whether it is a supply of food for the remainder of their lives or assured yearly payment of a child's school fees. In the absence of male support, women, whether married with an absentee husband, divorced, abandoned or widowed have limited options in the rural areas. As custodians of their husbands' lands they make a whole range of decisions about the homestead, however they are not able to make legal decisions about land, e.g. convert Allocations into Leaseholds, without male proxy. This legal handicap has implications not only for women's access to the benefits promised by the Land Act but such a handicap may also slow down the full implementation of its provisions. For example, introducing leasehold in rural areas among families whose male head is absent could be delayed owing to the wife's junior legal status. Judith Gay, in her USAID sponsored report on *Women and Development in Lesotho* (1982), claims that:

> Rural Basotho women are often more eager to innovate than their husbands, more able to read and to understand the reasons behind the proposed changes, and more able to undertake the tasks of rural development. (Judith Gay 1982, p. 5)

Nonetheless women lack the independent legal capacity to initiate and follow through on changes of title to arable land.

Sharecropping and women

My fieldwork also suggests that sharecropping continues to be an important option for resource-poor rural women. Therefore it is useful to chronicle some of the ways sharecropping has been described and analysed. Comparisons can be drawn between my 1987 study of households in Mohale's Hoek and Berea with other studies of sharecropping in those areas, especially Judith Gay's work on Ha Sechaba in Mohale's Hoek (Judith Gay 1980), John Gay's work on Nyakallo and Ha Lethole (John Gay 1979, cited in Robertson 1987) and A.F. Robertson's (1987) re-analysis of John Gay's work and follow-up on Nyakallo. (All of the aforementioned authors follow the anthropological tradition of using pseudonyms for village names.)

Judith Gay's (1980) profile of Ha Sechaba shows how Basotho women's access to cash, homesteads, property and land is determined primarily by their marital status, 'thus marital condition provides the basis for analysing the options of women at various stages in their lives and in the developmental cycles of the households to which they belong' (Judith Gay 1980, p. 1). Elaborating on Murray's concept of the household and the importance of the developmental cycle in understanding the process of accumulation and decumulation that occurs in rural Lesotho, Judith Gay finds that typically sharecropping in Ha Sechaba in 1978 is usually an unwritten agreement, and that it follows a similar form all over the country and involves one party providing land, and either seed or food for the ploughmen. The weeding and harvesting is done jointly and the crop divided equally. If one partner provided more than half of all the factors of production then that party would get a proportionately larger share (Judith Gay 1980, p. 192). Judith Gay also found that no matter how much male labour, cattle, tractors or cash was available, no household cultivated more than four fields. This Judith Gay (1980, p. 192) attributed to women's inability and/or unwillingness to weed.

Investors (those who share in) were either landless or cultivating their own fields as well as participating in sharecropping. Those households able to do both, that is act as an investor and cultivate their own fields, were the more well off families usually with a good supply of labour available, cash from migrant earners, cattle. The next group, slightly less well off than the first, were landless investors, generally new households with migrant earners who have not yet been given land. Those who supply fields only are the most economically disadvantaged, lacking labour, cash, cattle, and were usually widows or elderly couples (Judith Gay 1980, pp. 194-7).

A widow may sharecrop, according to Judith Gay, with her daughter-in-law, thereby gaining access to the other woman's labour and allowing her son access to family fields in anticipation of intergenerational transfer. A wife may also sharecrop with her natal kin, lending her labour and perhaps cash, thus retaining some access to fields in case her marriage breaks down (Judith Gay 1980, pp. 195-6, see also Robertson 1983, p. 163).

Judith Gay, like Spiegal (1979) (cited in Judith Gay 1980, p. 197) does not represent these sorts of inter-household patterns as an incipient 'capitalist class' in formation or as an 'independent peasantry'. It is true that a few households may benefit from the disadvantage of other households but these well-off families are in their turn dependent on migrant earnings. Sharecropping at this level consists of informal contracts which help to maintain households' viability through the worst parts of the developmental cycle, which is in itself shaped by a pattern of oscillating migration.

For Judith Gay both the intention and the result of sharecropping is shown to be relatively benign. She also extrapolates from Ha Sechaba to Lesotho more generally in terms of her description of sharecropping. Although I have been unsuccessful in obtaining a copy of John Gay's (1979) *The Impact of the Ministry of Agriculture on Poverty in Lesotho,* Robertson's (1987) discussion of this work is thorough and important to this context. John Gay's study of two northern (Berea) villages, Nyakallo and Ha Lethole, confirm the general picture that has been drawn of rural Lesotho, but introduces evidence of considerable variations taking place in Berea. John Gay's overall survey of these villages provides some measure of the extent of sharecropping. In 1978 there were significant rates of adult males absent from their villages, 44% and 49% respectively. Women made up 39% and 27% respectively of all household heads. Thirty-one per cent of all households in Nyakallo were involved in sharecropping, 17% as landholders, those who 'share out' and 14% 'sharing in' or to use John Gay's term 'lessors'.

John Gay's work helps to confirm Duncan's finding (Duncan 1960, pp. 94-5) that sharecropping in Lesotho has many variations. This perspective is unlike Judith Gay's (1980, p. 192) and Morojele's (1963, pp. V-51) characterization of sharecropping strategies as being similar throughout the country (Robertson 1987, p. 203).

John Gay's surveys are also distinctive for revealing the complexity of inter-household agricultural co-operation. For any given field share arrangements could involve five or more households depending on the size and condition of the field and social circumstances of the households involved (Robertson 1987, pp. 174-177).

Therefore John Gay's work demonstrates the kind of variations that do exist in farming strategies and share agreements in an area of Berea.

Robertson's 1983 visit and subsequent re-analysis of Nyakallo explores the usefulness of the domestic cycle in helping to understand the 'reality of variation, among individuals and over time and space' of sharecropping practices in Lesotho (Robertson 1987, p. 128). Robertson characterizes the literature on sharecropping as polarized between accounts which emphasize the communitarian 'peasant mode of subsistence' face of sharecropping, as opposed to another school of thought which stresses the accumulative, entrepreneurial side of the arrangement which 'works mainly to the advantage of the supplier of individual inputs'. Robertson (1987, p. 203) maps out some of the key studies on sharecropping from 1954 to 1980 and finds significant variation in what is defined as sharecropping, and what the terms and conditions are. For Robertson (1987, p. 200), 'the question of who benefits from the share arrangement is very subtle ... until such time as lessees do acquire the power to dictate terms ... sharecropping cannot be construed as discriminating generally against poor landholders', thus revealing his position in the debate. However, Robertson acknowledges that the Technical

Operations Unit (TOU) 'has come very close to this.' I will discuss TOU in due course.

In comparing my work with Judith Gay (1980), John Gay (1979, cited in Robertson 1987) and Robertson (1987), some tentative comments can be made, because my own field work overlaps with all three authors in significant ways. First, although my work is not an intensive survey of one geographical area, like the villages of Ha Sechaba, Nyakallo and Ha Lethole, the villages I visited were in either Mohale's Hoek, like Ha Sechaba, or in Berea, like Nyakallo and Ha Lethole. Of 40 sharecropping respondents I spoke with, 17 were from villages in Berea and 23 from villages in Mohale's Hoek. John Gay's work on Nyakallo and Ha Lethole are distinguished by the fact that they are profiles of the villages and of the role sharecropping plays in those areas as a link between all households, although sharecropping may involve only 30% of a village at one time. My work cannot compare in this regard. I did not seek out nor stumble across households which had multiple and simultaneous share out agreements (John Gay 1979, cited in Robertson 1987, p. 178). However, like John Gay I did find that sorghum is the second most popular crop among those I spoke with and that green vegetables did not figure in share strategies.

I found this to be the case in both Berea and Mohale's Hoek. Unlike John Gay I cannot make any claims as to the *extent* of sharecropping taking place in any specific area, but looking at a sample of sharers *across* regions may help in illustrating further farmers' strategies.

A look at findings from Berea and Mohale's Hoek separately (See Table 1) reveals a difference between the two areas. In Berea out of 17 households I found 13 male heads of households, 5 among those who share out, 8 (the total) among those who share in.

In the South, which had a bigger sample, I found fewer male heads of households, 2 among those who 'share in' and 6 out of 21 among those 'sharing out' (and half of those 6 were engaged with TOU).

It is, given the literature, not surprising to find male heads of households 'sharing in'; this fits the pattern of younger, 'cash rich' households with little or no land. But these findings suggest that a significant number of male-headed households in Berea are involved in sharing land *out*. The male 'heads' range in ages between 56 and 72.

Is this an important variation? Is there a relationship between Mohale's Hoek sharecropping strategies and the extent of female-headed households? Does Berea have fewer female-headed households and more elderly couples who employ their fields in sharing-out arrangements?

As useful as individual village surveys can be, nonetheless I believe more work needs to be done on comparing regions in Lesotho.

Table 1
Percentage of males and females insharing/outsharing by region

Area	North	South
Total number outsharing	9	21
Number of males outsharing	5	6
Males outsharing as percentage	55.56	28.571
Number of females outsharing	4	15
Females outsharing as percentage	44.44	71.429
Total number insharing	8	2
Number of males insharing	8	2
Males insharing as percentage	100	100
Number of females insharing	0	0
Females insharing as percentage	0	0

My findings suggest that while female-headed households are a dominant type of 'sharing out' household in Mohale's Hoek, they do not seem to be the dominant type in Berea. In both Berea and Mohale's Hoek, male-headed households were 100% represented among those 'sharing in'. But whereas 6 out of 21 'sharing out' (29%) were male-headed households in Mohale's Hoek, 5 out of 8 or nearly 56% of sharing-out households in Berea were male-headed.

All of the above notwithstanding, I found that generally, as in Judith Gay's work (1980), sharecropping is in the majority of cases an agreement between women even in cases where they were not household heads. However, there were 4 cases of written contracts and 7 cases of witnessing, which seems to suggest that sharecropping agreements are becoming more formalized (see Appendix). Also unlike Judith Gay I found variation in the terms and conditions of sharecropping. For example, just under half of those who share out land managed to put some oxen into one or more of the agricultural operations of ploughing, planting, cultivation or traction, even if the oxen were obtained through hiring or *mafisa*. See Appendix.

Robertson says that John Gay's work fails to explore how the harvest is divided, but reads into the comments made by Judith Gay's respondents 'an insistence on the norm of precisely equal division' (Robertson 1987, p. 172).

My field work results sketch a slightly different story. Two of the 'share in' respondents took 60% of the harvest. Those who share out might have to pay additional expenses and so may receive less than half. One 'share in' respondent simply said that a fifty-fifty split was the usual practice. More interesting was the wide variation of practice with respect to the residue or stubble from cropping. Thirteen of the 40 respondents divided the stubble, or its income. Again there is significant regional variation. In the South, only 2 out of 23 respondents divided the stubble, while in the North 9 out of 17 split the residue or the proceeds from its sale (See Table 2).

Interestingly enough, differentials in labour availability in the household are so slight as to be insignificant between Berea and Mohale's Hoek.

Unfortunately comparisons in income are unreliable given the high reticence among respondents in the North (!) to answering the question on income.

Robertson's discussion of sharecropping is useful for its attempt to analyse Nyakallo with reference to the household development cycle model, but he found that leasing out correlated with larger land holdings and deficiency in movable resources. I found in the South (Mohale's Hoek) that of 21 households sharing land out only 4 had more than 2 fields. In the North (Berea), of the 9 households contacted only 2 had more than one field (see Appendix). Of the total number of households sharing out (30), 12 possessed one field, 3 had 3 fields and only one household had 4 fields. The remainder had 2 fields each. Therefore I cannot say that 'sharing out' correlates necessarily with larger land holdings, since 2 fields is thought to be the average. Comparisons are made even more difficult owing to the fact that field size and quality vary.

The picture that I have of sharecropping in Lesotho differs with Robertson in this respect. It is not that the 'share out' households have larger land holdings and a deficiency in movable resources. They possess average holdings and use cash to hire a plough/tractor team in order to engage in sharecropping on terms that will not disadvantage them. For a landholder to be totally dependent on the sharecropping partner for all ploughing and inputs could over time jeopardize the landholder's ability to collect half of the harvest. Even among those who share in, respondents were aware of their partner's oxen contribution. Five of the 10 who shared in did so with landholders who provided oxen or tractors to an agricultural operation.

All in all an exploration of the field studies of Judith Gay (1980), John Gay (1979, cited in Robertson 1987) and A.F. Robertson (1987) has been useful for discovering the kind of variations taking place within sharecropping agreements within villages. It has been useful, also, for helping to suggest that share strategies may differ between Mohale's Hoek and Berea in important ways. For instance households with female heads may very well dominate a

Table 2
Various factors by region

	North	South
Number of respondents interviewed	17	23
Number of respondents to income question	2	21
Average income	350	322
Income above M400	0	6
Labour: Total number of males	26	27
Mean per household	1.5	1.17
Total number of females	30	34
Mean per household	1.8	1.5
Households with cattle	16	11
owned	6	1
mafisa	0	2
hired	8	9
not specified	5	0
Male headed households	13	8
Female-headed households	4	15
Divide Stubble/Proceeds from sale	9	2

sample of landholders sharing land out in Mohale's Hoek. But this may not be the case in Berea. More work needs to be done to confirm this finding.

My main intention in interviewing individuals was not to compare results with other much more systematic anthropological work that was being done on sharecropping. Rather the intention was to focus on the ineffectiveness of leasehold provision within a social context that permitted more flexible ways of acquiring land. Therefore while the above mentioned studies have set out to understand households, the primary intention behind my work was to understand what could pre-empt leasehold. A look at sharecropping is, I believe, illustrative of processes at work that helped to make leasehold an unpopular solution to land hunger in rural areas ten years after the Land Act 1979.

In visiting villages and asking to speak with people who sharecrop, I found that the vast majority known to sharecrop were women (regardless of whether the households to which they belonged were male-headed or female-headed). The evidence shows and custom suggests that sharecropping is an activity that does not require a chief's permission as such although often a chief or headman will witness the agreement. Typically I found that female-headed households lacked adequate draught power, labour, cash for seed, insecticide and fertilizer. Some had adult offspring working in South Africa or Maseru but who were unable or unwilling to regularly support their mothers. Many women with absentee husbands had entered sharecropping agreements without consulting male guardians. I believe that this suggests that sharecropping remains important to women rural producers because they can help satisfy their requirements for livelihood, fulfil their obligations to husbands or other male guardians to have the land cultivated and prevent the land being taken away for failure to cultivate, all by exercising their own authority without requiring anyone's permission. And sharecroppers enjoy the ability to terminate sharing agreements without incurring any penalties.

The agreements are in practice made from year to year. There is, in short, minimal risk to either party in the customary sharecropping arrangement.

Other studies such as that of Judith Gay (1980, 1982), John Gay (1979, cited in Robertson 1987) and A.F. Robertson (1987) also confirm my own small study. All three surveys stress the 'feminization of farmers' (Robertson 1987, p. 151), its high risk nature, and the increasing range of agricultural arrangements devised between parties for crop production. The studies show that there are a range of agreements occurring between households, and between households and other groups, some of which bear a resemblance to traditional *seahlolo* and *lihalefote*. Other agreements borrow aspects of tradition and marry them to desires for expansion and accumulation. Along with the growth of entrepreneurial farmer-contractors is an increase in the need for cash to pay people for work which used to be done in exchange for food, drink or as a part of a community's pattern of social obligations (Robertson 1987, p. 173).

Although not approaching the scale of Robertson's research which includes in one volume studies on land tenure in Sudan, Ghana, Senegambia as well as Lesotho, my own work does confirm Robertson's view of share-cropping in Lesotho. Robertson's focus is also much more tightly centred on the variation of sharecropping type arrangements found. Whereas the primary focus for this work is an analysis of the Land Act 1979, nevertheless some knowledge of on-the-ground practices and agreements was deemed essential to observing and understanding the inoperability of the Land Act.

Robertson and I concur on the following:

1   We both found the flexibility in sharecropping arrangements is perceived to have advantages over the more technologically advanced, but contractually rigid, rural producer schemes.

2   We both failed to find evidence of chiefs benefiting through sharing arrangements.

3   We both link entrepreneurial success in rural areas with earning from outside agriculture, either from civil service employment or from construction, mining, tourism.

4   We both came into contact with the TOU (Technical Operations Unit) scheme which mimics sharecropping in some respects but which is qualitatively a state-run scheme.

Robertson finds that the flexibility associated with sharecropping is one of its most important advantages (from the point of view of the sharecropping parties) over the more technologically advanced rural producer schemes. The following discussion explores my sharecropping survey in detail. The data is from fieldwork, collected in lowland areas of Berea and Mohale's Hoek in February and March 1987.

Like Robertson, I set out to find sharecroppers and was therefore dependent on informants to help me.

I am as a result indebted to village chiefs and USAID officials and others for their help in identifying potential respondents.

While the sample is not random and is asymmetric (weighted more heavily to those who 'share out' and to respondents in Mohale's Hoek) it is nonetheless illustrative of share strategies which have been discussed comparatively with other studies in previous pages.

In general I found that sharecropping in Lesotho takes place between a landholder and a landless (or near-landless) party who usually provides some of the agricultural operations needed to produce a crop. Ploughing is usually the main agricultural operation the 'investor' provides, but it is not exclusively so. There are those who share out and provide ploughing oxen but the 'investor' does the planting and provides seed and fertilizer.

Typically the agreement lasts for the agricultural year, although parties do renew agreements if the experience has been satisfactory. Of the 40 farmers I surveyed in Moletsane, Berea District, all of whom volunteered to participate in the survey, and Mohale's Hoek (Maposeng) I found that 30 shared their land out, while 10 shared land in. Sharing land out means that one is allowing others to help cultivate one's land, while sharing land in means that being land-poor one cannot cultivate without sharing access to land with a landholder. I found that 63.3% of households sharing out their land were female-headed. These women were all widows. The average age of all those sharing land was 63. In contrast all those sharing land in were households headed by men (*de jure*). Their average age was 50.

I also spoke with village chiefs about sharecropping in order to get their assessment on the role of sharecropping in their villages, as well as to look for any signs that chiefs could benefit from sharecropping arrangements. Like Robertson I found no evidence that sharecropping benefited chiefs by virtue of their access to land. In general, access to land does not seem to be a major determinant of wealth in Lesotho. It is however for the overwhelming majority of Lesotho the premier source of social security. Those rural producers who are the most successful are those whose capital is derived from off-farm sources, as will be seen when I look at the characteristics of agricultural entrepreneurs.

Sharecropping: field survey

Of the 10 households who shared land in, 7 had household heads who had worked in RSA as miners. Of the 11 male household heads who shared land out, all were former mineworkers. Those sharing land out had low levels of cash income whether from farming or non-farming activities. The respondents averaged net income 292 *maloti* annually. (The Poverty Datum Line for the average rural household of 5.2 persons was calculated in 1984 to be 3,100 *maloti* [Bardill and Cobbe 1985, p. 93].). These households are also chronically short of enough healthy draught oxen with which to plough and plant. Without ready cash they are also unable to hire tractor services. Without oxen and/or cash these households are unable to farm independently. In contrast, those households sharing land in seem on the whole to have more available cash for farming. While only three respondents would answer the question regarding annual cash income, the average of those responses was 766 *maloti*. Out of all the households participating in the survey, only one male household head was reported as being absent, *specifically* for work. This is potentially an important finding. Conventional wisdom on absentee male household heads is that it is wage-related, e.g. migrants. But absenteeism of male household heads need not be wage-related.

Besides cash, another factor in agrarian production is labour. Labour availability is considered very important by some researchers in Lesotho and there is growing concern that this factor has remained so far under-explored (Tshabalala and Holland 1986, Low 1986). According to my study respondents sharing land out reported having an average of 2.76 persons over the age of 14 living in the household during the growing season. There were slightly more women then men, 1.53 to 1.23. Of those sharing land in there was an average of 3.7 persons available over 14, or 30% greater labour available to work in agriculture. In addition there were slightly more resident males than females, 2 to 1.7 among those households sharing land in.

Those sharing land out rarely have a great deal of land, on average 1.8 fields. While the size of a field is not standard, the average is about 1.8 hectares (Gattinara 1984, p. 147). Forty per cent of those sharing land out held one field, 43.3% held 2 while 13.3% held 3 fields. One case (3.4%) held 4. Only 2 households of the 10 sharing in had crop land. Both held one field each.

All of the respondents I spoke with grow 'traditional' field crops. Twenty-two out of 40 produced more than one crop over the past agricultural season. The most cited combination is maize and sorghum. Thirty-four respondents grew maize, 20 sorghum, and 5 beans. One field is on occasion parcelled to accommodate different crops. In general sharing land out is a low cost and minimal risk way to crop land for very low cash income older widows. Those who share land in tend to be former mineworkers, younger with some cash income but who are landless.

I asked all 40 sharecroppers and all 19 chiefs about the terms and conditions of sharecropping agreements. Eighty-nine per cent of the respondents described the agreement as usually an oral one, the remaining 11% described it as written. Among the chiefs, only one chief said that agreements were evenly divided between oral and written. The rest described them as oral. Of the sharecroppers, 25 said their agreements had not been witnessed, 9 had witnessed agreements in 6 cases by family member(s), 2 by neighbours, and one by the village chief. There were 6 non-responses. It is unusual for a chief to witness sharecropping agreements. Most of the chiefs I spoke with said that they had not been asked to witness. Agreements are made for the duration of the agricultural year, usually in 2-4 months in advance of the ploughing season which begins in October.

Respondents described how each party's resources were used in ploughing, planting, cultivation and harvest of the crop. (See Table 3 concerning traction services.) In brief I found that tractors are used for ploughing more often than oxen. All tractors are hired. Four out of 10 respondents sharing land in owned oxen. Half owned 2 beasts, the other half owned 4. In 11 cases seeds were broadcast owing to inadequate traction resources. Those who shared land in provided the oxen most frequently and/or tractor. However in one-quarter of the cases where oxen were used, it was the landholder who provided the oxen. Regarding the distribution of labour, respondents said labour tasks for ploughing and planting were shared equally in approximately half of the cases. In slightly over one third of the cases the party sharing land in is exclusively responsible for ploughing and planting, while cultivation and harvesting tasks are shared jointly.

Table 5 shows contributions of farming equipment made by the parties. We see that those sharing land in most frequently provide ploughs and planters. Seed in all cases was provided/paid for by the party providing ploughing or was supplied jointly. In keeping with the observation that those who share land out are generally cash-poor, we find that they are rarely the providers of fertilizer or pesticide.

All but 2 of those sharecroppers interviewed said that the harvest was equally divided. These 2 respondents share land in and received 60% of the crop. In both cases the respondents said that they had been responsible for more work done than the landholder. In one instance ploughing and cultivating operations had been shared jointly, but he and his household had done 100% of the planting and 80% of the harvesting. In the second example, ploughing and harvesting were shared equally, but the party sharing land in was 100% responsible for the planting and cultivating.

It is clear from the evidence that for those sharing land out there is usually a critical shortage of oxen and/or cash for tractor hire. Without ploughing capability they are not able to farm independently. The second most cited reason for their household not being able to farm on their own is a shortage of labour among those households sharing their land out. This is in keeping with what I observed time and time again, villages full of women and children, with very few young adults available for agricultural work.

I also interviewed chiefs and sharecroppers about disputes and trends in sharecropping. Although chiefs answered that they thought disputes were rare, sharecroppers themselves responded that disputes took place often and 25% of those sharing out said that disputes they had led to the breakdown of the sharecropping agreement. Most frequently disputes revolved around conflicts over the proper division of the harvest. Most of the chiefs and sharecroppers I spoke with thought sharecropping had become more frequent in their areas. In Ha Makaba (Moletsane area of Berea District) half of all farmers were engaged in sharecropping according to the village chief. In Majaneng, 40%, in Makhosi 50%, again according to the village chiefs. Eleven of the total 19 chiefs interviewed said sharecropping was increasing in their areas. Six said that the incidence had declined, and three reported the percentage to be unchanged. Reasons they gave for the increase in sharecropping arrangements were less land for reallocation to new households, more widows with little money, a decrease in livestock owners, fewer available oxen for ploughing in the areas, increasing farming costs, and increasing population pressure generally.

Table 3
Party providing traction for ploughing, planting and cultivating

	Ploughing		Planting	Cultivation
	Oxen	Tractor		
Share Out	3	4	7	8
Share In	16	22	18	7
Provided Jointly*	1	2	4	8
Average number of oxen used	4.4	-	2.9	2.0

* included in the total number of those who 'share in' and 'share out'

N.B. In 5 cases, both oxen and tractors were used in ploughing. Out of 30 'Share Out' respondents, 17 provided some traction. The remaining 13 provided none.

Table 4
Labour contributions of sharecropping parties

	Operation			
	Ploughing	Planting	Cultivating	Harvesting
Labour provided by:				
Share Out only	6	8	6	1
Share In only	15	15	6	1
Labour provided jointly *	19	17	28	38

* included in the total number of those who 'share in' and 'share out'

Table 5
Division of 'input' and equipment contributions

	Plough [a]	Planter	Seed	Fertilizer	Pesticides
Input provided by:					
Share out only	3	6	15	3	1
Share in only	16	16	14	10	11
Provided jointly [b]	-	3	11	8	6
Not used	-	15	-	19	22

[a] Oxen plough.
[b] included in the total number of those who 'share in' and 'share out'

One third (6) chiefs interviewed said sharecropping arrangements in their areas are declining. Half of them cited TOU, the Technical Operations Unit (the implementation arm of the Food Self-Sufficiency Programme) as the main reason. The FSSP helps landowners to raise credit so as to be able to hire contract farming services from TOU contractors. Three other chiefs said that income from grown children working in Maseru or South Africa led to a decrease in sharecropping, since landholders could live off that income. The remaining 2 chiefs said sharecropping was declining in their areas because more landholders were buying their own equipment to farm independently.

I also asked chiefs if they knew of any incidences of landholders renting fields in their areas. Seven of the 19 said that they knew of land being rented in their villages, although they regarded the practice as uncommon. Nine chiefs said that they were unaware of cropland being rented in their villages and 3 interviewed said they were not sure if land was being rented in their areas.

Most, i.e. 80%, of the sharecroppers themselves, said that sharecropping arrangements were increasing. Half of the respondents who shared land out cited lack of money as the main reason for the increase in such arrangements. Other causes cited for the increase were greater incidences of landlessness, declining oxen ownership, and the fact that many landless people had the cash to pay for farming expenses as well as being 'interested' in farming.

Survey work done with such a small sample while certainly not conclusive does help illuminate the preliminary figures from the 1986 census (*Lesotho Today* 11 March 1987). It has been estimated that 25.4% of all rural households own no land. This is an increase from 23.7% in 1970 and 20.7% in 1980. The number of rural households between 1970 and 1986 grew by

30.8%. Lowland rural households without land in 1986 are estimated to be 28.6%. Of even greater concern, the number of rural households reported to have both land and livestock is estimated to be only 46.7% for Lesotho as a whole and 41.2% for the lowland areas. The problem of being able to farm independently is deeper than the numbers would suggest since the criteria for land and livestock ownership is a household having at least one small-stock unit. (Four oxen are needed for traction). The picture that is evolving then is that the majority of rural households do not have sufficient oxen for ploughing, even in the cases where they have some land and beasts. Sharecropping then continues to be crucial to Lesotho's farm economy offering the one available prospect whereby a large proportion of landholders lack other assets to farm independently. According to the 1986 census 30.3% of households own no livestock at all.

Extra-customary forms of land transactions

Although it remains illegal to buy or sell land in Lesotho the sale of Form C Customary allocations (Form C is the 'title' landholders get from chiefs for cropland) on cultivated land is considered common practice among people in and around the capital, Maseru. Typically the buyer of land is someone working in Maseru, usually a member of the civil service who wants the land for residential purposes. As a general rule though, land is bought, houses are built and those houses are rented out. It may be quite a while before the land owner actually resides on the land. Maybe never at all. Sales of land come about when a prospective buyer initiated negotiations with the landholder. After the prospective buyer and the landholder agree on the sum to be paid for the transaction, both parties then approach the area chief where the landholder requests that his allocation be transferred to the buyer. The chief and buyer also come to an agreement, and the buyer then is reallocated the plot.

Others who have gained control over land in this way are the new breed of commercial farmers found in other parts of Lesotho. Their numbers are not yet significant, but most of these men have enormous influence. Some are former civil servants (high level), some are businessmen from other industries like construction and retail.

In this study I interviewed seven commercial farmers, most of whom have not bought land but who rent from landholders unable to farm on their own.

Farmer A is a former civil servant and has been making leasing agreements with some landholders in his area since 1980. These agreements are not written nor witnessed. Renewals for longer than the first year are possible and encouraged. There are three forms of payment available to the landholder. The first is in grain with the amount determined by the average annual amount

141

previously produced by the landholder on his/her own. Farmer A told us that there can be problems for him with this kind of arrangement. There was a case when a man wanted his land back after Farmer A had used fertilizer and lime to upgrade the quality of the soil, thereby increasing the average yield from 35 bags to 75. For this reason Farmer A prefers long-term agreements so that he can get maximum return on his investments. The second form of payment is cash rent in advance. The third form of payment is the farming of one field, i.e. ploughing, seed, fertilizer, etc., on one field in exchange for use of the other field.

In addition Farmer A also has multiple year agreements, for a three to five year period. These agreements allow the farmer to greatly increase soil fertility, he says. These agreements also differ from the annual arrangement in that they are written, reproduced in triplicate, and witnessed by the village chief. The terms of the multiple year agreement vary. The rent may be paid entirely in advance or annually. The discretion is left with the landholder. Payments are also made in kind, or with cattle, or in farming services for another field.

Farmer A also engages in sharecropping although he finds the arrangement the least profitable of the three types of transactions he is involved in. The arrangement differs from the traditional arrangement in that Farmer A performs all of the operations on the land. The crop is also divided differently in that Farmer A's expenses are deducted from the produce before the remainder is divided equally. Farmer A feels vulnerable to premature harvesting on the part of the landholder, and the ambiguity involved in the division of a crop. His perception is that the landholder's preferences are ranked in reverse order to his own.

Farmer A acquires land through contacts who know of fields that are fallow or idle for some time. Most frequently his clients are widows or others who are unable to plant on their own or who have lost interest in farming. Farmer A says that some of his clients are those who have not been able to recover from the last drought.

Farmer B is a well-known businessman. He divides his interests among farming, vegetable marketing, and retail sales. His farming activities are concentrated in the area around his home village in Maseru District. He has 100 separate agreements with landholders for renting cropland. This amounts to approximately 500 acres. The agreements are all written, witnessed by the chief. The landholder receives a duplicate with the terms of the contract specified. Farmer B employs a full-time clerk to keep these details in order. Most of Farmer B's agreements are for five years. The terms vary according to the specified need of the landholder. He distinguished five different kinds of agreements. The first, a service agreement, is made when, in exchange for

142

use of cropland, Farmer B agrees to perform a service, for instance he will provide the costs of funeral services. These contracts are two-three years rather than the usual five. Funerals cost as much as 1500-2000 *maloti*. He may agree to provide ploughing services and other farming inputs to the rest of the landholder's cropland for the duration of the contract.

The second type of contract he provides is 'sharecropping.' This again is a written five year contract. It differs from the traditional model in that the crop is divided in thirds, one for expenses, one for profit, and the final third to the landholder. The landholder is guaranteed a minimum regardless of crop performance. The minimum is one third of the expected total yield in a good-rainfall year. In the event of total crop failure the landholder may be paid in cash equivalent at current prices.

Another type of arrangement Farmer B makes is use of cropland in exchange for building a house for the landholder. (Farmer B is also in the construction business). Still another arrangement is for cash, paid either in advance or in annual increments.

Finally, Farmer B also has a few lifetime agreements wherein he provides basic food and clothing requirements in exchange for being made heir to the land. Farmer B said that every landholder he contracts with is entitled to a job on their land. Few however take up the offer. He has 120 people working on the farms and in produce marketing. They are mostly women and come from the local area. The field crops that he acquired through lease agreements are turned into irrigated operations producing vegetable 'cash crops', cabbage, potatoes, beetroot, lettuce. He expands his irrigation operations by bringing in neighbouring land under his five-year lease agreements. Farmer B says he is able to farm 1000 acres but does not want to go much further because management costs would be much higher, especially if he began to farm outside his local area. Farmer B says that he has not had land reallocated to him.

Farmer C is a retired civil servant who lives and farms in his home district of Matsieng. He has a contract operation. His main client is the Technical Operations Unit (TOU), a government programme. However apart from acting as TOU contractor, he also uses his equipment and expertise to sharecrop privately with 15 other landholders. This amounts to approximately 30 acres. Farmer C provides ploughing, planting, and discing by tractor and provides harvesting with the use of a combine harvester. He also provides seed and fertilizer. The landholder is responsible for weeding and applying the pesticide. The landholder receives one third of the harvest with Farmer C taking one third to pay for expenses and one third for profit. These agreements are made orally and without formal witnessing. They are annual arrangements which are renewed from year to year. Some of these agreements go back to

1974. Farmer C says there have been some disputes, stemming from the fact that he takes an extra bag of the harvest as compensation if the landholder has failed to weed properly and apply pesticide.

Farmer C says that these agreements are instigated by the landholder. Most landholders have to be turned away as he is not able to expand much further. Although access to land is not a problem, access to suitable finance is.

Farmer D has a dairy farm in Berea plateau near Maseru. Because of the high costs of dairying equipment, he says he needs clear title for his operation. As a result he has had cropland 'reallocated' to him. It would be difficult for him to expand further since it is becoming increasingly difficult for non-village residents to buy land. This is because others who have had land reallocated to them reneged on their promises regarding an increase in agricultural production leading to more jobs for local people. From 1983 through to 1986 Farmer D negotiated a reallocation of land; in exchange he built a two-room house for the previous allottee. Farmer D says that at present good-quality plots and those of lesser quality can get the same price. If however there was a legal market in land then professional assessments could be made for the true market value of any plot of land. In addition Farmer D believes that public support for land sales could include limits on the amount of land an individual could accumulate.

All of the farmers interviewed saw themselves as making a contribution to society. They saw themselves as pioneers and perceived their efforts as contributing to Lesotho's aims for self-sufficiency. Frequently they talked in terms of having a social obligation to help those landholders who are not able to farm on their own and who have little or no regular income, such as widows. They recognize that cropland is not being used to its full potential. One farmer estimates that only 10% of the landholders are able to farm the land effectively or productively. They all say that they have been able to increase yields. At the same time the farmers accept that the Basotho are tied to the traditional tenure system, not through sentiment or 'culture' necessarily, but because their cropland provides a modest form of social security which is not available from any other sector of society.

In short, the entrepreneurs I spoke with would like to see a change in the tenure system towards more secure individual title but recognize that there is strong political resistance to such a move. A properly functioning leasehold system they suggest could work to the advantage of landholder and commercial farmer alike. A system of monthly pensions to widows could be created. Rents from long term leases could be used to improve living conditions for the poor. One farmer in giving his ideas stipulated that above all else the desire for change must come 'from the people' and not from the government. Only one of the farmers had applied for leases as provided for

144

under the Land Act 1979. It was such a lengthy procedure and so full of delays that he lost interest.

The farmers claim that an increase in agricultural production, employment, and income can be realized through commercial agriculture. Farmer C says that the Basotho need not give up traditional ideas of equity in the process:

> Equity should not be expressed in terms of land ownership but in terms of the benefits of new jobs accruing to those without land.

In addition some farmers expressed the view that soil conservation goals would be best served where land is consolidated in single holdings. Diversions, waterways, etc., would not be as subject to the variable interests and capabilities of smallholders.

I also asked respondents, i.e. chiefs, sharecroppers and commercial farmers about the Land Act 1979. I found that few of the sharecroppers knew about the Act's provisions and therefore could not say how or whether they would be affected by the Land Act of 1979. Most village chiefs, on the other hand, were aware of some of the provisions of the Act. Most did not care for the inheritance provision, as to be expected, and preferred that fields be returned to chiefs' custodianship after the death of the landholder to be reallocated, even if that reallocation is to be the next generation of the deceased's family. Some chiefs expressed concern that the inheritance provision of the Act will mean that while 'Some families will have many fields, other families will not have any at all'.

Because some families do not have land at present, there is the perception on the part of some chiefs at least, that inheritance of fields will deprive those families without land from ever being able to acquire any. I asked chiefs if they thought there should be any changes to the Land Act 1979. Of those who said it should be changed, most said that the inheritance provision should be changed: 'The words that say that land is an inheritance should be removed'.

Others said that some way of redistributing land from those who have many fields to those who have none should be guaranteed by law: 'The person who has the power to inherit land should first be introduced to the chief, and the chief should authorize (the title)... if the person owns ten fields the chief should not authorize all the fields to the inheritor. They should divide (the surplus) among others who own no fields.'

Again, 'I think the law should change, it should say "if one person possesses more than four fields, he should spare one of his fields"'.

Some chiefs expressed concern that 'the (political) hierarchy has in the past misused the Land Act ... which has led to a lot of confusion'.

Finally at least one chief thought not enough information had been made available about the Land Act for the general public: 'It is only the civil servants who know about it'.

Similar attitudes about the Land Act's likely effects on land distribution are expressed among 'commoners' in Gattinara's survey on the Land Act in his FAO Report on Lesotho: 'I do not like this new law because even if somebody has left the place and cannot plough his field, the chief has no right to take them and reallocate to others — as a result there are many fields in this area which have not been ploughed and many people without land'.

Gattinara (1984, p. 114) remarks that while the main justification for the introduction of the Land Act 1979 was to ensure that landholders had more security of tenure, he found that paradoxically the Land Act had caused a new kind of insecurity: 'Young people will have a problem living as new fields will not be allocated any more'. 'I do not know what this young generation is going to live on.' 'Young people will live around the towns in search of jobs'.

Without access to land or the promise of such access, there will be the insecurity associated with the absence of a social security 'safety net'.

Gattinara also found, as in my own case study on agricultural entrepreneurs, evidence that 'migrant farmers, widows or otherwise occupied persons willingly give their fields to large owners in exchange for a share of the products' (Gattinara 1984, p. 104). Gattinara believes that this new kind of sharecropping 'increases the existing differentiation in the distribution of land and its use' (ibid.). On the other hand Robertson (1987) claims that entrepreneurs, whom he terms 'contractors', 'cannot monopolize land or labour', at this time ... 'their advantage rests essentially in investment in movable capital ... but this in turn depends on earnings from outside agriculture' (Robertson 1987, p. 200). Our evidence is similar in that I found like Robertson that initial capital invested by agricultural entrepreneurs comes from civil servants' income and/or savings, and secondly from commercial enterprises associated with tourism, mining or construction (Robertson 1987, p. 200). With respect to the special category of resource-poor female-headed households, Robertson rejects the view that sharecropping with entrepreneurs *per se* worsens their plight:

> At the most some contractors succeed in cashing in on the predicament of relict women, but that predicament is neither caused nor perpetuated by sharecropping, nor by the power of some incipient rural class. Its primary cause is continued dependence on the highly imperfect market for mine labour in South Africa. (Robertson 1987, pp. 200-201)

The plight of rural households headed by women requires an analysis that is sensitive to the ways in which increased immiseration and dependence can occur for them as a group, and especially within the context of the Sotho domestic cycle In my fieldwork female-headed households in both Berea and

146

Mohale's Hoek were sharing out land. They had less income and less available labour than male-headed households. Most male heads were married, with the wives frequently involved in generating income, e.g. brewing and selling beer (see Appendix Spreadsheet).

Female-headed households, many of whom are over 65 (although the mean is 54), dependent on remittances from children, frequently possess only one or two fields which they share out in order to receive some produce (and possibly prevent land being taken from them for failure to cultivate over several seasons). Sharecropping gives them access to labour, cattle and other inputs such as seed, fertilizer and herbicide.

Robertson has said, following Guma (Robertson 1987, p. 148), that *seahlolo* was a means of putting under-used land to work. The female-headed households in my survey were not sharing out surplus land; simply the land that they had would not get cultivated by any other means. Those sharing out who have access to traction and inputs over those sharing in are few and far between. Their only obstacle to cultivating on their own is a shortage of labour.

The findings confirm and contribute to those produced by Judith Gay (1982). Interviewing female household heads in Mohale's Hoek in 1977, she found that as a matter of course rural women 'use a variety of traditional mechanisms ... whereby households without cattle can obtain ploughing apart from cash hire'. For example, if a woman 'has sorghum she may prepare beer and food and then invite willing ploughmen to join in a *letsema la lipane*, a co-operative work group of ploughing spans' (Judith Gay 1982, pp. 38-39).

Judith Gay also found sharecropping to be one of the most important ways in which households without cattle can obtain traction. But the main drawback to such arrangements from the perspective of the women is, according to Judith Gay, that one must give up half the yield.

Government sponsored programmes enabling women to farm without having to give up half the produce can benefit female-headed households, says Judith Gay, 'if the weather is good, the yields are sufficient to cover the costs of inputs and the credit and payment arrangements are promptly fulfilled' (Judith Gay 1982, p. 39). She also found that women much preferred food self-sufficiency programmes over those which encouraged cash crop and fodder production. The women I interviewed were all involved in food crops and like Judith Gay's sample were planning, organizing, delegating — in short, managing the crop production process.

We can see then that while sharecropping is popular it does represent a last resort effort at food crop production for resource-poor female-headed households. Most women, according to Judith Gay, would prefer to engage in arrangements that allow them to reap a good yield without having to cede half to a partner. Most of the traditional ways of getting temporary use of labour and cattle for specific food production tasks, e.g. the provision of food and drink in exchange for ploughing, are being transformed by a preference for cash over food, grain or reciprocal obligations. Female-headed households tend to be cash poor, dependent on remittances. At the same time they frequently shoulder responsibilities which call for lump sums of significant amounts of cash, e.g. school fees, funerals. In point of fact, women managing rural households on their own are the ones most likely to pledge land for a year or longer in exchange for cash to pay for such items previously mentioned. If such households could be helped to keep their full yield, any surplus over subsistence needs could be sold for cash.

Households headed by men, especially in Berea, whether sharing in or out, do not appear to be dramatically better off than female-headed households. Only with respect to cash income is there a significant male advantage. The only significant difference between the men who share in and those who share out is age. Men who share out in my sample have a mean age of 60, while those who share in have a mean age of 48. This reflects what is known about the Sotho domestic cycle wherein 'young' males must wait increasingly longer for the allocation of fields (Murray 1981).

As outlined by Judith Gay in her 1982 work *Women in Development in Lesotho,* I found that those who share in are sharecropping 'investors', young landless families of migrant workers or men employed in Lesotho (Judith Gay 1982, p. 34). While I am aware of another type of investor, the land-holding family with resident husbands owning ploughing teams or tractors who thus increase the number of fields they cultivate, but nevertheless provide female hand labour to harvest and weed, I did not encounter many families of this type in sample. Most were sharing in only one field, although there was one family who did share in five fields.

Still another type of 'sharecropping' arrangement discussed by Robertson and which I found in the field was the government-sponsored Technical Operations Unit (TOU) scheme, which has been called a 'financial disaster' by the United Nations Development Programme and which seems to further Lesotho's 'dependence on technical inputs bought in South Africa'. TOU officials were, according to Robertson, not sure whether they should consider their operations *seahlolo,* i.e. 'traditional sharecropping' or 'were better described as a short lease or credit arrangement' (ibid., p. 195). In determining who benefits from sharecropping, I believe it is necessary to take into account the flexibility of the arrangement, the division of input and output, the degree of risk incurred, the sources of inputs, the destination of outputs and opportunities for expansion and accumulation.

In my section on entrepreneurial farmers I found that over time they were able to benefit from leasing-type arrangements above and beyond the benefits accrued to those who leased their land. Compared with the customary arrangement, agreements with entrepreneurial farmers are more rigid. Such farmers prefer longer contracts so that they can build up the soil's fertility and increase the yield. Some entrepreneurial farmers contract to turn over half of what the landholder would 'normally' produce in an average year. However, over time as the overall yield increases but the number of bags the landholder receives remains the same, the landholder may perceive him/herself as disadvantaged by the agreement. An entrepreneurial farmer spreads the risk by encouraging longer contracts than conventional sharecropping. He also sharecrops with many households. Finally his capital does not as a rule come from agriculture and profits can be used to finance forays into other sectors of the economy. In contrast the conventional agreement is made among rural producers who are producing mainly for their household's own consumption and only secondly for marketing. Profits are minimal.

I asked entrepreneurial farmers their opinions on the Land Act. I considered their views to be especially important given that at first glance it would appear that the leasehold mechanism would create opportunities to acquire land to expand their agricultural enterprises. At the same time it is important to emphasize that these commercial farmers are not typical of most Basotho farmers who produce mainly for subsistence and not for commercial purposes. Contrary to most Basotho rural producers, the commercial farmers I spoke with said that they could put into production much more land than they presently cultivate. Some of the entrepreneurial farmers I spoke with thought of themselves as 'pioneers' intent on helping to build up some degree of national self-sufficiency on food; 'If they are self-sufficient across the border,' said one farmer, 'why can't we do it here?'. However the pioneers accept that Basotho landholders will not easily forfeit their fields despite the low average yields and the better incomes offered by migrant labour. They recognize that land holding and agriculture (however poorly resourced) does indeed provide a degree of economic security not provided elsewhere in the economy. One commercial farmer explains:

> The tendency is for people here to cling to the land. They are not ready to forfeit it all together. It is a sort of security. People mostly rely on working in the mines, and one starts thinking about the time he will be coming home, and having nothing to live on. He will just get a few bags of grain (from his land) but its much better than getting nothing. That is the problem.

The farmers I spoke with were also mindful of the political resistance which would result from radical measures to quickly introduce land markets in rural areas. Such an introduction of a market in land would threaten the social security aspect of current Basotho practices on arable land in the rural areas. Farmers themselves frequently talked of their relationship with needy landholders as a kind of social obligation. They stress their desire and ability to offer security against unemployment and old age. Another farmer expressed the hope that under a properly functioning leasehold system, rents accruing to Government revenues could be used to improve poor people's lives. With one exception, none of the commercial farmers' enterprises were contingent on the leasing mechanism introduced by the Land Act 1979. One farmer said he had attempted to get a lease but had lost interest after having waited for over five years for permission. The farmers have nevertheless been able to get access to land without the Act's provisions and while their 'extra-customary' contracts are written simply and witnessed by the local chief they feel that the language and procedures associated with most formal legal documents can deter the ordinary landholder.

6.2   Class in Lesotho

I turn now to assess the impact trends in individualized tenure may have on various classes in Lesotho at a more general level than uncovered in the previous discussion.   Inasmuch as the main theoretical assumptions and categories of this work are Marxist then the discussion of class will proceed along that trajectory. I provide a general discussion on the proletariat and the petty bourgeoisie. The latter class category is crucial in any attempt to understand class in Lesotho because of its broad and politically ambivalent character. I also include a subsection on multinational corporations. I believe this is relevant for trying to deduce the interests of the bourgeoisie with regard to land issues in Lesotho, in particular with regard to trends in policy and practice. This section 'Class in Lesotho' is not meant by any means to be an exhaustive nor original look at class in Lesotho. Instead its purpose is to provide a class context within which the Land Act 1979 might be understood and to raise issues about what groups stand to benefit from the provisions of the Land Act and trends towards individualized tenure.

A general model

Bardill and Cobbe (1985, pp. 113-121) have provided a useful outline of class formation and consolidation in Lesotho, and it is an adequate base on which to build. Of special interest are the authors' derivation of class struggles and the stress on the degree of overlap between classes. In general this is due to the formative/transitional nature of all classes.

The Marxist concept of class is defined by relationships to the means of production. Capitalist society, according to Marx is that society where capitalist relations of production dominate. In such a society two great classes with differing and opposing interests struggle for societal control, i.e. capitalists — owners of the means of production — and the proletariat — those without ownership of the means of production (Marx 1983a, p. 93). If I apply this model to Lesotho there is an uneasy fit. First I would be hard-pressed to find the owners of the main means of production among the Basotho population. Invariably Lesotho's bourgeoisie are among the South African, British and American capitalists (Winai-Strom 1986, pp. 95-130). Secondly Marx's model has underestimated the staying power of the petty bourgeoisie (Poulantzas 1976), a class category that he doomed to transience (Marx 1983a, pp. 95-98). In the Lesotho case it is not so much the staying power of the petty bourgeoisie that interests us, as the large overlap between this class category and the proletariat. Bardill and Cobbe (op.cit.) point to the horizontal and vertical divisions among the petty bourgeoisie which account for its politically ambivalent character. And thirdly, in defining the working class in Lesotho, it is necessary not to be bound by conventional urban-rural distinctions, nor be confused by the fact that some have land and/or cattle, for the proletariat in Lesotho is essentially rurally based.

The rural-based proletariat

The origins of Lesotho's present day proletariat can be traced to the rise and fall of the Basotho peasantry. The creation of the peasantry itself owes its beginnings to the mercantile network that evolved regionally in the second half of the last century. A Basotho peasantry, as we have seen in the historical chapters, rose answering the need for food and livestock in the region during the middle to late 19th century. Its decline was a consequence of a number of factors: South African protectionist policies, the South African preference for Australian grown wheat to make up their demand for food, decline in the availability of Basotho labour for Basotho agriculture. By 1930 Lesotho was no longer self-sufficient in food. This remains the case. Evidence from national censuses and smaller scale intensive research indicate that only a small minority is able to live 'off the land', the vast majority rely to varying extents, directly or indirectly on migrants' wages. In particular Spiegal's (1979) work, and that of Murray (1980a, 1980b and 1980c) dismiss the idea of a present-day peasantry, instead they offer the phrase of rural-based proletariat. This is because the people in the rural areas of Lesotho are part of the regional South African working class. Using this as a point of departure, it is important

151

then to take into account Murray's further qualification of the picture, by his extensive work on differentiation in the rural areas. He has shown that social stratification is closely linked to the life cycle of the household with key points in that cycle affording opportunities to improve life chances and conversely key points of special vulnerability where access to opportunities is blocked. However, these key points, taken or not, involve secular as well as cyclical trends (Murray 1981).

There is in addition a small urban working class, which because of its location is potentially better placed for organization, consciousness-raising and agitation. Wage differentials among the working class are related to skills, with unskilled workers, whether urban or rural based, earning less than migrant workers. And finally there are the growing numbers of structurally unemployed and underemployed. As South Africa continues to internalize its work force Lesotho suffers grave effects throughout its economy, while the government of Lesotho tries to find ways of absorbing the surplus labour (Bardill and Cobbe 1985).

Both Mosaase and Phororo, who, as we have seen in the last chapter, have opposing views on the desirability and efficacy of the Land Act 1979, recognize the importance of cropland and pasturage as the only resource of social importance as proportions of Basotho workers decrease in South African mines.

Overlap with the petty bourgeoisie

The petty bourgeoisie is a broad although quantitatively small class in Lesotho comprising a commercial section, a bureaucratic section, and finally an agricultural section. Bardill and Cobbe (1985, p. 115) observe, and their observation is supported by my own fieldwork, that there is much overlap among these groups; members run the gamut from senior civil servants through primary school teachers, and throughout this range there is frequent use of salaries to invest in agriculture, or to open small shops. Prosperous farmers and rural contractors (who at one time were important civil servants) further expand their capital base by starting construction firms.

The bourgeoisie

And now we turn our attention to the vexed question of the bourgeoisie in Lesotho. First I see every reason to echo the words of Bardill and Cobbe on the debate around the potential growth of a national bourgeoisie, versus the constraints and limitations pointed to by key Dependency theorists; 'the evidence from Lesotho is unlikely to prove conclusive on this debate' (ibid., p.

116). For as we have seen some members of the petty bourgeoisie are accumulating capital and some are expanding their base. However these gains do not intrude on the general pattern of foreign ownership and control in the private sector (Winai-Strom op.cit.).

Crucial for our purposes is not just the existing classes but how they relate to the state. We need to examine not only its class character but also its typically expansive character and the role of its personnel. Is it relevant to talk of a Bureaucratic Bourgeoisie (Shivji, p. 1976) in the Lesotho case?

Certainly in the area of land use and administration it is the case that civil servants are in a position to control on behalf of the state an increasing amount of a very important resource, namely, land. Furthermore by virtue of civil servants' knowledge, expertise and contacts, they are in a prime position to take advantage of the provisions of the Land Act 1979 to benefit themselves and others in their network. We do not need to answer that question, however, because it is possible to determine some of the interests of the bourgeoisie or at least some fractions of that class by referring to multinational involvement in Lesotho.

6.3   Multinational companies

I turn now to consider the place of multinational firms for the purpose of determining what their interests might be with regard to land tenure. I conclude that an 'open economy' alone failed to attract investment. Rather sanctions on South Africa coupled with an open economy has allowed Lesotho to diversify its transnational links.

With respect to the 1979 Land Act there is no evidence that the leasehold provision nor any other provision of the Land Act was *decisive* in attracting foreign investment.

Labour has formed the basis of foreign business interest in Lesotho. British mining firms which set up in South Africa in the latter half of the last century created subsidiaries which in collusion with colonial authorities monopolized labour recruitment and set wages at artificially low rates for African employees. Basotho labour was among the first to be attracted to the gold and diamond mines owned by Anglo-American and DeBeers, owing mostly to the fact that, as we have seen in Chapter 2, the best and most arable of Basotho lands had been taken from them by Afrikaner trekkers. As a result modern day Lesotho is one-third its original size, and is predominantly mountainous — for the most part unsuited to agriculture. Other factors pushing labour into South Africa were the hut tax instituted by the British colonizers (and which had to be paid in cash from 1872), the encouragement of chiefs, missionaries and colonial officials who all in some way stood to gain by migrant labour (Winai-Strom op.cit.). Over the years few other multinationals have taken an interest in Lesotho. Anglo-American and DeBeers account for the mass majority of oscillating migrant labour. Frasers and Sons have cornered the market in retail trade since the earliest days of Lesotho's protectorate status. After independence in 1966 British Barclays and Standard banks have played an increasingly important role in the country's economic affairs, particularly with the introduction of financial regulations in 1974. In 1975 Anglo-American/DeBeers invested in diamond mining in Lesotho, an enterprise which lasted only 8 years. Another South African company, the Rembrandt Corporation, is also very important. According to G. Winai-Strom, it 'supplies managers to LNDC (Lesotho National Development Corporation) subsidiaries and has ownership in the Economic Development Bank for Equatorial and Southern Africa (EDESA) which was established in 1973 in Lesotho' (Winai-Strom 1986, p. 103). The LNDC or Lesotho National Development Corporation is a parastatal established in 1966 to service foreign investors. Lesotho Government has not received any capital transfers from either EDESA or the Rembrandt Corporation. In the expanding field of tourism, Holiday Inn had the monopoly from 1970 until 1974, when the government signed an agreement with the Hilton Corporation. This was until 1987 the extent of multinational corporate involvement.

On the surface this comes as something of a surprise given the Lesotho state's policy of fostering an open economy since independence. The package offered to foreign investors includes: tax shelter for foreign investors wishing to establish themselves in tourism, manufacturing, or construction, encompassing complete exemption from company income tax for the first six years of operation or deduction of specified allowance from company income for the purpose of calculating company income tax. A manufacturer can as a result deduct from his taxable income 145% of the cost of machinery and equipment brought into use and can deduct 75% of new building costs with an additional 5% during the next 20 years of operation. Moreover other perks are to be had with the cost of new housing for employees, wages to Basotho workers, educational costs, and infrastructure, i.e. water, sewerage, transport and electricity. According to Winai-Strom (op.cit.) the Lesotho government's policy toward the creation and maintenance of an open economy emerged from the view that Lesotho had not developed owing to colonial interference from the British and South Africans which prevented the establishment of capitalist enterprise in the country. As a consequence of this view the government created the LNDC to partner foreign investors with the aim of increasing economic growth in the country. Hence joint ventures have figured prominently in Lesotho's quest for economic advancement. These joint ventures are structured so that Lesotho provides the capital while the foreign investor supplies the expertise. Lesotho is also able to provide an impressive array of markets; access to Southern and East Africa is assured through the Southern Africa Development Committee Conference (SADCC), the Southern African Customs Union and the Preferred Trade Area agreements as well as the European Economic Community through the Lome Convention Agreement. Despite all the Lesotho government's emphasis on the creation and maintenance of an ideal climate for foreign business interests, meaningful diversification of business contacts has been unsuccessful until recently.

Conclusion

Since independence in 1966 Lesotho has been trying, through its parastatal the Lesotho National Development Corporation, to attract foreign investment with a package that allows for a 15-year tax holiday, government subsidies for training, favourable terms on loans, and security for investment through its membership in the Multilateral Investments Guarantee Agency. Lesotho also provides foreign investors with free access to foreign exchange and allows for the repatriation of investment capital and earnings. But it has only been in the context of a military takeover of the Lesotho government on the one hand and a climate of limited international sanctions on South Africa on the other hand that significant foreign investment has increased, and most of that from South Africa.

There is in Lesotho a huge rural-based proletariat and a small-urban based counterpart. The vast majority of the former are directly or indirectly reliant on migrants' wages. Most often the migrant works on a contractual basis for a South African gold, diamond or coal mine. Usually but not always the migrant is male. If married he is entitled to arable land and the use of pasturage, but he may have to wait for several years before he is allocated land for his household. In this case the Land Act of 1979 provides for an automatic right to inherit the father's land if the migrant is the eldest son. If the migrant is not the eldest, presumably (not stated in law but what has been interpreted by the law's advocates) he may be able to come to an arrangement, i.e. borrow, rent, or sharecrop with the heir. This would not be so very different from the actual pre-1979 situation. Fields were frequently reallocated to the eldest son upon the death of a landholder and it was considered a part of the new landholder's customary obligations to help needy junior members of the family. If the migrant is an heir then potentially he can acquire a lease for his arable land. Should implementation of the optional conversion of a traditional tenure to leasehold be effected in rural areas then he could obtain a lease and

155

enjoy the benefits thereof. Before that happens though our migrant landholder would have to accumulate enough savings and assets to hire a battery of lawyers to impress the banks that the land is worth developing. Once the land is considered developable then application can be made for a lease. However we must be reminded that as of 1987 the Ministry of Agriculture has not allowed agricultural land in rural areas to be leased.

Nevertheless the inheritance provision is thought by some supporters of the Act to be an important milestone in Lesotho law, inciting migrants to use their considerable wages in developing their fields in the full certainty that improvements made will be enjoyed by the eldest son or other designated heir.

However, for the vast majority of households the expectation of every household customarily being 'entitled' to land for crop cultivation has been jettisoned.

Statistical evidence shows that the vast majority do not have enough land or beasts to cultivate profitably and that this has been the case for generations. Therefore the Act can be seen as legal acknowledgement of a process of enclosure that has been under way for some time. Inasmuch as the working class is/will be split between landholders and landless, the various fractions of the petty bourgeoisie will also fare differently under the impact of social trends towards privatized tenure. With respect to the government bureaucracy, university lecturers and school teachers, it is apparent that senior members of these groups have benefited from the Land Act and will continue to do so. Living and working in the urban areas of Lesotho where all land has been converted to leasehold, this class fraction has been able to accumulate leases not only on their own urban residential land but also on lands that individuals have obtained illegally through sale. Some of this land is being hoarded, but recently there have been private sector moves to develop much of this land into housing estates. There is a chronic shortage of housing in urban Lesotho, specifically Maseru and especially now that the Highland Water Scheme has been agreed. The alternative for many expatriate staff on the scheme would be to live in one of the South African cities close to the Lesotho border like Bloemfontein.

On the other hand the agricultural fraction has not necessarily benefited from the leasehold provision of the Land Act 1979. As we have seen, obtaining a lease can be a long and frustrating process. And it is by no means clear when and/or if agricultural land in the rural areas will be open to optional conversion. Prosperous farmers and rural contracts who wish to expand cannot as yet rely on the official leasehold. 'Entrepreneurial' types that I spoke with in the field had found other less cumbersome ways of getting access to arable land. They found out who was likely to need help in cultivating their fields, approached those people, usually widows, and offered

156

farming services in exchange for rent, a proportion of the produce, or even school fees, a house, funeral arrangements. Of the entrepreneurs I spoke with only one, a dairy farmer, actually possessed leased title to the land he had under production.

The commercial sector comprises the third major fraction of the petty bourgeoisie. This sector, unlike the others, has a strong race element which is a potentially divisive feature of this group. While I was in Lesotho there was strong public protest and concern over the Land Act's encouragement of (or inability to control) non-Basotho accumulation of land. Given the visible nature of commercial enterprises and the growing (Taiwanese) Chinese and South Asian presence in commerce and land transactions, publicity and debate on the Land Act was frequently confined to this issue. So great is the symbolic importance of land in Lesotho as a birthright of the Basotho people which they have maintained in the face of enormous odds, that the spectre of non-Basotho being able to accumulate land while so many Basotho are landless fuels resentment. Publicity around the issue also has the effect of obscuring other debates related to the Land Act.

Multinational interest in Lesotho has increased dramatically since 1986. However the timing of these gains and the reasons given by business representatives suggest that South African, U.S. and East Asian companies are attracted to a market which most South African businesses dominated before the advent of sanctions on apartheid. These observations are significant, I believe, inasmuch as the Land Act 1979 can be seen to be (among other things) yet another plank in the government's overall 'open economy' platform.

Conclusion

The central aim of the book has been to explore the relationship between land law and actually existing social relations on land in Lesotho. Using a method that combined two paths of inquiry I explored the Land Act 1979. The first path involved defining its nature and significance through consideration of:

1   the main provisions of the Act, which I consider to be the introduction of leasehold tenure and inheritance;

2   the views of leading proponents and opponents of the Act;

3   the more general debate on the role of tenure and its relationship to agrarian development in Africa and the region;

4   the role of the institutions, i.e. the chieftaincy, the Department of Lands, Surveys and Physical Planning, the Ministries of Interior and Agriculture, in the implementation and non-implementation of the Land Act.

The second level of inquiry explored actually existing transactions of arable land and found that the Land Act is not the avenue being used by entrepreneurial farmers, as intended by the Act. Instead new unofficial tenurial forms are being created. Although these new tenurial forms partake of customary language and involve the co-operation of local traditional authority, they are nonetheless not regulated by 'custom'. In that these new tenurial forms are not those proscribed by law, they are also, I argue, not regulated by law. This is not to say that all of the unofficial tenures I found evidence for are illegal, (although land sales are prohibited by law) but that law in this instance has failed to capture and regularize social relations which left unfettered can lead to greater impoverishment of people who are already poor and marginalized in Sotho society.

While some of the arrangements taking place among households in Lesotho share most of the characteristics of traditional *seahlolo* and *lihalefote,* some of the increasingly more popular agreements take place between an entrepreneurial farmer and several resource-poor landed households headed by women. There is some indication that such households may get drawn into increasingly passive relationships with contractors who may win long-term access to land in exchange for cash.

Leasehold, as stipulated by the 1979 Land Act, has not been implemented in the rural areas of Lesotho. Publicly stated reasons given for the lack of implementation include inadequate resources, human and financial, necessary to carry out the provisions for rural land. Less publicized reasons focus on interministerial disagreement between the Ministries of Interior and Agriculture over the desirability of the Land Act as a keystone of land policy. Nonetheless the absence of such implementation has not stopped the emergence of a small group of entrepreneurial farmers from acquiring land for production from the more vulnerable rural and peri-urban households, i.e. female-headed households.   Agreements between these households and entrepreneurial farmers, while seemingly mutually beneficial, in the end mask fundamental social inequalities between the two parties. In short they do not bargain from equal strength. This argument differs from that espoused by Robertson, wherein he fails to clearly distinguish the qualitative differences between what I would consider, advisedly though, as customary sharecropping (between for instance co-equals from the same area and class, sharecropping with another) and the newer tenurial forms (wherein a former civil servant, for example, acquires the use of several widows' fields in exchange for a fixed sum of cash, or a service). Government has not or cannot intervene in such transactions, and without some sort of regulation and protection for the more vulnerable households, there will be greater impoverishment of the poorest. In the end, I believe, sharecropping options will be more and more conditioned by the presence of entrepreneurial farmers.

Since the mid-1970s a body of literature has been developed on law in Third World countries informed by Marxist, dependency and/or underdevelopment perspectives. Despite theoretical differences the best works from these perspectives find an historically nuanced approach to the study of law to be the most useful. Studies borrowing from these perspectives stress the economic and other social forces which shape and condition the adoption and implementation of legal rules. Law as a discrete area of concern is not central to the framework I adopted in this work, rather I have been concerned to analyse the relationship law, in this case the 1979 Land Act, has within the social, economic and political context provided by Lesotho and its relationship with the global capitalist economy as mediated through South Africa.

159

The book is mainly informed by a Marxist political economy perspective on the study of the Southern African region which notes the role African agrarian systems have played in the creation, maintenance and reproduction of an inexpensive supply of labour for South African mining, farming and manufacturing industries. Selected works from recent Southern African historiography which focuses on the creation and depletion of African peasantry systems provides the base on which the book has been built. The formation of the colonial state and the various adjustments made by the colonial and post-colonial state for the maintenance of Basutoland as a labour reserve has been crucial in the following areas: first, in helping to illustrate the changing role of chiefs in the administration of land and thereby maintaining them as an institution of social control in colonial and post-colonial structures; second, in tracing the codification and modification of custom, both processes which narrowed the rights of subordinate classes and other social groups *vis-à-vis* state-supported chiefs.

Women form an important group disadvantaged by the colonial construction of customary law in particular and the attempt to freeze 'tradition' generally. In the Southern African context women also do the bulk of rural production work and act as caretakers and managers of smallholdings at the household level. The book confirms a great deal of what has been found by other authors concerned with similar questions relating to domestic labour, the subordination of women and the effect on them of law and state policies aimed at development. To those writers who would stress the importance of integrating women into the development process, I present evidence that such an integration already exists. The question is what kind of integration will best unburden already 'double-burdened' poor rural women.

Legal reforms to women's status suffer from all the limitations associated with any attempt to change social relations solely through law. Women's status in Lesotho is not only handicapped by law. Most rural women with limited and/or unreliable sources of off-farm income occupy the weaker bargaining positions in their agreements with entrepreneurial farmers. It is precisely these female-headed households which provide entrepreneurial farmers with fields for commercial expansion.

Whether through recourse to leasehold tenure or any of the unofficial tenurial forms in operation on arable land, contracts feature prominently. These contracts, at the ideological level, serve to mask social inequality between the parties and create the illusion that both parties are bargaining from similar positions of strength.

Contract, along with private property and the notion of the legal personality, are three of the most important concepts of law as it has developed during the capitalist era. Certainly then these contracts, whether of the official leasehold variety or of the various unofficial tenurial forms, indicate a transformation of relations on the land from non-commoditized to commoditized.

I have borrowed Seidman's (1978) category by characterizing the 1979 Land Act as 'facilitative' law. This is because the leasehold mechanism in the rural areas is primarily an optional provision to ease land transfer. Individuals are not compelled to obtain a lease, although government has done a considerable amount of public relations to encourage interest in leasehold by emphasizing the lessee's right to sublease the holding, and thereby increase income.

Despite its 'optional' (and individualist) nature I would also characterize the legislation as 'instrumental' in the sense used by Shivji (1986) as well because the intent of the Act is to effect a transfer of land use from those without the working capital and labour to maximize production to those who do possess such capital. Such an intention fits with Shivji's and others' definition of the instrumental use of law as being a tool of the state to promote and manage capitalist accumulation and expansion. The process of the commoditization of male labour has been continuous for a century. The process of the commoditization of land has only recently begun. There is already a *de facto* market in land which is unregulated. The Land Act is an official alternative that allows the state to collect revenue from the process and has some potential for regulating land transactions. In addition the Land Act calls for leasehold and not freehold, reflecting in some sense the populist ideas that Lesotho land is for the Basotho people.

That the Act has not been implemented in the rural areas can also be seen as a concession to some subordinate classes who, in the context of mass landlessness, would pose a political threat to government. Nevertheless the Land Act lease has not proven popular with entrepreneurial farmers, the very types it was meant to encourage. Unofficial tenurial forms are devised because commercial farmers seek to limit the kind of state involvement which can cost them a lot of time and money before production has even begun. Smallholders co-operate with entrepreneurial farmers because by turning over their crop land to contractors for production the smallholder minimizes risk of crop failure from year to year. The problems associated with lack of labour, adequate traction, seed, herbicides and pesticides, even the problems with transport, are no longer the problems of the landholder, but are solved by the contractor. Other tenurial forms are likely to be affected by entrepreneurial farming, which will tend to undermine conventional sharecropping and government programmes.

At the same time, a great part of the Land Act should also be seen as political, in the sense that the law is part of an attempt by state power holders to neutralize chiefs' powers over arable land, and represents in a sense another

161

attack by the post-colonial state on chiefs' control over land. While the early colonial state boosted the power of chiefs in order to create and maintain a labour reserve system to supply labour to South African mines, farms and industries, the late colonial and most of the post-colonial state has been geared to crushing the power base of chiefs. Over time judicial and land administrative duties have been turned over to 'secular' bureaucratic authorities. This has proved to be a long and complex process wherein some of the more senior level chiefs have become a part of the bureaucracy, and some of the more junior and de-gazetted chiefs still have *de facto* power and influence at the village level and remain unpaid.

The introduction of inheritance, of leasehold, and of provisions for the re-creation of democratic structures of village development at the local level, all threaten the basis of chiefly authority over land. Nevertheless chiefs have on the whole successfully side-stepped attacks on their power in the past mainly because they have acted as *de facto* sources of access to land, both arable and grazing. While their power to allocate fields has diminished over the years because of a dwindling resource base, they still until the advent of inheritance possessed the right to re-allocate land outside of the original holder's family.

It is unlikely that the Land Act 1979 will be successful in laying to rest the power of local chiefs. Chiefs still have the power to confirm or deny a landholder's rightful possession of a field. They are still mandatory members of land allocation committees in the villages. Chiefs maintain considerable administrative rights over grazing land, act as witnesses to some forms of land transactions, and are in a position to totally subvert the first canon of land law in Lesotho by colluding in the sale of land and as such enjoy fairly wide and regular opportunities for petty corruption.

The Act can however be seen as embodying partial (and maybe only temporary) successes for the subordinate classes in Lesotho as well as for women. For the former, leasehold may be seen to be a concession over the threat of freehold in that a leaseholder can derive some income from the land by subleasing it to someone interested in commercial farming. For the latter there is the possibility of daughters inheriting land in rural areas via wills, the potential for widows to inherit land from their husbands and possess full title rights to it, including the right to bequeath it as they wish. But law is not the only social regulation circumventing women's abilities in Sotho society, although women are particularly disadvantaged in some areas of the economy by their minor jural status which has a limiting effect on many women's ability to be an independent party to a legal contract. I have presented evidence that entrepreneurial farmers are finding much of their land from female-headed households. Moreover the fact that the state is unwilling or unable to require regulation of these transactions is typical of what so often happens where women and production relations are concerned. It is possible that some of the vulnerability of economically marginalized women may be lessened under the Land Act where many of the female household heads may inherit and bequeath land.

Inheritance is also a fillip to some rural producers who may decide to improve their land holdings, confident that the land would have to pass on to the next generation of their family. But the inheritance provision brings with it its own problems as the 'new' concept of a single individual landholder with exclusive rights conflicts with the older (and popularly considered more Sotho) concepts of collective rights, and the obligations of the landholder to his juniors and dependants. It may be in the area of helping to settle family disputes over the re-definition of what obligations a landholder has to junior siblings and dependants that local chiefs may still have the last word.

Bibliography

Afshar, H. (ed.) (1985), *Women, Work and Ideology in the Third World,* Tavistock, London.

Aitken, C. (1987), 'Experiences in the Implementation of the 1979 Land Act' in *Proceedings: Land Act Policy Seminar, January 27-30, 1987,* Quthing.

Alavi, H. (1982), 'The Structure of Peripheral Capitalism', in *Introduction to the Sociology of Developing Societies,* Macmillan, London.

Alavi, H. and Shanin, T. (ed.) (1982), *Introduction to the Sociology of Developing Societies,* Macmillan, London.

Allott, A.N. (1970), *New Essays in African Law*, Butterworth, London.

Amin, S. (1972), 'Underdevelopment and Dependency in Black Africa: Origins and Contemporary Form', *Journal of Modern African Studies,* vol.10, no.4.

Armstrong, A. (ed.) (1987), *Women and Law in Southern Africa,* Zimbabwe Publishing House, Harare.

Arrighi, G. and Saul, J. (1973), *Essays on the Political Economy of Africa,* Monthly Review Press, New York.

Ashton, H. (1946), *The Social Structure of the South Sotho Ward*, Cape Town School of African Studies.

Ashton, H. (1952), *The Basuto,* Oxford University Press for the International African Institute, Oxford.

Aubert, V. (1969), *Sociology of Law*, Penguin, Harmondsworth.

Bachofen, J.J. (1967), *Myth, Religion and Mother Right: Selected Writings of J.J. Bachofen,* Princeton University Press, Princeton, New Jersey.

Banaji, J. (1973), 'For a Theory of the Colonial Mode of Production' *Economic and Political Weekly,* vol. 7, no. 52, pp.2498-2502.

Bardill, J. (1980), 'Dependence and Development in Lesotho: A Critique of Winai-Strom', *South Africa Labour Bulletin,* 6(4), November, pp.79-90.

Bardill, J. and Cobbe, J. (1985), *Dilemmas of Dependence in Southern Africa*, Westview Press, Boulder, Colorado.

Beckman, B. (1979), Editorial: 'Peasants, Capital and The State', *Review of African Political Economy*, no. 10 pp.1-6.

Beinart, W. (1984), 'Soil Erosion, Conservation and Ideas About Development: A Southern African Exploration, 1900-1960', *Journal of Southern African Studies*, vol. 11, no. 1, January, pp.52-83.

Beinart, W. (1989), 'Introduction: The Politics of Colonial Conservation' *Journal of Southern African Studies*, vol. 15, no. 2.

Beinart, W., Delius, P. and Trapido, S. (ed.) (1986), *Putting a Plough to the Ground: Accumulation and Dispossession in Rural South Africa 1850-1930*, Ravan Press, Johannesburg.

Bennett, J., Lawry, S.W. and Riddell, J.C. (1986), *Land Tenure and Livestock Development in Sub-Saharan Africa*, Aid Evaluation Special Study, No.39, United States Agency for International Development, Washington D.C.

Bentsi-Enchill, K., Cowen, D.V., Dunnam, A. and Fallers, L. (1963), *Recommendations and Reflections on Some of the Problems of Land Tenure in Basutoland*, University of Chicago, Chicago.

Bernstein, H. and Campbell, B. (ed.) (1985), *Contradictions of Accumulation in Africa: Studies in Economy and State*, Sage Publications, London.

Bernstein, H. (1979), 'Notes on Capital and Peasantry' in *Review of African Political Economy*, no. 10, pp.60-73.

Bernstein, H. (1985), *For Their Triumphs and Their Tears: Women in Apartheid South Africa*, International Defence and Aid Fund for Southern Africa, London.

Blaikie, P. (1981), 'Class, Land-use and Soil Erosion' in *ODI Review*, 2.

Boserup, E. (1970), *Women's Role in Economic Development*, George Allen and Unwin, London.

Bottomore, T. and Goode, P. (1983), *Readings in Marxist Sociology*, Clarendon Press, Oxford.

Bozzoli, B. (1983), 'Marxism and Feminism and Southern African Studies', *Journal of Southern African Studies*, vol.9, no.2.

Breytenbach, W.J. (1975), *Crocodiles and Commoners - Continuity and Change in the Rulemaking System of Lesotho*, Africa Institute, Pretoria.

Briffault, R. (1952), *The Mothers*, George Allen and Unwin, London.

Brown, M.B. (1984), *Models in Political Economy: A Guide to the Arguments*, Penguin, Harmondsworth.

Bruce, J. (1984a), 'A Layman's Guide to the Land Act 1979' in *Proceedings: Land Act Policy Seminar*, Ministry of Agriculture, Government of Lesotho.

Bruce, J. (1984b), 'A Report on the Land Act Policy Seminar' in *Proceedings: Land Act Policy Seminar*, Ministry of Agriculture, Government of Lesotho.

Bruce, J. (1986), *Land Tenure Issues in Project Design and Strategies for Agricultural Development in Sub-Saharan Africa*, University of Wisconsin-Madison, Madison.

Bruce, J. (1987), *Review of Quthing Seminar,* unpublished.

Bruce, J. (1988), 'Indigenous Land Tenure and Land Concentration', in Downs, R.E. and Reyna, S.P. (ed.), *Land and Society in Contemporary Africa*, University Press of New England, Hanover and London.

Bujra, J. (1978), 'Introduction: Female Solidarity and the Sexual Division of Labour', in Caplan, P. and Bujra, J. (ed.), *Women United, Women Divided: Cross Cultural Perspectives on Female Solidarity*, Tavistock, London.

Bundy, C. (1978), *The Rise and Decline of the South African Peasantry*, Heinemann, London.

Bundy, C. (1984), 'Land and Liberation: The South African National Liberation Movements and the Agrarian Question, 1920s-1960s', *Review of African Political Economy*, no. 29, pp.14-29.

Bunting, B. (1964), *The Rise of the South African Reich*, Penguin, Harmondsworth.

Burawoy, M. (1980), 'Migrant Labour in South Africa and the U.S.' in Nichols, T. (ed.), *Capital and Labour: Studies in the Capitalist Labour Process*, Fontana.

Burman, S. (1976), *The Justice of the Queen's Government: The Cape's Administration of Basutoland 1871-1884*, African Studies Centre, Cambridge.

Burman, S. (1981), *Chiefdom Politics and Alien Law: Basutoland under Cape Rule, 1971-1884*, Macmillan, London.

Bush, R. and Cliffe, L. (1984), 'Agrarian Policy in Migrant Labour Societies: Reform or Transformation in Zimbabwe?', *Review of African Political Economy*, no. 29, pp.77-94.

Callinicos, A. (1983), *Marxism and Philosophy,* Oxford University Press, Oxford.

Caplan, P. and Bujra, J. (1978), *Women United, Women Divided: Comparative Studies of Ten Contemporary Cultures*, Tavistock, London.

Casalis, E. (1971), *My Life in Basutoland*, C. Struik, Capetown (originally published in 1889 by the Religious Tract Society).

Chakela, Q. (1981), *Soil Erosion and Reservoir Sedimentation in Lesotho*, Scandinavian Institute of African Studies, Uppsala.

Chanock, M.L. (1982), 'Making Customary Law: Men, Women and Courts in Colonial Northern Rhodesia' in Hay, M. and Wright, M. (ed.), *African Women and the Law: Historical Perspectives*, Boston University Papers on Africa, vol. 7, Boston University Press, Boston.

Chanock, M.L. (1985), *Law, Custom and Social Order: the Colonial Experience in Malawi and Zambia.*

Cliffe, L. (1982), 'Class Formation as an Articulation Process: East African Cases', in Alavi, H. and Shanin, T. (ed.), *Introduction to Sociology of Developing Societies*, Macmillan, London.

Cliffe, L. and Lawrence, P. (1988), 'The Dynamics of Land Tenure and Agrarian Systems in Africa' (to be published by the Food and Agriculture Organization [FAO], Rome).

Coontz, S. and Henderson, P. (ed.) (1986), *Women's Work, Men's Property: The Origins of Gender and Class*, Verso, London.

Cowen, D.V. (1967), 'Land Tenure and Economic Development in Lesotho', *South African Journal of Economics*, vol.35, pp. 57-74.

Davies, R., O'Meara, D. and Dlamini, S. (1985), *The Kingdom of Swaziland: A Profile*, Zed Books, London.

Davis, A. (1981), *Women, Race and Class*, Women's Press, London.

Dorner, J. (1972), *Land Reform and Economic Development*, Penguin, Harmondsworth.

Duncan, P. (1960), *Sotho Laws and Customs*, Oxford University Press, Capetown.

Dwyer, D.H. (1987), 'Gender, Law and Control of Property' in Ghai, Y., Luckham, R. and Snyder, F. (ed.), *The Political Economy of Land: A Third World Reader*, Oxford University Press, Oxford.

Eckert, J. (1980), *Lesotho's Land Tenure: An Analysis and Annotated Bibliography*, Lesotho Agricultural Sector Analysis Project, Ministry of Agriculture, Kingdom of Lesotho and Department of Economics, Colorado State University.

Edgar, R. (not dated), *Prophets with Honour: A Documentary History of Lekhotla la Bafo*, Ravan Press, Johannesburg.

Edholm, F., Harris, O. and Young, K. (1977), 'Conceptualizing Women', *Critique of Anthropology*, vol. 3, issue 9-10, 1977, pp. 101-130.

Ellenberger, D.R. (1969), *History of the Basuto: Ancient and Modern*, (first published in London 1912, translated by J.C. MacGregor), Negro Universities Press.

Engels, F. (1987), 'Determinants of Legal Development: The Economic Element' in Ghai, Y., Luckham, R. and Snyder, F. (ed.), *The Political Economy of Land: A Third World Reader*, Oxford University Press, Oxford.

Engels, F. (1978), *The Origin of the Family, Private Property and the State*, Foreign Languages Press, Beijing.

Fallers, L. (1969), *Law Without Precedent*, Chicago University Press.

Food and Agriculture Organization of the United Nations (FAO) (1985), *Women in Agricultural Production: Selected Papers*, FAO, Rome.

167

Food and Agriculture Organization of the United Nations (FAO) (1985), *Lesotho: Report of the WCAARD Follow-up Rural Development Team*, vol. I, II and III, FAO, Rome.

Foster-Carter, A. (1978), 'The Modes of Production Controversy', *New Left Review*, 107, pp.44-74.

Gattinara, G.C.C. (1984), *Basotho Culture and Lesotho Territory*, Ministry of Agriculture and Marketing, Kingdom of Lesotho.

Gay, J.S. (Judith) (1980), *Basotho Women's Options: A Study of Marital Careers in Rural Lesotho*, unpublished Ph.D. thesis, University of Cambridge.

Gay, J.S. (Judith) (1982), *Women and Development in Lesotho*, United States Agency for International Development, Maseru.

Germond, R.C. (1967), *Chronicles of Basutoland*, Morija:Sesuto Book Depot.

Gluckman, M. (1945), 'African Land Tenure', *Human Problems in British Central Africa*, no. 3, pp. 1-12.

Gordon, E. (1981), 'An Analysis of the Impact of Labour Migration on the Lives of Women in Lesotho', *Journal of Development Studies*, 17(3), pp.59-76, April 1981.

Gray, R. and Gulliver, P.H. (ed.) (1964), 'The Family Estate in Africa: Studies in the Role of Property' in *Family Structure and Lineage Continuity*, Routledge and Kegan Paul, London.

Griffin, K. (1981), *Land Concentration and Rural Poverty*, 2nd Edition, Macmillan, London.

Hamnett, I. (1975), *Chieftainship and Legitimacy: An Anthropological Study of Executive Law in Lesotho*, Routledge and Kegan Paul, London.

Hanlon, J. (1986), *Apartheid's Second Front: South Africa's War Against its Neighbours*, Penguin, Harmondsworth.

Hanlon, J. (1986), *Beggar Your Neighbours*, Catholic Institute for International Relations, and James Currey, London.

Hay, M.J. and Wright, M. (ed.) (1982), *Women and Law in Africa: Historical Perspectives*, Boston University Papers on Africa, vol. 7, Boston.

Heyer, J. (1981), *Rural Development in Tropical Africa*, Macmillan, London.

Hirschon, R. (ed.) (1984), *Women and Property, Women as Property*, Croom Helm, London.

Holm, J.D. (1972), 'Political Stability in Lesotho', *Africa Today*, vol. 19, Issue 4, 1972.

Hooks, B. (1981), *Ain't I a Woman*, South End Press, Boston.

Interministerial Task Force (1983), *Lesotho Country Report on Progress in Agrarian Reform and Rural Development with Selected Rural Development Indicators*, Government of Lesotho, Maseru.

International Bank for Reconstruction & Development (1974), *The Economy of Lesotho*, Report no. 331 a-LSO 1974, p. 1.

Jacoby, E.H. in collaboration with Jacoby, C.F. (1971), *Man and Land: The Fundamental Issue in Development,* Andre Deutsch, London.

Jingoes, S. (1975), *A Chief is A Chief of The People*, Oxford University Press, London.

Jones, G.I. (1966), 'Chiefly Succession in Basutoland', in Goody, J. (ed.), *Succession to High Office,* Cambridge University Press.

Kane-Berman, J. (1979), *South Africa: The Method in the Madness*, Pluto Press, London.

Kanel, D. (1984), 'Land Tenure and Agricultural Development', in *Proceedings: Land Act Policy Seminar, March 18-22, 1984,* Quthing.

Kea, R. (1982), *Settlements, Trade and Politics in the Seventeenth Century, Gold Coast*, Baltimore.

Khaketla, B.M. (1971), *Lesotho 1970: an African Coup under the Microscope*, C. Hurst, London.

Kimble, J. (1979), *Towards an Understanding of the Political Economy of Lesotho: Origins of commodity production and migrant labour 1830 circa to 1885*, M.A. Dissertation, National University of Lesotho.

Kimble, J. (1982), 'Labour migration in Basutoland, circa 1870-1885', in Marks, S. and Rathbone, R. (eds), *Industrialization and Social Change in South Africa: African Class Formation, Culture and Consciousness 1870-1930*, Longman, London.

Kimble, J. (1983), *Runaway Wives: Basotho women, chiefs and the Colonial State c. 1890-1920*, unpublished paper, National University of Lesotho.

Kimble, J. (1985), 'Clinging to the Chiefs: some contradictions of colonial rule in Basutoland c. 1890-1930', in Bernstein, H. and Campbell, B.A. (eds), *Contradictions of Accumulation in Africa,* Sage, London.

Kimble, J. (1986), 'The Lesotho Coup', *West Africa*, 3rd February 1986, pp.235-236.

Kitching, G. (1980), *Class and Economic Change in Kenya: The Making of an African Petite Bourgeoisie 1905-1970*, Yale University Press, New Haven.

Kowet, D.K. (1978), *Land, Labour Migration and Politics in Southern Africa: Botswana, Lesotho and Swaziland*, Scandinavian Institute of African Studies, Uppsala.

Kuper, A. (1982), *Wives for Cattle: Bridewealth and Marriage in Southern Africa*, Routledge and Kegan Paul, London.

Laclau, E. (1979), *Politics and Ideology in Marxist Theory: Capitalism, Fascism, Populism*, Verso, London.

Land Act Administration Group (1984), 'Working Party Recommendations on the Land Act 1979' in *Proceedings: Land Act Policy Seminar,* Ministry of Agriculture, Government of Lesotho.

Land Policy Review Commission (1987), *Land Policy Review Report,* Lands Surveys and Physical Planning, Ministry of Interior, Government of Lesotho.

Lawrance, J.C.D. (1966), *Report on the Mission in Land Consolidation and Registration in Kenya* (The Lawrance Report), Government Printer, Nairobi.

Lawry, S.W. (1986), *Livestock and Range Management in Sehlabathebe: A Study of Communal Resource Management,* Land Conservation and Range Development Project, United States Agency for International Development, Range Management Division, Ministry of Agriculture, Kingdom of Lesotho.

Legassick, M. and Wolpe, H. (1976), 'The Bantustans and Capital Accumulation in South Africa', *Review of African Political Economy,* 7, pp.87-107.

Leistner, G.M.E. (1966), *Lesotho: Economic Structure and Growth,* Africa Institute, Pretoria.

Lesotho Government Printer (1959), *1959 Gazette, The Laws of Lerotholi.*

Lesotho Government Printer (1979), *1979 Gazette, Land Act 1979 (Act 17 of 1979).*

Letsoalo, E. (1988), *Land Reform in South Africa,* Skataville Publishing, Johannesburg.

Levin, R. (1987), 'Traditional land tenure in Swaziland', in Neocosmos (ed.), *Social Relations in Rural Swaziland,* Social Science Research Unit, University of Swaziland.

Leys, C. (1976), *Underdevelopment in Kenya: The Political Economy of Neo-colonialism 1964-1971,* Heinemann, London.

Leys, R. (1979), 'Lesotho: Non-Development or Underdevelopment: Towards an Analysis of the Political Economy of the Labour Reserve' in Shaw, T. and Heard, K. (ed.), *The Politics of Africa: Dependence and Development,* African Studies Series, Longman & Dalhousie University Press, Dalhousie, New Brunswick.

Little, K. (1973), *African Women in Towns,* Cambridge University Press, Cambridge.

Lonsdale, J. and Berman, B. (1979), 'Coping with Contradiction: the development of the colonial state in Kenya 1895-1914', *Journal of African History,* vol. 20, pp. 487-505.

Lonsdale, J. (1981), 'States and Social Processes in Africa: A Historiographical Survey', *African Studies Review,* vol. 24, pp. 139-225.

Low, A. (1986), *Agricultural Development in Southern Africa: Farm Household Economics and the Food Crisis,* James Currey, London.

Louw, L. (1985), 'Towards resolving the new confusion about land tenure', *Reality*, vol.18.

Lowe, R.G. (1986), *Agricultural Revolution in Africa? Impediments to Change and Implications for Farming, for Education and for Society*, Macmillan, London.

Lye, W.F. (1969), 'Ndebele Kingdom South of the Limpopo River', *Journal of African History*, vol. 10, no.1, pp. 87-104.

Lye, W.F. and Murray, C. (1979), *Transformation on the High Veld: The Tswana and the Southern Sotho*, Barnes and Noble, Totowa, New Jersey, (also published 1980 by David Philip, London).

MacPherson, C.B. (1978), 'The Meaning of Property' in MacPherson, C.B. (ed.), *Property: Mainstream and Critical Positions*, University of Toronto Press, Toronto.

MacPherson, C.B. (ed.) (1978), *Property: Mainstream and Critical Positions*, University of Toronto Press, Toronto.

Magubane, B.M. (1979), *The Political Economy of Race and Class in South Africa*, Monthly Review Press, New York.

Mahomed, I. (1985), 'The future of Roman-Dutch law in Southern Africa' in *Lesotho Law Journal: A Journal of Law and Development*, Special Issue about Modern Perspectives on Roman-Dutch Law, vol. 1, no. 2, pp.191-216.

Maine, H. (1861), *Ancient Law*, (ed. F. Pollack), Oxford University Press, Oxford.

Makhanya, E.M. (1979), *The Use of Land Resources for Agriculture in Lesotho*, Department of Geography, National University of Lesotho, Roma, Lesotho.

Malinowski, B. (1935), *Coral Gardens*, Princeton University Press, Princeton, New Jersey, U.S.A.

Mandel, E. (1976), 'Introduction' in *Capital: A Critique of Political Economy, vol. 1*, by Karl Marx, (translated by Ben Fowkes), Vintage Books, New York.

Maqutu, W.C.M. (1985), 'Contemporary Problems in the Family Law of Lesotho' in *Lesotho Law Journal: A Journal of Law and Development.*, Special Issue about Modern Perspectives on Roman-Dutch Law, vol.1, no. 2, pp.191-216.

Markowitz, I.L. (1977), *Power and Class in Africa*, Prentice-Hall, Englewood Cliffs, New Jersey.

Marquard, L. (1969), *The Peoples and Policies of South Africa*, Oxford University Press, Oxford.

Marx, K. and Engels, F. (1968), 'Manifesto of the Communist Party', in *Karl Marx and Friedrich Engels: Selected Works in One Volume*, Lawrence & Wishart, London (first published 1848).

Marx, K. (1983a), 'A Historical Science of Society' (excerpt from *The German Ideology*, 1846) in Bottomore, T.B. and Goode, P. (ed.), *Readings in Marxist Sociology*, Clarendon Press, Oxford.

Marx, K. (1983b), 'Modes of Production and Forms of Property' (excerpt from *The German Ideology*, 1846) in Bottomore, T.B. and Goode, P. (ed.), *Readings in Marxist Sociology*, Clarendon Press, Oxford.

Marx, K. (1983c), 'The Classes of Modern Society', (excerpt from *Capital*, vol. 3, Chapter 52, 1873), in Bottomore, T.B. and Goode, P. (ed.), *Readings in Marxist Sociology*, Clarendon Press, Oxford.

Marx, K. (1987), 'Determinants of Legal Development: The Guiding Thread' in Ghai, Y., Luckham, R. and Snyder, F. (ed.), *The Political Economy of Land: A Third World Reader*, Oxford University Press, Oxford.

Maseru Development Plan (1980), *Working Paper No.4*, Kingdom of Lesotho.

Mashinini, I.V. (1982), *Land Tenure in Basutoland*, MA dissertation, The Hague, Netherlands, unpublished.

Mashinini, I.V. (1983), *Land Tenure in Lesotho*, Food and Agriculture Organization, Roma.

Mashinini, I.V. (1986), 'La Difficile Réforme Foncière au Lesotho' in *Politiques Africaines*, no. 21, pp.54-62.

Mateka, B. (1987), 'Lesotho Urbanization and Land Policy: Future Prospects', in *Proceedings: Land Act Policy Seminar, January 27-30, 1987*, Quthing.

May, J. (1987), *Changing People, Changing Laws*, Mambo Press, Gweru, Zimbabwe.

McEachern, D. (1975), 'The Mode of Production and Socio-Economic Formations', *South Asia Marxist Review*, 1,2, pp. 444-57.

Meillassoux, C. (1972), 'From Reproduction to Production: A Marxist Approach to Economic Anthropology', *Economy and Society*, vol. 1, no. 1, pp. 93-105.

Meillassoux, C. (1975), *L'Esclavage en Afrique Pré-Coloniale*, Maspero, Paris.

Meillassoux, C. (1981), *Maidens, Meal and Money: Capitalism and the Domestic Community*, Cambridge University Press, London.

Middleton, J. (1988), 'Foreword' in Downs, R.E. and Reyna, S.P. (ed.), *Land and Society in Contemporary Africa*, University Press of New England, Hanover and London.

Moll, P. (1988), 'Transition to Freehold in the South African Reserves', *Ceres*, no. 113.

Moore, S.F. (1986), *Social Facts and Fabrications: 'Customary' Law on Kilimanjaro 1880-1980*, Cambridge University Press, Cambridge.

Morgan, L. (1963), *Ancient Society* (edited by E. Leacock), World Publishing, Cleveland.

Morojele, C.M.H. (1963), *The 1960 Agricultural Census of Basutoland,* Reports (6 Parts: Part II - 1962, Parts I, III, IV, V & IV - 1963), Agricultural Development, Government of Basutoland, Maseru.

Mosaase, A. (1982), *Lesotho's Land Policy under the Land Act 1979 and Implications on Agricultural Sector,* Department of Lands, Surveys and Physical Planning, Ministry of Interior, Kingdom of Lesotho.

Mosaase, A. (1984), 'Experiences from the implementation of the Lesotho Land Act 1979, in Urban Areas', in *Proceedings: Land Act Policy Seminar, March 18-22, 1984,* Government of Lesotho.

Mosaase, A. (1985), *National Land Policy in Lesotho with Specific Reference to the Land Act 1979,* Department of Lands, Surveys and Physical Planning, Ministry of Interior, Kingdom of Lesotho.

Mosaase, A., (1987), *Agricultural Land Tenure Issues: Debate Leading to the Land Act 1979,* Department of Land, Survey and Physical Planning, Ministry of the Interior, Chieftainship Affairs and Rural Development, unpublished.

Mueller, M. (1977), 'Women and Men, Power and Powerlessness in Lesotho', in Wellesley Editorial Committee (ed.), *Women and National Development: Complexities of Change,* Chicago University Press, Chicago.

Muller, K. and Khabele, J. (1985), *Land Tenure - The Effect on Women's Participation in Agricultural Development,* National University of Lesotho, Roma.

Murray, C. (1980a), 'From Granary to Labour Reserve', *South African Labour Bulletin,* vol. 6, no. 4.

Murray, C. (1980b), 'Effects of Migrant Labour', *South African Labour Bulletin,* vol. 6, no. 4.

Murray, C. (1980c), 'Migrant Labour and Changing Family Structure in the Rural Periphery of Southern Africa', *Journal of Southern African Studies,* vol. 6, no. 2.

Murray, C. (1981), *Families Divided: The Impact of Migrant Labour in Lesotho,* Cambridge University Press, Cambridge.

Murray, C. (1984), 'Land, Power and Class in the Thaba 'Nchu District, Orange Free, 1884-1983', *Review of African Political Economy,* no. 29, pp. 30-48.

Mvunga, M.P. (1982), *Land Law and Policy in Zambia,* Institute of African Studies, University of Zambia, Lusaka.

National University of Lesotho (1985), *The Situation of Women in Lesotho,* Department of Social Anthropology/Sociology, UNICEF.

Nelson, N. (1981), *African Women in the Development Process,* Frank Cass, London.

173

Neocosmos, M. (1987), *Social Relations in Rural Swaziland: Critical Analyses*, Social Science Research Unit, University of Swaziland, Kwaluseni.

Noronha, R. and Lethem, F.J. (1983), *Traditional Land Tenures and Land Use Systems in the Design of Agricultural Projects*, The World Bank, Washington, D.C.

NUL, See National University of Lesotho.

Obbo, C. (1980), *African Women: Their Struggle for Economic Independence*, Zed Press, London.

Palmer, R. and Parsons, N. (1977), 'Introduction' to *The Roots of Rural Poverty in Central and Southern Africa*, UCLA, Berkeley, and Heinemann, London.

Palmer, R. and Parsons, N. (1977) (ed.), *The Roots of Rural Poverty in Central and Southern Africa*, UCLA, Berkeley, and Heinemann, London.

Palmer, V., and Poulter, S. (1972), *The Legal System of Lesotho*, Michie Co., Charlottesville, Virginia.

Pashukanis, E.B. (1987), 'The Specificity of Law', in Ghai, Y., Luckham, R. and Snyder, F. (ed.), *The Political Economy of Land: A Third World Reader*, Oxford University Press, Oxford.

Paulme, D. (ed.) (1963), *Women of Tropical Africa*, University of California Press, Berkeley.

Perry, J.A.G. (1983), 'Land and Politics in Lesotho', *Journal of African Studies*, 42(1), pp. 57-66 .

Phororo, D.R. (1979), *Crop Farming in Lesotho, Analysis and Suggested Policy*, Ministry of Agriculture, Co-operatives and Marketing, Kingdom of Lesotho, Maseru.

Phororo, D.R. (1987), Closing Speech of the Land Policy Review Seminar in *Proceedings of the Land Policy Review Seminar*, 27th-30th January, 1987.

Picard, L. (1980), 'Land Tenure Changes in Botswana' in *Comparative Political Studies*, October 1980, pp.313-356.

Poulantzas, N. (1976), 'The Capitalist State: A Reply to Miliband and Laclau', *New Left Review*, 95, pp.63-83.

Poulter, S. (1976), *Family Law and Litigation in Basotho Society*, Clarendon Press, Oxford.

Poulter, S. (1981), *Legal Dualism*, Morija Sesuto Book Depot, Morija, Lesotho.

Prah, K. (ed.) (1988), *Food Security Issues in Southern Africa*, Institute of Southern African Studies, National University of Lesotho, Roma.

Quinlan, T.K.C. (1983), *The Transformation of Land Tenure in Lesotho*, M.A. Dissertation, University of Cape Town.

174

Qunta, C. (ed.) (1987), *Women in Southern Africa*, Allison and Busby, London.

Ranger, T.O. (1983), 'Tradition and Travesty: Chiefs and the Administration in Makoni District, Zimbabwe 1960-1980', in Peel, J.D.Y. and Ranger, T.O. (ed.), *Past and Present in Zimbabwe*, pp.20-41, International African Institute, Manchester University Press, Manchester.

Renner, K. (1969), 'The Development of Capitalist Property and the Legal Institutions Complementary to the Property Norm', in *Sociology of Law*, Penguin, Harmondsworth.

Rey, P.P. (1971), *Colonialisme, Néocolonialisme et Transition au Capitalisme*, Maspero, Paris.

Rey, P.P. (1973), *Les Alliances de classes: sur l'articulation des modes de production*, Maspero, Paris.

Rey, P.P. (1976), 'L'esclavage lignager chez Tsangui, Punu et les Kuni du Congo-Brazzaville', in Meillassoux (ed.), *L'esclavage en Afrique Pré-Coloniale*, Paris, Maspero

Richard, A.J. (1939), *Land Labour and Diet in Northern Rhodesia*, London.

Roberts, P. (1984), 'Feminism in Africa: Feminism and Africa' in *Review of African Political Economy*, nos. 27-28, pp.175-184.

Roberts, S. (ed.) (1977), *Law and the Family in Africa*, Mouton, The Hague.

Robertson, A.F. (1987), *The Dynamics of Productive Relationships; African Share Contracts in Comparative Perspective*, Cambridge University Press, Cambridge.

Rogers, B. (1979), 'Women and Land Rights', *Isis International Bulletin - Women, Land and Food Production*, no. 11, Spring 1979.

Rosaldo, M. and Lamphere, L. (ed.) (1974), *Women, Culture and Society*, Stanford University Press, Stanford.

Rousseau, J.J. (1978), 'The Origin of Inequality' in MacPherson, C.B. (ed.), *Property: Mainstream and Critical Positions*, University of Toronto Press, Toronto.

Roxborough, I. (1979), *Theories of Underdevelopment*, Macmillan, London.

Rugege, S. (1986), *Ideology and Land Tenure in Lesotho*, (unpublished).

Russell, M. (1988), 'Communal Tenure in Swaziland', *Ceres*, no. 113.

Rutman, G. (1969), 'Innovation in the land tenure system of the Transkei, South Africa', *Land Economics*, vol. 45.

Sacks, K. (1979), *Sisters and Wives: The Past and Future of Sexual Equality*.

Safilios-Rothschild, C. (1985), 'The Persistence of Women's Invisibility in Agriculture: Theoretical and Policy Lessons from Lesotho and Sierra Leone', *Economic Development and Cultural Change*, 33(2), pp. 299-318.

Sanders, P.B. (1975), *Moshoeshoe: Chief of Lesotho*, Heinemann, London.

Santho, S., Mabbs-Zeno, C., Mashinini, V., Hoohlo, S.G. and Kimane, I. (1984), *Report on the Dynamics of Land Tenure and Agrarian Systems in Africa, Lesotho Country Study*, National University of Lesotho, Roma, Lesotho.

Santos, B. de S. (1977), 'The Law of the Oppressed: The Construction and Reproduction of Legality in Pasargada', *Law and Society Review,* vol. 12, 1.

Santos, B. de S. (1985), 'On Modes of Production of Law and Social Power', *International Journal of the Sociology of Law*, no. 13, pp.299-336.

Santos, B. de S. (1987), 'The Law of the Oppressed', in Ghai, Y., Luckham, R. and Snyder, F. (ed.), *The Political Economy of Land: A Third World Reader,* Oxford University Press, Oxford.

Saul, J.S. (1974), 'The State in Post-Colonial Societies: Tanzania', in Miliband, R.A. and Saville, J. (ed.), *The Socialist Register,* Merlin Press, London.

Saul, J.S. and Gelb, S. (1981), *The Crisis in South Africa: Class Defence, Class Revolution,* Monthly Review Press, London.

Schapera, I. (1943), *Land Tenure in the Bechuanaland Protectorate*, Oxford University Press, Oxford.

Schwager, D. and C. (1974), *Lesotho, Dirk Schwager Photographic Illustrations*, Mazenod Book Centre, Mazenod.

Seeiso, S.M. (1986), 'Legal Constraints of Women' in *Proceedings at the Seminar/Conference on the Evaluation of Lesotho Women's Achievements during the Women's Decade*, Ministry of Rural Development, Co-operatives, Women and Youth Affairs, Government of Lesotho.

Seidman, R. (1968-69), 'The Reception of English Law in Colonial Law Revisited', *Eastern Africa Law Review,* vol. 1-2.

Seidman, R. (1978), *State, Law and Development*, Croom Helm, London.

Seidman, R. (1987), 'The Reception of English Law in Colonial Africa', in Ghai, Y., Luckham, R. and Snyder, F. (ed.), *The Political Economy of Land: A Third World Reader,* Oxford University Press, Oxford.

Senga, W.M. (1976), 'African land tenure reform', in *Agricultural Development in Kenya,* Heyer, J., Maitha, J.K. and Senga, W.M., OUP, Nairobi.

Sheddick, V. (1954), *Land Tenure in Basutoland*, HMSO, London.

Shivji, I. (1976), *Class Struggles in Tanzania*, Heinemann, London.

Shivji, I. (1986), *Law, State and the Working Class: c. 1920-1964*, James Currey, London.

Showers, K. (1980), 'A Note on Women, Conflict and Migrant Labour', *South African Labour Bulletin*, 6(4) November 1980, pp.54-57.

Showers, K. (1989), 'Soil erosion in the Kingdom of Lesotho: Origins and Colonial Response, 1830s to 1950s', *Journal of Southern African Studies*, vol. 15, no. 2, 263-286.

Sinha, R. (1984), *Landlessness: A Growing Problem*, Food and Agriculture Organization of the United Nations, Rome.

Snyder, F.G. (1977), 'Land Law and Economic Change in Rural Senegal: Diola pledge transactions and disputes', in Hamnett, I. (ed.), *Social Anthropology and Law*, pp.713-157, Academic Press, London.

Snyder, F.G. (1981), 'Labour Power and Legal Transformation in Senegal', *Review of African Political Economy*, vol. 21.

Sorrenson, M., (1967), *Land Reform in Kikuyu Country*, Oxford University Press.

Spence, J.E. (1964), 'British Policy Towards the High Commission Territories', *The Journal of Modern African Studies*, vol. 2, no. 2, pp.221-46.

Spiegal, A. (1979), *Migrant Labour Remittances, Rural Differentiation and the Development Cycle in a Lesotho Community*, (Master's thesis, University of Capetown)

Spiegal, A. (1980), 'Rural Differentiation and the Diffusion of Migrant Labour Remittances in Lesotho', in Mayer, P. (ed), *Black Villagers in an Industrial Society*, Oxford University Press, Cape Town.

Spiegal, A. (1981), 'Changing Patterns of Migrant Labour and Rural Differentiation in Lesotho', *Social Dynamics*, 6(2), pp. 1-13.

Sumner, C. (ed.) (1982), *Crime, Justice and Underdevelopment*, Heinemann, London.

Swantz, M.-L. (1985), *Women in Development: A Creative Role Denied? The Case of Tanzania*, C. Hurst and Co., London.

Swynnerton, R.J.M. (1955), *A Plan to Intensify the Development of African Agriculture in Kenya* (The Swynnerton Report), Government Printer, Nairobi.

Terray, E. (1972), *Marxism and 'Primitive' Societies*, Monthly Review Press, New York.

Thomas, C.Y. (1974), *Dependence and Transformation: The Economics of, the Transition to Socialism*, Monthly Review Press, New York.

Thompson, L. (1975), *Survival in Two Worlds: Moshoeshoe of Lesotho 1786-1870*, Oxford University Press, Oxford.

Thompson, E.P. (1987), 'Capitalism and the Rule of Law', in Ghai, Y., Luckham, R. and Snyder, F. (ed.), *The Political Economy of Land: A Third World Reader*, Oxford University Press, Oxford.

Tshabalala, M. and Holland, D. (1986), *Agricultural Research Technical Information Bulletin - Recommendation Domain: Some Considerations for the Design of On-Farm Research and Extension in Lesotho.*

Van Apeldoorn, G.J. and Turner, S.D. (1984), *Research on the Rural Poor in Lesotho: Preliminary Indicators and Future Directions*, Research Report no. 5, Institute of Southern African Studies, National University of Lesotho.

Van der Wiel, A.C.A. (1977), *Migratory Wage Labour: Its Role in the Economy of Lesotho*, Mazenod Book Centre, Mazenod.

Van Onselen, C., (1978), *Chibaro*, Pluto Press, London.

Verhelst, T. (1968), *Safeguarding African Customary Law: Judicial and Legislative Processes for its Adaptation and Integration*, Occasional Paper no. 7, African Studies Center, University of California, Los Angeles.

Vogel, L. (1983), *Marxism and the Oppression of Women: Toward a Unitary Theory*, Pluto Press, London.

Von Freyhold, M. (1977), 'The Post-Colonial State and its Tanzanian Version', *Review of African Political Economy*, no. 8.

Walker, C. (1982), *Women and Resistance in South Africa*, Onyx Press, London.

WCARRD (1982), *World Conference on Agrarian Reform and Rural Development*, Food and Agriculture Organization of the United Nations, Rome.

Weisfelder, R. (1973), 'The Basotho Monarchy: A Spent Force or a Dynamic Political Factor', *Papers in International Studies, Africa Series*, no. 16, pp. 11-29, Athens, Ohio.

Weisfelder, R. (1977), 'The Basotho Monarchy' in Lemarchand, R. (ed.), *African Kingships in Perspective: Political Change and Modernization in Monarchical Settings*, Frank Cass, London.

Wellings, P.A. (1983), 'Making a Fast Buck: Capital Leakage and the Public Accounts of Lesotho', *African Affairs*, 82(329) October 1983, pp. 495-508.

Werbner, R. (1980), 'Introduction', *Journal of African Law*, vol. 24, no. 1, School of Oriental and African Studies, University of London.

Williams, J.C. (1972), *Lesotho Land Tenure and Economic Development*, Africa Institute of South Africa, Pretoria.

Winai-Strom, G. (1978), *Development and Dependence in Lesotho the Enclave of South Africa*, University of Uppsala, Uppsala.

Winai-Strom, G. (1986), *Migration and Development, Dependence on South Africa: A Study of Lesotho*, Scandinavian Institute of African Studies, Uppsala.

Wolpe, H. (ed.) (1980), *The Articulation of Modes of Production*, Routledge and Kegan Paul, London.

Wolpe, H. (1988), *Race, Class and the Apartheid State*, James Currey, London.

Women's Bureau, The (1986), *Report on Proceedings at the Seminar/Conference on the Evaluation of Lesotho Women's Achievements during the Women's Decade*, Ministry of Rural Development, Co-operatives, Women and Youth Affairs, Government of Lesotho.

World Bank, The (1975), *Assault on World Poverty: the problems of rural development, education and health*, Johns Hopkins Press, Baltimore.

World Bank, The (1989), *Sub-Saharan Africa: From Crisis to Sustainable Growth*, Johns Hopkins Press, Baltimore.

Newspapers

Financial Times, 4th October 1989.
Lesotho Today, 11 March 1987.
Work for Justice, April 1986.
Work for Justice, September 1987.
Work for Justice, December 1988, no. 20.
Work for Justice, December 1989.

Miscellaneous

Lesotho Law Journal: A Journal of Law and Development, Special Issue about Modern Perspectives on Roman-Dutch Law, vol. 1, 1985, no. 2, National University of Lesotho, Roma.

Presentation to Donor Round Table, May 15, 1984, Government of Lesotho, Ministry of Agriculture and Marketing and Ministry of Co-operatives and Rural Development, Maseru.

Proceedings: Land Act Policy Seminar, Quthing, Lesotho March 18-22 1984, Government of Lesotho, Ministry of Agriculture.

Proceedings: Land Act Review Commission Workshop, 27th-30th January 1987.

Appendix

Source: *Santho et al. (1984): iv*

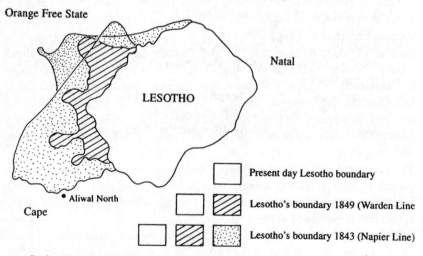

Source: *Redrawn from Bardill and Cobbe (1985):14*

180

Household data

Key to table on the following pages

Each respondent is identified on the vertical axis by region, (N)orth [villages in the district of Berea] or (S)outh [villages within the district of Mohale's Hoek] and by whether they share land (o)ut from their holdings or they share land (i)n to supplement their holdings. Finally each respondent also has an identifying number. Thus SO1 refers to the first respondent from the South who shares land out and NO9 refers to the 9th respondent from the North who shares land out and in a final example, NI8 indicates the 8th respondent from the North who shares land in. A household's involvement with the government-sponsored Technical Operations Unit is indicated by 'T.O.U.'

A range of factors are featured along the horizontal axis. First, general data regarding the sex of the respondent, marital status, age and whether the household head is normally resident within the household. An absent household head is indicated by an 'A'. Education, abbreviated as 'E', indicates the standard level acquired by the household head. 'Miner' refers to whether or not the household head had been employed as a miner. Principal resources of income, abbreviated by 'Prin. Inc.' include such examples as brewing and selling beer, remittances, cash help from adult children and gathering and selling wood. Respondents' estimates of the households' cash income figures under the column headed 'Cash Inc'.

Several factors on the horizontal axis feature responses to questions about labour and field availability within households and the circumstances surrounding sharecropping agreements. The labour category indicates the number of adults of both sexes available in the household for agricultural labour. 'Fields' indicates the number of fields a household has access to independently. 'Crops' column names the main products from the fields identified in the previous category. 'Init. Agr.' is an abbreviation of initiated agreement and indicates whether it was the respondent who initiated the share agreement or the other party. 'Agr. in Adv.' indicates how long in advance the agreement was made prior to co-operation starting. The 'Written/Oral' column indicates whether or not the agreement between parties to sharecrop was written or oral, while the next column shows whether or not it was witnessed and if so by whom. The length of the agreement is estimated in the next column.

The next set of factors concern the use of oxen in sharecropping. Under 'Your Oxen' respondents were asked how many oxen they supplied (whether owned or hired) for the operations of ploughing, planting,

181

cultivation and traction. Respondents were also asked to supply the same information with regard to the other parties ('Their Oxen'). Similarly, the division of labour in the operations of ploughing, planting, cultivation and harvesting between parties' households is indicated under 'Me' and 'Th' (Them).

In addition there are three columns which feature responses to the questions of who provides seed, fertilizer and pesticide. 'Crop ratio' indicates how the crop is divided between parties, while the next column asks if the residue (or proceeds from the sale of the residue, which is used to feed cattle) from harvest is divided and if so, to indicate the ratio. 'Con. Works' refers to which party has been responsible for conservation work on the land. 'Crop Again' provides responses to the question of whether the respondent would enter into agreement to sharecrop with this party again. 'Prin. Dec.' is an abbreviation for principle decision maker and refers to the respondent's answer to the question: 'Who is the main decision-maker in your household?'. The final column indicates whether or not the household is in possession of a Form C land title.

Household Data

Share Out

No.	Sex	Mar Stat	Age	Res.	E		Miner	Prin. Inc.
SO1	F	W	73	R	1		Yes	Other wages
SO2	F	W	69	R	1		Yes	Other (remitt)
SO3	F	W	75	R	1		Yes	Other (remitt)
SO4	F	W	79	R	1		Yes	Other (brew) (remitt)
SO5	F	W	69	R	1		Yes	Other (remitt)
SO6	F	W	37	R	1		Yes	Other (brew)
SO7	F	W	71	R	1		Yes	Crops Other (brew)
SO8	F	W	61	R	1		Yes	Other (brew) (remitt)
SO9	M	Ma	40	R	1		Yes	Crops
S010 1 field w/ (T.O.U.)	M	Ma	67	R	1		Yes	Other (piece jobs)
SO11	F	W	43	R	1		Yes	Other wages
SO12	F	W	60	R	1		Yes	Other (piece jobs)
SO13	F	W	69	R	1		Yes	Crops Other
SO14 T.O.U.	M	Ma	47	R	1		Yes	Other (brew)
SO15	F	W	58	R	1		Yes	Other wages

183

Household Data

Share Out

No.	Sex	Mar Stat	Age	Res.	E	Miner	Prin. Inc.
SO16	F	W	54	R	1	Yes	(Other) children
SO17 1 field T.O.U.	M	Ma	82	R	1	Yes	Other (brew) (wood)
SO18	M	Ma	61	A	1	Yes	Wages RSA, brew
SO19	F	W	66	R	1	Yes	(Other) Brew, Wood
SO20 2 fields T.O.U.	M	Ma	57	R	1	Yes	Crops Pigs
SO21	F	W	69	R	1	Yes	Crops, Livestock Other
NO1	M	Ma	56	R	1	Yes	Other wages
NO2	F	W	66	R	1	Yes	None
NO3	M	W	61	R	1	Yes	Livestock
NO4	F	W	65	R	1	Yes	Livestock
NO5	M	Ma	69	R	1	Yes	None
NO6	M	Ma	56	R	1	Yes	Other wages
NO7	F	W	59	R	1	Yes	-
NO8	M	Ma	72	R	1	Yes	Crops, Other
NO9	F	W	82	R	1	Yes	Other wages

Household Data

Share In

No.	Sex	Mar Stat	Age	Res.	E	Miner	Prin. Inc.
SI1	M	Ma	60	R	univ dipl	No	Crops, Livestock Other wages
SI2	M	Ma	32	R	'E' form agr. dipl	Yes	Other wages
NI1	M	Ma	40	R	-	No	Crops
NI2	M	Ma	58	R	none	Yes	Other
NI3	M	Ma	32	R	Std 1-5	Yes	Other wages
NI4	M	Ma	32	R	Std 2	Yes	RSA wages
NI5	M	W	58	R	none	Yes	None
NI6	M	Ma	56	R	Std 3	Yes	Livestock
NI7	M	Ma	76	R	Std 6-7	No	Other wages
NI8	M	Ma	45	R	Old Std 5	Yes	Crops Livestock

Household Data

Share Out

No.	Cash Inc.	Labour M	Labour F	Fields	Crops
SO1	150	1	1	2	Sorghum
SO2	200	1	1	2	Maize Sorghum
SO3	-	4	2	2	Maize Sorghum
SO4	100	1	1	3	Maize, Sorghum Beams
SO5	200	1	1	2	Maize Sorghum
SO6	100	2	2	3	Beans, Maize Sorghum
SO7	20	1	1	2	Maize
SO8	100	2	1	2	Maize Sorghum
SO9	100	1	1	2	Maize
S010 1 field w/ (T.O.U.)	1200	2	2	2	Maize
SO11	720	0	1	1	Sorghum Maize
SO12	240	1	3	2	Sorghum Maize
SO13	120	1	1	2	Maize Sorghum
SO14 T.O.U.	360	1	3	1	Maize
SO15	240	1	1	1	Maize or Sorghum

186

Household Data

Share Out

No.	Cash Inc.	Labour M	F	Fields	Crops
SO16	600	1	1	1	Sorghum
SO17 1 field T.O.U.	120	1	1	3	Sorghum Beans, Maize
SO18	-	1	3	4	Maize Sorghum
SO19	20	0	2	1	Maize Pumpkin
SO20 2 fields T.O.U.	600	2	2	3, 1 share 2 T.O.U.	Sorghum Maize
SO21	350	2	1	2 1 T.O.U.	Maize Sorghum
NO1	-	1	1	1	Maize
NO2	-	0	1	1	Maize Sorghum
NO3	-	2	1	1	Sorghum
NO4	-	0	1	1	Maize
NO5	-	1	5	2	Beans
NO6	-	2	2	2	Maize
NO7	-	2	2	1	Maize
NO8	200	1	1	1	Maize
NO9	-	1	1	1	Maize

Household Data

Share In

No.	Cash Inc.	Labour M	F	Fields	Crops
SI1	1000	3	1	1/5	Maize Sorghum
SI2	800	1	1	0/1	Maize, Sorghum Beans
NI1	-	1	1	?/3	Maize
NI2	-	6	4	?/1	Maize Sorghum
NI3	-	2	1	?/1	Maize
NI4	-	1	1	?/1	Maize
NI5	-	1	1	?/1	Sorghum
NI6	-	3	3	0/?	Maize
NI7	-	1	3	0/?	Maize
NI8	500	1	1	?/2	Sorghum

Household Data

Share Out

No.	Init Agr	Agr. in Adv.	Written /Oral	Witness	Length
SO1	me	4 mo	oral	No/ -	Not stated
SO2	me	2 mo	oral	No/ -	Not stated
SO3	me	2 mo	oral	No/ -	5 years
SO4	me	2 mo	oral	No/ -	4 years
SO5	me	2 mo	oral	No/ -	Not stated
SO6	me	2 mo	oral	No/ -	2 years/ not stated
SO7	me	2 mo	oral	No/ -	1 year
SO8	me	4 mo	oral	No/ -	Not stated
SO9	DK	2 mo	D.K.	D.K.	D.K.
S010 1 field w/ (T.O.U.)	me	2 mo	oral	No/ -	1 year
SO11	me	in winter	oral	No/ -	1 year
SO12	me	during plough season	written	Yes/ daughter	1 year
SO13	me	during plough season	oral	-/ -	1 year
SO14 T.O.U.	me	3 mo	written	No/ -	1 year
SO15	-	-	oral	No/ -	Not stated

Household Data

Share Out

No.	Init. Agr.	Agr. in Adv.	Written /Oral	Witness	Length
SO16	me	during plough season	oral	-/ -	1 year
SO17 1 field T.O.U.	me	during plough season	oral	-/ -	Not stated
SO18	me	before harvest	-	No/ -	1 year
SO19	them	during plant season	-	-/ -	Not stated
SO20 2 fields T.O.U.	me	3 mo	written	-/ -	Not stated
SO21	me	2 mo	oral	No/ -	Not stated
NO1	me	-	oral	No/ -	Yearly
NO2	me	-	oral	No/ -	Yearly
NO3	them	-	oral	Yes/ neighbour	Yearly
NO4	me	-	written	Yes/ chief	Not stated
NO5	me	-	oral	No/ -	Yearly
NO6	me	-	oral	No/ -	Yearly
NO7	me	-	oral	No/ -	Not stated
NO8	-	-	oral	No/ -	Not stated
NO9	them	-	oral	No/ -	1 year

Household Data

Share In

No.	Init. Agr.	Agr. in Adv.	Written /Oral	Witness	Length
SI1	me	4 mo	oral	Yes/ wife	Not stated
SI2	them	3 mo	oral	Yes/ wives	Not stated
NI1	them	-	oral	Yes/ neighbour	1 year
NI2	them	-	oral	No/ -	Not stated
NI3	me	-	oral	Yes/ kin	Yearly
NI4	me	-	oral	Yes/ kin	Yearly
NI5	me	-	oral	No/ -	Not stated
NI6	me	-	oral	No/ -	Not stated
NI7	me	-	oral	No/ -	Not stated
NI8	me	-	oral	Yes/ Yes	Not stated

Household Data

Share Out

No.	Plough	Plant	Your Oxen Cult	Trac
SO1	-	-	3	-
SO2	-	-	-	-
SO3	-	-	2 hired	-
SO4	-	-	2 hired	-
SO5	-	-	3 hired	hired
SO6	-	6 hired	2 hired	-
SO7	-	-	1 hired	-
SO8	-	3 mafisa	-	hired
SO9	3 mafisa	-	2 mafisa	hired (share exp)
SO10 1 field w/ (T.O.U.)	-	-	-	-
SO11	-	-	-	-
SO12	-	-	-	-
SO13	-	-	-	-
SO14 T.O.U.	-	-	-	-
SO15	-	-	-	-

192

Household Data

Share Out

No.	Plough	Plant	Your Oxen Cult	Trac
SO16	-	-	-	-
SO17 1 field T.O.U.	-	-	-	-
SO18	-	-	-	-
SO19	-	-	-	-
SO20 2 fields T.O.U.	-	-	-	-
SO21	-	-	-	-
NO1	-	-	-	-
NO2	-	-	1	-
NO3	2	2	2 hired	-
NO4	-	1	1	-
NO5	-	2	2	-
NO6	-	2	-	-
NO7	-	2 hired	2 hired	-
NO8	4 own	4 own	-	-
NO9	-	-	-	hired

193

Household Data

Share In

No.	Plough	Plant	Your Oxen Cult	Trac
SI1	6 own	6 own	2 own	hired
SI2	-	6 hired	-	hired
NI1	6	2	2	hired
NI2	1 own	1 own	-	hired
NI3	-	-	-	hired
NI4	-	-	-	X
NI5	-	2 own	2 own	hired
NI6	-	2 own	2 own	hired
NI7	4 own	2 own	-	-
NI8	4 own	4 own	-	-

Household Data

Share Out

No.	Plough	Their Oxen Plant	Cult	Trac
SO1	4 own	4 own	3 people	-
SO2	4 own	4 own	-	-
SO3	-	6 hired	2 owned	-
SO4	-	4 own	2 own	hired
SO5	-	-	3 hired	hired
SO6	2 own	2 own	3 own	-
SO7	-	6 hired	1 hired	-
SO8	-	-	-	hired
SO9	-	-	2 own	-
SO10 1 field w/ (T.O.U.)	4 own	-	-	-
SO11	-	4 borrowed	-	hired (share exp)
SO12	8 own	-	-	hired
SO13	4 borrowed	-	-	-
SO14 T.O.U.	-	-	-	T.O.U.
SO15	6 own	-	-	-

Household Data

Share Out

No.	Plough	Plant	Their Oxen Cult	Trac
SO16	4 own	1 own	-	-
SO17 1 field T.O.U.	-	-	-	hired
SO18	6 own	-	-	-
SO19	4	2	-	-
SO20 2 fields T.O.U.	-	-	-	T.O.U.
SO21	-	-	-	hired
NO1	2	2	2	hired
NO2	-	2	1	hired
NO3	2	2	-	-
NO4	-	2	2	hired
NO5	-	-	-	hired
NO6	-	-	2	hired
NO7	-	-	-	hired
NO8	-	-	-	-
NO9	-	2	2	-

Household Data

Share In

No.	Plough	Plant	Their Oxen Cult	Trac
SI1	-	-	5	-
SI2	-	-	-	-
NI1	-	-	-	-
NI2	-	-	-	hired
NI3	-	X?	X?	-
NI4	-	2	2	-
NI5	-	-	-	-
NI6	-	-	-	-
NI7	4	2	2	-
NI8	-	-	-	-

Household Data

Share Out

No.	Plough Me	Plough Th	Plant Me	Plant Th	Cult Me	Cult Th	Harvest Me	Harvest Th
SO1	1	0	1	0	2	2	3	2
SO2	1	0	1	0	2	2	3	2
SO3	1	1	1	1	3	3	2	2
SO4	1	1	1	1	2	2	2	2
SO5	1	0	1	0	3	3	3	3
SO6	2	2	2	2	2	2	2	2
SO7	1	1	1	1	1	1	2	2
SO8	2	2	2	2	1	1	1	0
SO9	4	-	4	-	2	2	2	2
S010 1 field w/ (T.O.U.)	-	2	-	-	1	1	1	1
SO11	-	1	-	1	1	-	DK	DK
SO12	-	2	-	-	1	2	DK	DK
SO13	-	2	-	-	1	1	1	1
SO14 T.O.U.	-	T.O.U.	-	T.O.U.	-	-	-	-
SO15	-	2	-	-	-	1	-	2

Household Data

Share Out

No.	Plough Me	Plough Th	Plant Me	Plant Th	Labour Cult Me	Labour Cult Th	Harvest Me	Harvest Th
SO16	-	2	-	2	x	X	X	X
SO17 1 field T.O.U.	-	1	-	-	1	1	1	1
SO18	-	3	-	-	x	X	2	2
SO19	-	4	-	2	1	-	X	x
SO20 2 fields T.O.U.	-	T.O.U	-	T.O.U.	-	-	-	-
SO21	2	2	2	2	1	1	2	2
NO1	50	50	.50	.50	.50	.50	.50	.50
NO2	0	100	-	100	-	100	-	100
NO3	50	50	100	-	100	-	.50	.50
NO4	50	50	.50	.50	-	100	.50	.50
NO5	50	50	.50	.50	.50	.50	.50	.50
NO6	50	50	100	-	100	-	.50	.50
NO7	50	50	.50	.50	.50	.50	.50	.50
NO8	0	4	0	4	2	2	.50	.50
NO9	50	50	.50	.50	.50	.50	.50	.50

Household Data

Share In

Household Data

Share Out

No.	Plough		Plant		Labour Cult		Harvest	
	Me	Th	Me	Th	Me	Th	Me	Th
SI1	2	0	2	0	2	2	4	4
SI2	0	2	0	2	0	2	1	2
NI1	50	50	100	-	.50	.50	50	50
NI2	50	50	.50	50	50	50	50	50
NI3	50	50	100	-	50	50	50	20
NI4	50	50	100	-	100	-	50	50
NI5	100	-	100	-	100	-	50	50
NI6	50	50	100	-	100	-	50	50
NI7	-	100	-	100	-	100	-	100
NI8	1	1	1	1	5	5	.50	.50

Household Data

Share Out

No.	Plough Me	Plough Th	Plant Me	Plant Th	Seed Me	Seed Th	Fertilize Me	Fertilize Th	Pesticide Me	Pesticide Th
SO1	-	X	-	-	X	-	-	-	-	-
SO2	-	X	-	-	X	-	-	-	-	-
SO3	-	X	-	-	X	-	-	-	-	-
SO4	-	X	-	-	X	-	-	-	-	-
SO5	X	X	-	-	X	-	-	-	-	-
SO6	-	X	-	X	X	X	-	-	-	-
SO7	X	X	-	-	X	X	-	-	-	-
SO8	X	X	-	-	X	X	-	-	-	-
SO9	X	-	X	-	-	X	-	2	-	-
S010 1 field w/ (T.O.U.)	-	X	-	-	X	-	-	-	-	-
SO11	X	X	-	X	-	X	-	-	-	-
SO12	-	X	-	-	X	-	-	-	-	-
SO13	-	X	-	-	-	X	-	-	-	-
SO14 T.O.U.	-	X	-	X	-	X	-	X	-	X
SO15	-	X	-	-	X	-	-	-	-	-

Household Data

Share Out

No.	Plough Me	Plough Th	Plant Me	Plant Th	Seed Me	Seed Th	Fertilize Me	Fertilize Th	Pesticide Me	Pesticide Th
SO16	-	X	-	X	X	-	-	-	-	-
SO17 1 field T.O.U.	-	?	-	-	X	-	-	-	-	-
SO18	-	X	-	-	X	-	-	-	-	-
SO19	-	X	-	X	X	X	-	-	-	-
SO20 2 fields T.O.U.	-	T.O.U	-	T.O.U	-	T.O.U	-	T.O.U	-	T.O.U
SO21	X	X	-	-	X	X	-	-	-	-
NO1	X	-	-	-	-	X	-	X	-	X
NO2	-	X	-	X	-	X	-	X	-	X
NO3	-	X	-	X	-	X	X	-	-	-
NO4	-	-	-	X	100	-	-	100	-	100
NO5	-	-	X	-	X	X	X	X	X	X
NO6	-	-	X	X	X	X	X	X	X	X
NO7	-	-	X	-	-	X	X	X	X	X
NO8	X	X	X	X	-	X	-	-	-	-
NO9	-	-	X	-	-	X	-	X	X	X

Household Data

Share In

No.	Plough Me	Plough Th	Plant Me	Plant Th	Seed Me	Seed Th	Fertilize Me	Fertilize Th	Pesticide Me	Pesticide Th
SI1	X	-	X	X	X	X	X	X	X	-
SI2	X	-	X	-	-	X	-	X	X	-
NI1	X	-	X	-	X	-	X	-	X	-
NI2	X	-	X	-	X	X	X	X	X	X
NI3	X	-	-	X	-	X	X	-	X	-
NI4	-	-	X	-	X	-	X	X	X	-
NI5	-	-	X	-	X	-	X	X	-	-
NI6	-	-	X	-	X	-	X	-	X	-
NI7	-	X	-	X	-	X	-	X	-	X
NI8	X	-	X	-	X	X	X	X	X	X

Household Data

Share Out

No.	Crop Ratio	Resid Div	Con. Works	Crop Again	Prin. Dec.	Form C
SO1	50-50	No	Me	Yes	Me	No
SO2	50-50	No	Me	Yes	Me	No
SO3	50-50	No	Me	Yes	Me	No
SO4	50-50	No	Me	Yes	Me	No
SO5	50-50	No	Me	Yes	Me	No
SO6	50-50	No	Me	Yes	Me	No
SO7	50-50	inc from sales 50-50	Me	DK	Me	No
SO8	50-50	No	Me	DK	Me	No
SO9	50-50	No	Me	DK	Husband	DK
SO10 1 field w/ (T.O.U.)	50-50	50-50	Me	-	Me	No
SO11	50-50	No	No Con Works	-	Me	No
SO12	50-50	No	Me	-	Me	No
SO13	50-50	No	Me	-	Me	No
SO14 T.O.U.	Other expenses	-	No Con Works	-	Me	No
SO15	50-50	No	No Con Works	-	Me	No

204

Household Data

Share Out

No.	Crop Ratio	Resid Div	Con. Works	Crop Again	Prin. Dec.	Form C
SO16	50-50	No	Me	-	Me	No
SO17 1 field T.O.U.	50-50	No	No Con Works	-	Me	No
SO18	50-50	No	No Con Works	-	Husband /me	Yes (on 2 fields)
SO19	50-50	No	Me	-	Me	No
SO20 2 fields T.O.U.	Other expenses	-	No Con Works	-	Me	No
SO21	50-50	Yes, for sale	Me	-	Me	No
NO1	50-50	Yes, 50-50	No one	Yes	Me 'H.H.'	No
NO2	50-50	No	-	Yes	Me 'H.H.'	Yes
NO3	50-50	No	No one	Yes	Me 'H.H.'	-
NO4	50-50	No	No one	Yes	Me 'H.H.'	Yes
NO5	50-50	No	No Con Works	Yes	Me 'H.H.'	Yes
NO6	50-50	Yes, 50-50	No One	Yes	Me 'H.H.'	No
NO7	50-50	Yes, 50-50	No-One	Yes	Me	No
NO8	50-50	Yes, 50-50	Me	Yes	Me	No
NO9	50-50	Yes, 50-50	No One	No	Me	No

Household Data

Share In

No.	Crop Ratio	Resid Div	Con. Works	Crop Again	Prin. Dec.	Form C
SI1	Usually 50-50	No	Me/ Them	-	Me	Yes
SI2	50-50	No	Them	Yes	Me	-
NI1	50-50	No	No One	Yes	Me H.H.	-
NI2	50-50	No	The Govt	Yes	Me H.H.	No
NI3	60-40	No	-	Yes	Me H.H. (Son)	-
NI4	50-50	50-50 Yes	-	Yes	H.H. (Father)	-
NI5	50-50	No	-	Yes	H.H.	No
NI6	60-40	50-50 Yes	No One	Yes	H.H. + Wife	-
NI7	50-50	50-50 Yes	No One	Yes	H.H. Father	-
NI8	50-50	No	-	Yes	Me	No